Crying Blue Tears

Story of a Fallen Hoodstar

Written by:
Marlon Evans

Cadmus Publishing
www.cadmuspublishing.com

PROLOGUE

I'd like to start by saying that the people, names, and events mentioned in this book are real. I was careful to not discuss any event or situation which could incriminate anyone. The crimes that are mentioned are either due to someone being incarcerated for them and serving their time, the real perpetrators are dead, or the statute of limitations has expired. This book is a true story of my life and more importantly my wrongful conviction and incarceration for a quadruple homicide I had absolutely nothing to do with. My hope is that the injustices done to me will come fully to the light and people (especially young boys and men) will learn from my experiences and make better decisions in their lives than I did. My purpose is not to glamorize the gang and criminal lifestyle but to show the reader what transpired in my life to push me to the dark side.

This book is written in loving memory to my stepfather, Michael, and my brothers, Deon and Pookie. I dedicate this book to my mother, Bertha Mae Garner, because she has given me life and taught me resilience and perseverance through all of our struggles. Momma, you are a superwoman. I'd be remiss if I didn't mention Glynnis Imani Payne-Smith for believing in me and encouraging me to tell my story. This is part one of two books.

"Back in elementary I thrived on misery, left me alone I grew up amongst a dime breed inside my mind couldn't find a place to rest, until I got that thug life tatted on my chest . . ." So many tears by 2Pac.

CONTENTS

CHAPTER ONE

I almost didn't make it into this world. Before I was conceived, one day my father and his father had a heated argument while at my grandparent's home. My grandfather pulled out his .32 Revolver and shot at my father. However, the bullet missed him, but struck my mother in the head. My mother gave birth to me on May 7, 1973 at the age of 21 years old. I was her third child. My mother's maiden name is Bertha Mae Nelson. She married my father Ernest Edward Evans a few years before I was born, but they separated months after I was born due to my father being physically abusive towards her. My mother is from Little Rock, Arkansas. My father is from California although his parents moved here from Louisiana.

My grandfather, Ernest Evans was born in 1907. Those were difficult times for black people in America. White racism and discrimination was the norm and many brothers and sisters struggled to find even menial jobs. My grandfather grew up in that environment which made him bitter towards whites. He and my grandmother, Vergie Evans fled Louisiana in the 1940's after he killed a white man. They had seven children together. Bobby, who was the oldest and someone I knew nothing about until I was 43 years old, because allegedly he disowned our family years ago.

My father, Edward, Robert, Jessica, John, Paula and Paul who were twins. Edward was a race car driver, a great mechanic, and a member of the "Royal Aces" motorcycle club which was located on 66th Street and Normandie Avenue. Edward used to work for Mc Donald Douglas and Northrop. His nickname was "Wild Man." He had a good sense of humor, was headstrong, and intelligent. However, he didn't raise me nor did he fulfill the father's role in my life. I'd see him for the most part whenever I was at my grandparents home and he popped up. I never knew where he actually lived nor did I ever have a phone number to reach him.

Aside from my uncle George I never met any of my father's cousins and relatives. George was an elderly man, slender, dark skinned, with short hair and steely eyes. He was allegedly a former pimp and was unapproachable. Whenever he visited my grandparents home he didn't speak much. I assume that he did like being around family though. George didn't have any children and his lovely wife. Aunt Hattie was a pleasure to be around. They lived across the street from my grandparents on 91st Street and Stanford. Hattie was never a prostitute so I didn't know how uncle George got her to marry him. Hattie was the most gentlest, kind hearted, and sweetest woman I'd ever met in my life. I loved her.

I have a host of cousins from my uncles and aunts. Bobby has a daughter named Karen. Robert and Paul didn't have children. Jessica had four children: Kim, Sharonda, Stephanie, and Frank. John had multiple children: John Jr, Jermaine, Usef, Andre, Jonathan, Josh, Shameka, Alicia, and a stepdaughter named Cashmere. Paula has four children: Duane, Nikki, Edwin Jr., and Paulette. Paul was gay and hilarious. He taught himself martial arts and became a third degree black belt in Tae Kwon Do. He also had his own school where he taught martial arts.

My grandfather Ernest loved to go fishing. He had a lot of fishing poles. He was suffering from an illness which kept him bedridden and required him to wear an oxygen mask. Every time we went to visit my grandparents I'd kiss my grandmother and then go into their bedroom to see my grandfather. He'd get excited and start smiling. He'd tell me to come closer to him. When I did he'd pinch my cheeks. He loved me. I didn't like my cheeks being pinched but I didn't complain because I saw how it made him feel. I liked to see him happy. In 1979, he became fed up with living like he was and allegedly went into the bathroom and prayed to God to end his life and within the hour he died. That was the first time I'd experienced death in my family. Prior to that my brothers and I thought death wasn't permanent. We were still waiting for Bruce Lee to come back to life in 1983. My grandfather had a brother named Otis who died in California. My grandfather was first cousins with Ida Little. Ida was Malcolm X's first cousin as well. Although I share family ties with Malcolm X, I don't talk about it because I've never met any of his family members.

As for my mother's side of the family, my grandfather's name was Pete Nelson and my grandmother's name was June. They had ten children. Ernest, Alvin, Odell, Robert, Sammy, Peter, my mother, Lena, James (Ledell), and Rosetta. I never met any of their relatives either with the exception of one of my grandmother's sisters. I found it strange that my family didn't keep in contact with their relatives. We never had family reunions so there was always a question in my mind of where do I come from and who am I? My grandparents lived in Watts in a two bedroom house on the corner of 109th Street and Willow Brook right across the street from the train tracks. My grandfather was distant and didn't speak much. He didn't spend any time with me whenever I visited and he wasn't affectionate so I stayed out of his way. He wasn't mean either. My grandmother on the other hand was affectionate. She used to hum songs in her head. She was soft spoken and rarely raised her voice.

My mother got pregnant with my brother Deon at the age of 15. He was born on December 1, 1968. My grandparents put her out. Deon's father abandoned my mother and never came back around. My mother met Edward, married him and had my brother Pookie and I. Pookie's birthday was November 4, 1970. Edward embraced Deon as his own son and Deon called him daddy. After my parents split my mother met Michael Garner. Michael was a former drug dealer and a player in the streets. He had a daughter named Trivette (pronounced, "Tray-Vee-Ette"). Her and Deon were the same age. Trivette lived with her mother but would periodically spend weekends with us. Therefore my brothers and I embraced her as our sister.

In a short time Michael and my mother became an item and we moved in with him on 61st Street and San Pedro. I was around six months old when these things occurred. Michael raised my brothers and I as his own sons. In 1980, he and my mother got married in Las Vegas, Nevada. The house I grew up in used to belong to Michael's parents, Charles and Doris Garner whom people respectively referred to as "Big Daddy and Big Mama." They once owned the front and back house on the property but due to financial hardship the property went into foreclosure. Michael stepped in and took over the mortgages. He and my mother would eventually pay off the mortgages to both homes. The front house we lived in was placed in Michael's name while the back house was placed in his parent's name to ensure that they always had a roof over their heads. Michael's siblings were Diane, Doug, Alfreida, Eddie (Spark), and Jeanette. Doug was murdered in front of the house before I was born.

My early childhood years were filled with joy, happiness, learning right from wrong, and getting acquainted with my environment. I was introduced to my parents' house parties where I'd hear oldies such as "Do it till your satisfied" by B. T. Express, "When you smile" by Leroy Hutson, "Say the word" by the Dramatics, and "Just my imagination" by the Temptations blaring from the 8 track stereo. My brothers used to call me "Boo-Boo" which didn't stick as a nickname. I loved socializing and playing with our friends. We used to play tag, hide and seek, shoot marbles, wrestle, ride big wheels and bikes, climb trees and roofs, as well as cops and robbers. I loved guns too due to watching t.v. shows like "Swat" and "Starsky and Hutch." I didn't like "CHIPS" because they never pulled out their guns no matter what the situation was. Michael and his friends loved me. They would toss me in the air and catch me. Sometimes I'd cry out of fear. I didn't like for anyone I didn't know to touch me or pick me up. My parents called me a crybaby.

The back house was rented out to a Mexican family. My best friend at the time was Felipe. His family lived in the back house. They were a close knit family who was generous, kind, and respectful. Felipe had two older brothers named Guillermo and Himey. He had a little sister named Miraina. Our families were close. On occasion Felipe's mom would give my mother a pan of enchiladas for our family. In those days neighbors looked out for one another. It was common for parents to send their kids to a neighbor's house to borrow a cup of sugar, flour, a stick of butter, or some milk. People didn't despise one another but instead helped each other. They understood that we all were in the same boat subjected to the same conditions thus we were all one. Race didn't matter much. Michael used to say that the best friend a black man could have was a Mexican. I saw some truth in that statement because Felipe and I were like blood brothers. We would fight one minute and be playing the next. No one else better lay a hand on either of us cause we'd jump him. We didn't care how big the person was. Our birthdays were the same day but he was a year older.

There were also other people in our neighborhood who became family to us because we were so close. Michael was well known and respected in the hood. His nicknames were "Touche" and "Tuda-Ray." Damon Campbell was an only child. His mother moved him to Los Angeles from New Jersey. His father wasn't in his life. Mrs. Campbell was Godfearing and a devout Christian. She was humble and kind hearted. She was older than my mother and played the big sister role to her. Damon was two years older than Deon and became a big brother to us. We spent nights and ate meals at each other's houses. We were also close with the Lang family. Eddie, Edward, Frog, Danny, Tony, Leslie, Jackie, Ella, Wilbur, Burbanks, Carl Jr., Otis, Leroy, Darcy, Jerome, Dave Jr., Fanny Mae, Scottie, Kemo, Charlie, Tammy, Creshinda, Shane, Arkillis, Denise, Shawntang, and Dre were just a few members of the Lang family. Darcy was like an uncle to my brothers and I while Scottie, Kemo, and Charlie were like cousins so we called each other family from childhood. Darcy was from Six Deuce Neighborhood East Coast Crips at the time. He was a few years older than Deon. His nickname is Lil Dee. There were rumors that Scottie's uncle Wilbur was actually his father. Allegedly when he found out he was devastated and became a functional alcoholic.

The Taylor family lived next door to us and became family as well. John D., Ernest (Popcorn), Linda, Barbara, Elizabeth (Liz), Roscoe, Andrew, Candy and Cookie. The matriarch of the family was Magdeline which everyone pronounced as, "Maggaleen." Maggaleen was an alcoholic divorcee who drank most days from sunup to sun down. She loved her grand babies though. She had a reputation for getting angry at her children and others and throwing alcohol bottles at them. The vacant lot on the corner was filled with broken bottles which people attributed to her. Her brother was uncle Sugar. Sugar loved the liquor too. He sold joints of marijuana, rode around on a bike, and was a comedian. He drank so much that he walked with his hands behind his back for balance. His favorite lines were calling someone a "goat mouth ass bitch or nigga!" or telling someone to get their "goat smelling ass out of his face!" Linda had three children: Eddie Ray, Maya, and Jolie. Popcorn had sons named Osmond, Ernest Jr., and Poppa Doo and a daughter named Triecy. John D. had a son and an older daughter named Donna who was fine and thick. They also had a cousin named Charlie Mac. Barbara had two kids at the time named Monique and Shavonda. Barbara was married to Ronnie Rivers who was nicknamed "Double R." Monique was conceived in a previous relationship before Barbara met Double R. Double R.

and Michael were close friends. Double R. also sold PCP in those days.

Maggaleen's ex husbands often came around. Their names were Daddy Rock and Mr. Graves. Mr. Graves was quiet and laid back. Daddy Rock was vibrant with a good attitude and a big smile. Both of them were good men. I remember one day Mr. Graves had the whole block crying in laughter. I don't know what happened to piss him off but he stood up and loudly said, "fuck all of you dick sucking bitches!" He was talking about Maggaleen and her daughters. The Taylors became family to us as well.

CHAPTER TWO

As a kid I saw a lot of violence, drama, and turmoil in my neighborhood. There seemed to be something happening all the time. There was never a dull moment. My parents used to let Quake and Bulla Cow from 62NHC take my brothers and I swimming up at Bethune Park on 61st and Hooper. They protected us and made sure we had a good time. In those days Quake had a reputation on the East Side for knocking dudes out. My parents were young with no experience in raising children. Them allowing Quake and Bulla Cow to take us to the swimming pool was a way for them to get some alone time. But it also had another unforeseen effect too.

My brothers and I were exposed to gang members and their culture. We knew many of the Six Deuces by name such as: Snow, Sad, Bubble, Fish, Bruce, Wooder, Sike, Ric Rat, C. L., Black Jesus, Flux, Boo, Insane Wang, Crazy Larry, Lil Oscar, Termite, K. K., Lil Cavers, Bob, Mr. Lil Cee, Peanut, Pounds, Too-Tall, Billy Bird, Cowboy, Ric ROC, Ghost, Big Ed, Limes, Lil Bam, Kev, T-Dog, Lil Sike, Hulio, Leroy, Tank, Will, C-Bone, Snake, Green Giant, Art, and Boxer. We knew the homegirls from 62NHC too. I witnessed fights, robberies, drug dealings, and shootings. For example, next door to my house (opposite the Taylor household) was a vacant house the 62's used as a shack.

One night, I was in my yard and saw a man I didn't know high off of PCP standing in front of the shack. He could barely keep his balance. Boo walked over to him and said something to him. The guy mumbled something then Boo walked away about the space of two houses where two other 62's were waiting. They conversed briefly then Boo walked up to the dude high off PCP and socked him hard in the face dropping him to the ground. The other two 62's ran over and they began beating, kicking, and stomping him as they robbed him of his money. They left the dude unconscious as they ran away. I couldn't have been no more than 5 years old when that happened.

Another time I saw Sike and Kev walking down 61st Street headed towards San Pedro. It was around 3:00 p.m. in the afternoon when a pickup truck with about 5 Mexican men pulled up on them and jumped out. They began fighting. Sike beat up 3 of them while Kev was struggling with the other two. They fought for about 4 minutes then stopped fighting. The Mexicans ran back to their truck. But one Mexican asked Sike if he could fight Kev head up. Kev said he didn't want to fight anymore. Then Sike got upset and yelled at Kev, "nigga you better get down with him, you don't let no Mexican call you out!" Kev and the Mexican fought and he beat Kev up. I was standing about 15 feet away from them watching the whole ordeal. That situation filled me with a sense of black pride and showed me that if I was ever confronted by someone of another race to a fight I must perform like Sike not Kev. I admired Sike from that day.

Another incident I witnessed was when Bruce and this black cop who lived in the neighborhood had a fight in broad daylight. I was walking down the street and just happened to stumble up on it. They were both fighting hard and had bruises. That was a trip. Michael used to tell us we don't see or hear any evil. Snitching could get you killed. My parents didn't shield us from life's rawness. This guy named O.C. from the neighborhood got into it with Crumb at a motorcycle club and Crumb beat him to death. Crumb was a boxer. They found O.C. a couple of days later in a neighbors back yard with flies on his dead body. O.C. and Michael were friends. I remember my parents going around the corner to view his body still lying in the backyard and asking me if I wanted to go see him. I refused but Pookie went.

One thing was clear growing up in my neighborhood, one couldn't be weak or soft if you planned on surviving. My parents loved us and would go out of their way to make sure we had what we needed. They both were disciplinarians. My mother was low on patience and high on attitude. We kept nice furniture and clothes and the yard was neat and clean thus we may have had the appearance of doing far better than what we really were. My parents didn't have bank accounts and they struggled with money. Every dollar my mother saw she already had it spent.

My parents had their flaws. I remember seeing my parents snorting lines of cocaine off of an album cover with one of Michael's friends. I recall the police raiding our house looking for drugs and taking Michael to jail. He got released a few months later. I witnessed domestic violence between them too. I remember walking home from a neighbor's house one day around 5 o'clock in the evening. I was 5 years old. I heard yelling and cursing coming from within my home. Neighbors were outside listening to my parents fight. In those days people didn't intervene in other people's relationships. I entered the house from the back door and walked into the kitchen. From there I could see into my parents bedroom. I saw my mother standing on the bed holding a glass A and W root beer mug which she was using to defend herself. Michael was on the floor trying to get to her. When my mother saw an opportunity she ran out through the kitchen and out the back door. The kitchen back door had a glass window.

Michael didn't pursue her as she ran away. My mother stopped in the washroom, turned around and hurled the mug through the back door window shattering the glass all over the floor. Michael was livid. He chased her outside and caught up with her in the driveway. He held her down with one hand while hitting and slapping her with the other hand. My brothers had gone over to Mrs. Campbell's apartment to call my uncles and my father Edward. I on the other hand walked up to Michael while he held my mother in a headlock and punched him in the mouth. He stopped fighting my mother and said, "you gone hit me!" I just looked at him as the neighbors broke out in laughter. They applauded me for intervening. Michael respected me for helping my mother. My mother told me not to intervene again. I couldn't sit by and watch him hurt my mother. This incident taught me that it was wrong for a man to put his hands on his woman.

I experienced police brutality during that time as well. It was early Christmas morning 1978. My parents bought us a bunch of toys. Pookie used to love race tracks and cars that plug in, I'm assuming because Edward was a race car driver. Damon, Deon, and Pookie were outside playing and hanging out but in the front yard. Damon had on some brand new skates his mother bought him. All of a sudden we heard screaming and crying coming from outside. Michael opened the front door to see what happened and saw Damon and my brothers on their knees with their hands on their head. Damon was curled up on the ground because an officer had kicked him in his crotch area. I was peeking out the door watching. These officers were white. Michael was fuming as he cursed the police out for assaulting children. Damon was 12, Deon 10, and Pookie 8 years old at the time. One of the officers said that they looked like gang members. At that time joining a gang was the furthest thing from their minds. Michael standing up to the police showed me that I must stand against injustice and not be silent. That situation also taught me that cops don't always uphold the law nor were they all good. I stopped accepting baseball cards from cops driving through the neighborhood.

When I was 7 years old, Liz died from an overdose. Allegedly her boyfriend had given her a deadly concoction of angel dust laced with PCP. They found her dead one morning lying naked in her bed. She lived across the street from us in a one bedroom house situated behind a two unit apartment Double R and Mrs. Campbell's family lived in. Liz was a young mother of two children: Tone-Tone and Bib-Bib. Her death rocked our community. Bib-Bib's father's name is Calvin. Leroy from 62NHC and Calvin were brothers. A short time after Liz's demise Calvin saw Liz's boyfriend and shot at him in broad daylight. To make matters worse for Tone-Tone is the fact that both of his parents died within a year of each other leaving him to be raised by his grandmother Maggaleen. I empathize with him because I couldn't imagine growing up without my parents. Life was too raw and scary thus I found myself being afraid at times from seeing so many traumatic events at a young age.

Another incident occurred when I was a child which left an indelible image in my mind. One night my parents took us to the drive-in movie theatre. When we got home our front door was opened and all of the lights were on in the house. Our house had been burglarized. When we walked inside I saw that the house was ransacked and every room had been rifled through. A lot of things were missing from clothes to silverware. Michael was upset about it. I was afraid and personally I felt a sense of betrayal because my family seemed to be liked and respected in the community. I wondered who did it and hoped that it wasn't the Six Deuces. Michael did his investigation and the next day he found out that my mother's best friend's brother broke into our house while high off of PCP.

My mother's friend's name was Lajuana and her brother's name was Herbert. Herbert stashed all of the merchandise under the vacant house next door to us in some cardboard containers thus we recouped all of our belongings. Lajuana had a son named Dee-Dee who I was close to. They too would become family to us. Michael forgave Herbert because he understood that PCP was a powerful hallucinogenic drug which caused people to do things they most often wouldn't remember doing. Prior to this incident Herbert used to try to outrun cars as they drove down the street while high. Nevertheless, shortly after this incident Lajuana's family moved. Herbert had broken a street code which was you never break into your neighbor's or anyone you know home because that would result in violence. Lajuana and Dee-Dee still came around though. All of these aforementioned events occurred by the time I was 8 years old and no doubt played a role in the person I would become.

CHAPTER THREE

As a kid it seemed that fighting was normal and the way to solve one's problems. My parents took us to church and we learned the basics about the Lord Jesus Christ, his sacrifice for mankind, and we were taught to love our neighbors and to be forgiving. However, in the hood people were squabbling up. For example, one evening I saw my neighbors Andrew and Roscoe fighting like cats and dogs. For them to be brothers they fought like they were trying to kill each other. Andrew even picked up a pipe and hit Roscoe with it. Roscoe rushed him, took the pipe from him, and beat him up some more. Neighbors were all outside watching. One evening I saw Insane Wang chasing this dude from the hood named Burt whipping him upside the head with a gas can. Another day I saw Crumb knock out this dude from Hoover in the field a few yards away from our house. The Six Deuces and Hoovers used to set up fights between their homeboys, bringing some of their top fighters to go head up. I never saw Crumb lose. Deon had a bully in the hood named Duke they used to fight often. Me and Pookie would jump in hitting and kicking Duke to help Deon win the fight.

Another day I went outside after waking up from a nap. My mother and one of her girlfriends were sitting on the porch looking at something. I sat down and followed their heads to see what they were looking at and I saw Onion beating the hell out of Leroy from 62NHC. Leroy fought back but he was no match for Onion. Onion was an original east side Crip. In those days dudes could lose a fight and not come back with a gun. Home boys didn't kill each other over a fight. Raymond Washington was out of my neighborhood. He founded the Crips and he came up with the idea for all East Side Crips to turn East Coast Crips because he didn't like how the West Side Crips which Tookie is credited with starting began fighting among themselves.

At the same time Michael used to buy pairs of boxing gloves for Christmas and have me and Pookie fight as entertainment for him and his friends. I would lose the majority of the time but I fought back because I couldn't let nobody hit me and not hit them back. I didn't like to fight Pookie because he was my brother, but I can't say the same for him. We became rivals who constantly fought as children. Burbanks gave us nicknames, he called Pookie ("Poison") and called me ("Killer"). As we got older I would come to realize that these names had meaning to them. In the hood you were respected if you had "hands." Subconsciously I began to think fighting was cool.

Two sources of peace, unconditional love, and comfort for me during my childhood was Doc and my red nose pit bull name Sassie. Doc was the owner of the corner drug store on 61st and San Pedro. He was a pillar in the community and was respected by everyone. Doc was around 6'0" 180Ibs in his mid 50's in age. He was light skinned with short hair and wore glasses. The thing about him that stood out to me is that he was humble, confident, cordial, and had a graceful way of dealing with everyone. I never heard him yell, curse, or become disrespectful towards anyone. Kids in the neighborhood used to go there and spend hours inside reading the comic books. My mother used to send me to him with a note and some money for cigarettes. I felt like I could get anything from Doc, he never denied me anything especially whenever I came back from swimming and was hungry. I didn't take advantage of his kindness and I never stole from Doc. His personality made you want to be honest with him and not disappoint him. He was too good to the community as a whole. At times I would go in his store and work behind his counter for free whenever he was busy in the back. I loved and respected him. Doc gave everyone a tab if you asked for it. I don't believe that he kept his store open for the money. I think he kept it open because he was dedicated to serving the community.

Now, Sassie and I were like kindred spirits. Michael got her as a puppy when I was a toddler so we grew up together. Sassie loved me and obeyed me more than she did my parents. Michael raised her to be aggressive and she would attack if provoked, however, I could take her for a walk through the neighborhood unleashed and tell her not to bark or bite anyone and she would obey me. She wasn't aggressive with kids. We used to let her join us in water fights and some sports. But if she sensed that you were a threat to me or my family she would go on the offensive. Sassie was there to comfort me if I got a whipping, hurt myself while playing, or if I was feeling down. She would come up and lick me in the face with her tail wagging. She also knew to stay out of kids' squabbles too.

One day Feleipe and I were going a few rounds in the boxing gloves. I was winning until Deon went and whispered in Feleipe's ear. When we squared up again, he put hands on me. I was upset with Deon for that. I went and sat on the side of the house crying. Sassie watched the whole ordeal. She sat about 15 feet away from me and then got up and came to me rubbing her head against my chest and licking me in the face because she saw that I needed comforting. People used to say we looked alike. Truthfully, I miss those days and cherish those memories. Those were good times. My family was still intact and crack cocaine was yet to take over the community.

CHAPTER FOUR

It was December 13, 1992, about a quarter past 9 o'clock at night. I was with Kemo, Lil Greedy, Lil Mont, Tiny Bubble, and Quacc. We drove to Lala's apartment on 61st and Miramonte. Earlier that day the Six Deuces and members from other factions of the East Coast Crips had made plans to go to this club called "The Name of the Game" which was located on 120th and Western. We went to Lala's apartment to kick it for a minute and to find out whether or not he and Ric ROC were going to the club too. When we got there, he invited us inside as we all greeted him. He had recently moved in so the place wasn't furnished yet. Rap music was playing while we hung out for about 20 minutes. Kemo and Lil Mont conversed with Lala while the rest of us listened to the music.

I was thinking about the club and how the night was going to turn out. I wasn't really a club person but I'd go if my homeboys went. I normally didn't say much whenever we got together. I was business-like. I developed this demeanor when I was 15 years old. Big Casper from Six Deuce and I were riding in his Cadillac and I was just talking and talking because I felt comfortable with him and he was someone I respected. He waited for me to finish and said that I talked too much. He wasn't sarcastic or disrespectful, but he was just matter of fact. I accepted his constructive criticism. I thought about what he said, analyzed my ways, and made a change. Being talkative can lead to snitching. Cas was lacing me on how to survive in the streets. Later on, some people would take my silence as me being standoffish, (meaning those who didn't know me) however, my intention was to exercise discretion not to offend anyone. Lala said he couldn't go to the club with us because he and RicRoc had something going on. He didn't say what that was and moments later we all parted ways. Quacc and Tiny Bubble were driving their own cars while Kemo, Lil Mont, Lil Greedy, and I were riding 4 deep in Kemo's black Monte Carlo on I-Roc rims. We drove through our hood and dropped Lil Mont off on 61st and San Pedro. We were looking for the rest of our homeboys so we could caravan to the club together.

We drove up 61st Street to the corner of Main Street and turned right heading towards Slauson. By this time Quacc had separated from us but Tiny Bubble followed behind us. When we turned on Main Street, I saw a black and white police car driving past us in a southbound direction headed towards Gage. I was on the run for two attempted murders on Newton Division L.A.P.D. officers and Glynnis had just bailed me out of Vista County jail in San Diego County on December 10th for a dope case I caught. I had gone to jail on December 3, 1992, so quite naturally I wasn't trying to go back plus Christmas was right around the corner.

The trip part about Oceanside is that the police had no knowledge of me being on the run for the police shooting in Los Angeles. I saw the police car make a U-turn on 61st to follow us. I told Kemo to smash out which he did. Tiny Bubble turned the corner and got in between Kemo and the police car. Kemo made a left on 59th Place and Main heading westbound. He parked across the street from Crip Cal's house which was approximately 30 yards from the corner. Kemo cut his car lights out and we duck down so as not to be spotted by the cops. Seconds later Tiny Bubble turned the corner and parked about 20-25 feet in front of us. The police blocked his car in with theirs, got out of their car, and began conducting a traffic stop. Crip-Cal came outside of his parent's house and observed the traffic stop.

Moments later we heard multiple loud gunshots which to me sounded like they came from the freeway and possibly Five Nine ("59") Hoover hood. The weapon sounded like an assault rifle. Maniac from 62 NHEC walked up and also observed the traffic stop from across the street. Upon hearing the gunshots, the officers immediately terminated the traffic stop, got into their car and sped off towards Broadway. Then they turned left and headed towards Gage. They rushed away from the traffic stop so fast that they left with Tiny Bubble's driver's license. Tiny Bubble's real name is Larry Anderson. We all momentarily exited both cars and conversed about how we dodged a bullet with the traffic stop and the gunshots we all heard. Somebody was getting off (meaning, doing a lot of shooting).

We wondered who it was and where it was coming from but we didn't pay it too much attention because we had no knowledge of what had just happened. A couple of minutes after the cops sped off we got back into the cars and Maniac got into Kemo's car with us Crip-Cal stayed home. We drove to 59th and Inskeep to see if any homies were hanging out there. Lil Greedy also lived on Inskeep. He went into his house to grab something and came back out in a minute's time. We got back in the cars and drove back through the hood. When we came to the corner of Gage and San Pedro, we saw Lil Owl from Six Eight East Coast Crip ("68EC") parked in his '83 turquoise Cadillac on gold Dayton rims in front of the apartments. His car was shot up and someone was in the passenger seat. A police car had just arrived and the Fire Department was on the way.

We drove across Gage, parked on the side of the apartments, and got out of the cars to find out what happened. I saw a small crowd of about 10 people there standing around watching. More people started coming and the crowd got larger. Lil Mont and Mya (Maggaleen's granddaughter) called the ambulance for Lil Owl and his passenger, which we learned was Junebug from 68EC. They were best friends. Lil Mont and Mya came up to us and fed us the details about what they saw. They also heard the gunshots and walked from 62nd Street and San Pedro to Gage where they found Lil Owl's car parked and riddled with bullet holes. Lil Mont said that he went up to the Cadillac and looked inside. He stated that he saw Lil Owl lying back in the seat not saying much and Junebug slumped down in the seat gasping for air. He also said Junebug's uncle named Big Biscuit from 68EC pulled up in his black Grand National Regal, got out of his car and walked up to the passenger side of Lil Owl's car and said something to Junebug. Lil Mont said Biscuit handed him a .45 Glock with an infrared beam on it (which he showed us) and told him to watch out for Junebug. He said Biscuit got back into his car and drove off. Biscuit and his brother named Dog supplied much of Los Angeles with water (PCP). They were millionaires.

Lil Owl and Junebug were balling too. Someone in the crowd commented that there were other people shot at the Mobil Gas Station.

That's when we learned that the gunshots we heard came from the gas station on Gage and Grand Avenue. While in the crowd I stayed in the background due to my being wanted by the police. The police at the scene were preoccupied with the shooting victims so I wasn't nervous. We waited there until the ambulance drove both Junebug and Lil Owl away. At that time they both were still alive. We got back into the cars and drove to Fred's Liquor Store on Gage and Broadway. Lil Mont was riding with another one of my homeboys. From the liquor store's parking lot I could see into the gas station. There was yellow tape all around the gas station, but I couldn't tell how many victims there were. There were a lot of police cars on the scene too. This situation was somewhat surreal because I had just seen Lil Owl and Junebug at Locke High School earlier that evening. The Q102 East Coast Crips ("Q102EC") was playing the Eight Seven Gangster Crips ("87GC") in football. That was also the first time I'd seen Lil Owl's Cadillac. It was clean.

We went into Fred's Liquor Store and purchased some items. I purchased a black San Diego Padre hat. The Padre hat is worn by the Six Duces due to the "SD" emblem on the front of it. Plus, when dudes from other hoods see a group of Crips wearing SD hats they know that the individuals are from 62 NHEC. The hat also matched my outfit. I was wearing a white Pendleton long sleeve shirt with black checkerboard stripes, black Cross Color Jeans and black Hirachi Nike's. I went back outside and waited in the parking lot while my homeboys lingered in the store. There was a crowd of about 25 people in the parking lot looking into the gas station. Some were conversing loud enough for me to overhear them. I learned that the victims within the gas station were not members of EC. That was good news to me seeing that I was from EC.

I saw Buckwheat and Lil Smokey from Six Nine East Coast Crip ("69EC") about 10 feet in front of me talking to each other with low voices. I couldn't hear what they were saying. I wondered what rival gang was responsible for this shooting. The Five Deuce Broadway Gangster Crips ("52BGC"), 59 Hoovers, and Swans were all immediate suspects as far as I was concerned. One thing was clear, this shooting was going to result in the Six Pack going to war to avenge this shooting. Junebug and Lil Owl were reputable Lil homies who a gang of people had love for including myself. The Six Pack represent the four factions of East Coast Crips located between Avalon and Grand Avenue, from Slauson to Florence. The factions are 62, 66, 68, and 69 EC. The 69's was the first hood to turn East

Coast, then 62, afterwards 68, and 66 came last. Nevertheless whenever there was war with a rival gang we all came together to smash our enemies.

When my homeboys came out of the store we had a discussion in the parking lot and decided to still go to the club because the hood was swarming with police. We went and got strapped. I got my .44 Magnum and Lil Mont had the .45 Glock so we had enough firepower to get us out of a jam if some drama unfolded. I refused to go to any event where gang members attended without being strapped. This was the year of 1992. In '92, the city of Los Angeles kicked off riots over the police being acquitted for the Rodney King beating. Young black men had lost their minds the city was on edge. We despised law enforcement and people were looting and burning down the city. In '92, L.A. had the record for homicides. 1992 was the year of the peace treaty between the Crips and Bloods, yet gang related homicides were at an all time high. Some accused the L.A.P.D of having a hand in some of the killings to undermine the efforts of the peace treaty.

Black males between the ages of 16-25 were at the highest risk to be murdered being that age was like having a target on your back. That's why I kept a gun on me the majority of the time. By the time we got to the club it was around a quarter after 11:00 p.m. We walked into the club and it was jumping. Rap music was blaring, the place was crowded, people were socializing, females everywhere it was going down. While at the club we noticed that no other East Coastes was there. It was about a dozen of us that showed up. Some of us took a photo together which Lil Greedy paid for. I noticed that there were a lot of Main Street Crips ("MSC") there. MSC's are rivals to the East Coast, but sometimes they don't be trippin because they were more concerned with making money than gang banging.

We stayed at the club for a couple of hours and decided to leave. On our way to the cars I observed at least 25 MSC's in the parking lot. I presumed that they were strapped too. When we got to the cars two dudes approached us asking us what hood we're from. I could tell that the main speaker was drunk. We responded by saying, "Six Deuce East Coast!" They said that they were from MSC. We repeated what hood we were from and they reiterated where they were from. Personally I didn't care. The drunk one was mean mugging me and I was staring him down. He told his homie that he didn't like me and he wanted to get down with me. I replied, "We can do whatever." My bro Lil Ghost intervened by saying, " a nigga will beat your ass fool!" I wasn't concerned about him, I was more concerned with his homies in the parking lot.

They hadn't noticed what was going on. I slipped my hand on my burner because this situation could get ugly. While we were having words with these dudes their homeboy Dell-Dog walked up with his gun drawn but pointed at the ground asking us what's going on. Dell-Dog used to be from Eight Nine East Coast Crips ("89EC"). We told him where we were from. He told us who he was and Lil Flux startled him by getting close up on him and saying, "I'm Flux." Dell-Dog looked at him and said he's from MSC. Lil Flux repeated what he had said. Dell-Dog allowing Lil Flux to get that close up on him wasn't a smart move because Lil Flux had hands and was known for knocking dudes out and breaking jaws. Months prior to this incident he knocked out Lil Skull from Seven Six East Coast ("76EC") at a party while Lil Skull was strapped with a Uzi and took it from him. I had pulled my gun out and was ready to shoot Dell-Dog and his homies once I saw he had his gun out. Dell-Dog squashed the situation by telling his homies to come with him. We got in our cars and left.

CHAPTER FIVE

On December 14, 1992, I woke up at approximately 6 o'clock in the morning. I normally didn't sleep for more than 5 hours, living the street life can keep a person sleep deprived. Quacc and Lil Mont came through 61st Street and San Pedro in Quacc's black Malibu wagon with dark tints and picked up me and Pookie. They had the sound bumping "Colorblind" by Ice Cube. Me and Pookie got in the back seat, I was still strapped. They told us that we were going down to the 68's to see what they wanted to do about Junebug and Lil Owl getting busted on last night. Word was that Junebug died on his way to the hospital. That's when I officially knew that bug died. I was devastated upon hearing the news because me, Junebug, and Lil Owl went back years together. I went to 66th Street Elementary School with Lil Owl, and me and Junebug met at Bethune Jr. High School when I was in the 7th grade. At that time I was the smallest and youngest homie from the Six Pack. Junebug was bigger and older than me. Him and Scooby from 68EC embraced me as a little brother, we were close.

Plus me and Lil Ghost had not too long ago spent about 45 minutes with Junebug at Sherman Kim's Mechanic shop on 64th and Main Street. He had his blue '64 Chevy on Daytons in the shop and I had my Cadillac in the shop putting some new brakes on it. The "64" he had once belonged to my Mexican homeboy Ruben. Ruben was from Florence/62EC. I told Ruben to sell Junebug the Chevy. Junebug and I had never met each other's parents, but we knew each other's people who were from East Coast. We drove down to 68th and San Pedro. We saw E-Walk from 68EC out there by himself. We parked on the 8 and bounced out the car. He walked up to us and we greeted him and extended our condolences to him for the loss of Junebug. His face was filled with grief. We let him know that we were down to ride for Junebug. We also asked him who they think did it. He said he didn't know. None of us knew for certain who was responsible for the shooting. We wondered whether or not someone was trying to carjack Lil Owl for his car and he refused to give it up. We told him if the 68's wanted to put in some work on whoever (meaning EC rivals) just let us know and we can go together. E-Walk said that Biscuit had the guns and that they couldn't do anything until he showed up in the hood. I found it strange that one person possessed all of the guns for an entire hood. After about 5 more minutes we got in the car and left.

Quacc drove to the Mobile gas station where the shooting took place. He parked by the gas pumps closest to Grand Avenue. The gas station was crowded like the night before never happened. Quacc went to pay for gas and we got out of the car and began looking around the gas station to see if we could see traces of the shooting. I walked by the cashier window and noticed a crack in the window that I hadn't seen before. It looked like it could've been a gunshot. I saw a video camera in the cashier window facing towards the outside of the cashier window and the gas pumps nearest Gage. Anyone coming in the vicinity of the cashier window would be on video. I wondered if the camera was on the night before and if the shooting was caught on tape. I looked around to find yellow tape, blood on the ground, bullet holes, glass, or any other thing that might confirm that a shooting took place. I didn't see anything. There was an alley behind the gas station that ran in an east-west direction. Although this gas station was in my neighborhood, it was on the outskirts of my hood.

On occasion you might find enemies getting gas there as well as EC allies as a result of the peace treaty. The EC's didn't agree to a peace treaty with our adversaries. We saw it as an avenue for enemies to come through and learn the ins and outs of our hood so that they could double back and kill our homies. Homies from the entire Six Pack got gas there as well. We got back in the car and Quacc dropped us all back off on 62nd and San

Pedro. Pookie walked to my mother's apartment on 62nd and Wall Street while me and Lil Mont hung out briefly on the Pedro. I saw Scottie in C-Rag's yard posted up by the garage. Scottie's nickname was "Ice" from 62EC. However, Scottie wasn't gang banging anymore. He was just selling drugs to take care of his family. He had a wife and two kids. You could most often find him at C-Rag's house kicking it with Rag's uncle and aunts drinking alcohol and selling crack cocaine. Scottie was tall and skinny. He could never gain any weight. He was my family and I loved him. I saw him and spoke to him then I went and sat down on the curb in between two parked cars 3 houses down from C-Rag's house to gather my thoughts.

I was tripping off of the fact that I had only been out for 4 days and yet so much had happened. My second day out I went to my homeboy Ralph's funeral. He had gotten killed by a Jamaican while he was coming out of the store on 61st and Broadway. Ralph had stopped gang banging too in the 80's. His nickname was Roscoe (not my neighbor Roscoe). He got shot while I was locked up in Vista County Jail. Now Junebug is dead and Lil Owl is in critical condition. I needed to get back on my grind and make some money. I was giving serious thought to running up in a bank and robbing it. The Foe-Trays ('43GC') and Foe-Duces ("42GC") had been hitting bank licks and were balling. Some of my homies had been talking about doing the same thing. I was desperate and down to go get it.

My mother was a crack addict who was struggling to raise 5 young daughters with no help from their fathers. Pookie wasn't much of a help either. He wasn't hustling. I felt like I was the older brother who had to watch out for him. Pookie was impulsive and would do crazy things on the whim without giving it much thought. One day my girlfriend Glynnis was driving down Avalon to drop him off in the hood and he saw some Swans on 75th Street and without telling her anything, stuck a .357 Magnum out of the window and started busting on the Swans. Glynnis was terrified and shook up by that incident. I had to check him about that. Bottom line I felt like everything was on my shoulders. Scottie walked up to me and said, "Mar-Loon." That's a name only he would call me. My name is Marlon and most of my homies called me Marlo. My nickname from 62NHEC was Baby Bam. Deon was Lil Bam and the original Lil Bam bumped up to Big Bam. I replied, "what's up cuz." He wanted to know how I was doing. I told him that I was straight. In reality physically I was well, but financially I wasn't doing so well and that was bringing on stress. I couldn't stand being broke. We spoke about Junebug and Lil Owl getting shot up the night before. He felt bad for them too. We conversed for about 15 minutes then I stood up and we parted ways. I never knew that would be our last conversation.

Lil Mont and I walked through the Ascot Walk and came out on 61st Street. The Ascot Walk is a walkway that is situated in the middle of the block and goes from 61st, to 62nd, to Gage. We headed to my uncle Spark's house. As we were walking Lil Mont broke my train of thought by yelling out that a car that drove by was some Broadways. I pulled out the strap and shot at the car 3 times. The car sped off and turned the corner. We didn't tolerate our enemies driving down the streets we hung out on because they could be coming through to do a drive-by or to see if we were hanging out so that they could go back and tell their homies to come through shooting. A police helicopter appeared in the distance, it was time to get ghost. When we got to Spark's house I saw Lil Smokey from 69EC drive past in his blue Cadillac on Daytons. Buckwheat was in the passenger seat. I threw up the EC gang sign to them but they just looked at me with serious looks on their faces.

At the time I didn't think much of it, I thought they were just in a somber mood due to Junebug's death. We walked in Big Mama's yard and headed through the driveway to the back house where Spark lived. Now, I grew up in the front house but some underhanded tactics took place back in the 80's, which caused my mother to lose the front house. Big Mama now owned the property and lived there. I'll explain how this occurred later. I saw that Spark's door was open and went inside of his house. I unloaded the 3 spent shells and reloaded the .44 Magnum. Spark heard the shots. I greeted him and we briefly spoke about what the shooting was about outside and the shooting at the gas station. The helicopter was flying over the hood now because we could hear it. I stayed inside of his house for a few hours. Lil Mont kicked it over there too then left about 45 minutes later. Around 11:30 a.m. I went back outside and saw Lil Mont. I think he was selling dope.

We walked down the street to C-Bone's mother's house where C-Bone, Lil Ghost, Ruben, Tiny Mont, and Crip-Cal were in the front yard hanging out. About ten minutes after we got there I saw Lil Smokey's Cadillac turn the corner from Avalon and drive past us again. We threw up the Six Deuce gang sign to him and Buckwheat and they didn't respond. They still had those serious looks on their faces. I felt like something wasn't right because it was the second time they came through that I knew of where they didn't respond to us saying what's up. I didn't say anything because I wasn't certain.

After about 30 minutes we parted ways and I went back to Spark's house. I was there for a few more hours chilling watching the Box music videos and talking to Glynnis on the phone. Glynnis was crazy. She loved to argue with me when we ran out of things to say on the phone as opposed to just hanging up and talking to each other later. She was on the phone trying to pick a fight with me when my cousin Lil Pookie came into the house and asked to use my gun, but he didn't say why. I told him no. He left the house and came back 5 minutes later asking for my gun again, but this time there was urgency in his voice. I asked him what's going on, that he needed a gun so badly. He replied, "Scottie got shot!" I immediately hung up the phone with Glynnis in mid-sentence after I told her Scottie supposedly got shot.

I went outside and walked towards the Ascot Walk. I just assumed that Scottie got shot on 62nd Street because that's normally where he was at. I didn't hear any gunshots so I was assuming that it might not be that bad. When I got to the Ascot Walk I saw Jolie. She was from 62NHEC and went by the nickname Baby Quarter Pound. I greeted her and as I turned into the Ascot Walk I saw Lil Mont coming towards me from the other end. He saw me, stopped, jumped in the air, and said, "the Swans killed Scottie!" He began to cry and that's when I knew he was serious. I replied, "he's on 62nd?" He said no, he dead on 69th and Avalon right now in Lil Wolf's car. Lil Wolf is from 68EC and he was paralyzed due to a shootout he had with the Swans. I wondered what happened to Lil Wolf. I looked and saw Ruben bending the corner in his gray '85 Regal headed in our direction. I flagged him down as he got closer. He stopped and Lil Mont and I got inside of his car. He had a chrome .45 semiautomatic pistol sitting on the seat. I pulled out my gun and told him to drive to 69th and Avalon because allegedly Scottie was dead on that street in Lil Wolf's car. I needed confirmation of his death because this didn't seem real. We drove up 61st to Wall Street and made a left headed towards 62nd Street.

When we got to the corner of 62nd I saw Scottie's wife LaShawn Farrington walking across the street headed home to their apartment which was next to the corner house on Wall Street. I saw her and got out of the car. I called her name as I approached her. She stopped and turned around. I said, "LaShawn, have you heard what happened to Scottie?" She said, "no, what?" I didn't want to be the one to break the news to her, but I felt an obligation to share the information I'd just received. I looked her in the eyes and said, "LaShawn, Scottie got killed on 69th and Avalon, he's dead in Lil Wolf's car right now, get in your car and go down there, we're on our way down there now." She looked at me without saying anything to me. I could only imagine how she was processing the news because I was still having trouble doing the same. I got back into the car and we drove off. We drove up San Pedro to 69th Street and made a left.

We drove to the middle of the block and stopped when we saw Lil Wolf's car (a blue Nova) surrounded by police cars and yellow tape. Someone was in the passenger seat dead. We backed up, parked, and got out of the car. A small crowd was starting to form. I heard a female call Lil Mont. I turned around and saw that it was his half-sister Angie. She was with another thick dark skinned female who may have been in her early 30's in age. We went to their yard and Angie let us into her house. Come to find out she and the other female were living there together. We had her hold our guns while we were on 69th Street. Angie was from Eight Tray Hoover ("83 Hoover") so I was surprised that she was living in EC territory. We went outside and I saw my homeboy JC pull up with a couple of more of my little homeboys in the car with him. We watched from Angie's front yard as the police tended to the crime scene.

Realization that Scottie was actually dead began to set in and the tears started to fall. I put my hands over my eyes to hide my grief, but I couldn't hide it. I was hurt. My chest heaved up and down a few times as I cried. JC put his arm around my shoulder to comfort me. I became filled with rage. All I could think of was retaliation. A crowd began to form around us and Lil Chip from 69EC walked up and kicked it with us. He extended his condolences and didn't say much. A brown Chevy passed by with 3 people inside. I recognized two faces in the car: Big Skull and Lil Junebug from 68EC. Skull was Junebug's uncle and Biscuit's brother. I thought I might have been tripping at the time but Skull was mean mugging us as the car drove past us. After about ten more minutes we grabbed our guns and drove back to our hood. We drove on Inskeep and saw Lil Greedy with a few other homies standing in front of his house. When we parked and got out that's when Lil Greedy gave us the rundown. The Swans didn't kill Scottie, Buckwheat from 69EC did. Someone from 66EC was there when it took place. Scottie didn't get killed on 69th Street either. The 68's were having a vigil for Junebug in the daytime on 68th Street. Scottie went with Lil Wolf to go pay his respect. Shortly after they pulled up Buckwheat had a young cat from 68 or 69 lure Lil Wolf out of the car to supposedly holler at him about something. Lil Wolf went for it and once Scottie was alone in the car Buckwheat walked up to the car and shot Scottie in the head in front of about 30 people. Some young cat drove Wolf's car on 69th and Avalon and parked it. They then sent my homies from 62EC a bogus message that the Swans did it so that we would take it out on them. Hearing this left my mind scrambled. I couldn't believe it.

Now, everything made sense like the pieces to a puzzle. That's why Lil Smokey and Buckwheat were whispering in Fred's Liquor Store parking lot. They blamed the 62's for Junebug and Lil Owl getting shot. That's also why those same two dudes were driving through our hood early in the morning. They were looking to catch a 62EC slipping with no one else around so that they could blast on him and get away with it. That's also why Skull from 68EC was mean mugging us when they drove past us. It was on with all of them as far as I was concerned. Shortly thereafter we had a big meeting in the hood and some 62's went and lit 70th and Main up where the 69's hung out while the police were still on 69th Street at the crime scene. No one from 69EC got killed during that shooting but the war was on. I didn't believe Lil Wolf set Scottie up because he grew up in the 62's and should've been from 62EC. Plus we knew his whole family and they had always been close with the Lang family. Thus, we gave Lil Wolf a pass. Buckwheat and whoever else was involved did put him in a trick bag though. Good thing for him that we allowed the voice of reason to prevail in the midst of this turmoil otherwise he would've ended up dead too.

It was real in the field. Buckwheat killed Scottie for a couple of reasons. The first reason is because he had a child with Junebugs auntie named Helen. They may have been married thus he considered Junebug his nephew. The second reason is because he still harbored ill feelings towards the 62's due to a fight he lost to Lil Flux on June 2, 1992, which was the 62NHEC hood day. We threw a party at a hall my homies rented in our hood and Denny from 69 EC caused a riot when he hit Lil Duce brother name Larry in the face busting his eye. My homeboy Ruben came up to me at the party and told me that some dude just hit Larry in the face. He was excited and angry. I went with him and saw Larry dazed and holding his eye. Blood was dripping profusely on his royal blue suit. Ruben spotted Denny and said, "There he is!" I walked up behind Denny and socked him in the side of his face. I immediately felt somebody push me away. I caught my balance, looked, and saw Lil Flux knockout Denny. About five of us started beating and kicking him which led to the party erupting in violence. It seems some of everybody was fighting. I didn't know Denny at the time or that he was Buckwheat's brother. I thought he was from another hood. Afterwards my homies were pissed that the 69's messed up our hood day so we went on 70th Street and Main to get down with them.

Some of my homeboys were already out of their cars squabbling with the 69's when I pulled up. I saw Lil Duce and Lil Quake putting hands on Denny. I saw Lil Cookie walk towards Godfather's apartment in the middle of the block. I saw Lil Ducc Down from 69 EC hit Lil Duce and when Lil Ducc turned towards him to rush him, Lil Ducc Down pulled a .45 semiautomatic on Lil Deuce and pointed it at his face. I immediately stepped in and pointed a .357 Magnum in Lil Ducc Down's face. He was startled. I don't think he realized that I was right there. He pointed the .45 at me and we had a standoff with guns pointed in each other's faces. I was ready to shoot him. I was looking into his eyes and I could see that he was thinking the same way. I said, "Bust nigga" Lil Mont ran up on the side of him with a .38 snub nose and pointed it at him. He got spooked. He turned around and ran away. As he ran towards Main Street he yelled out, "Fuck 62!" I looked and saw a large crowd standing on the corner of 70th Street and Main looking at the fighting. The 77th Street police station was there watching. But it was so much fighting going on they couldn't see everything. I saw Lil Flux square off with Buckwheat. Buckwheat swung and actually dropped Lil Flux to one knee. He then ran to Marstein from 69 EC mother's house and twisted the door handle to get inside but the door was locked. Lil Flux ran up to him and when Buckwheat turned around to face him Flux knocked him out and proceeded to beat him while he was unconscious. Buckwheat was left with two broken jaws and internal bleeding. He spent 4 or 5 weeks in the hospital. Big Casper pulled Lil Flux off of Buckwheat and said, "That's enough!" Casper possibly saved Buckwheat's life.

Many speculated that Lil Flux did him like that in retaliation for his brother Roc getting murdered by the 69's in 1990. Allegedly one of their little homies lost all of his money to Roc in a dice game on 61st and San Pedro. The money he lost actually belonged to another one of their homies he was selling dope for. To avoid getting a beat down for losing all of his money shooting dice he lied to the 69's and said that Roc jacked him for the money. Some of the 69's drove on 61st Street in a few cars to confront Roc. Lil Duce and Roc allegedly were the only 62's on the block. Big Cokie from 69EC confronted Roc and allegedly shot Roc six times with a .357 Magnum killing him. The 62's and 69's didn't go to war at that time due to our close bond with each other and the 69's alleged that Cokie tripped out. They disagreed with what Cokie did, especially once the truth came out. The conclusion was that their little homie who lied and Big Cokie was going to get knocked down whenever the 62's caught up with them. However, both of them disappeared and stopped coming around. My homies ran off Kendog from 69EC at that time too. Nobody knew for certain why Lil Flux smashed Buckwheat the way he did; we just had our own suspicions.

Kemo and I drove to Compton to his grandmother's house in Nutty Blocc hood. We stayed there for a few hours then drove back to the neighborhood. We came to 62nd Street and Broadway saw a dark colored I-Roc at the stop sign waiting to turn the corner. Kemo thought that it might be Buckwheat in the driver's seat so we pulled behind the car and I got out with a snub nose .357 Magnum and crept up to the passenger window and looked inside. Good thing I didn't impulsively start shooting because when I looked inside the car I saw Lucky Kemo's father!

CHAPTER SIX

Lucky saw me at his passenger window and rolled the window down. I heard some Isley Brothers playing as we greeted each other and I smiled and told him that I thought he was someone else. I went and got in the car with Kemo and told him that was Lucky in that car. He blushed and shook his head. We drove down to 62nd and San Pedro and parked in front of Maniac's house. My uncle Clydell lived behind him with his wife Rhonda and their 4 daughters. Many of our family members were over there gathered together. About an hour later me and a few of the homeboys were hanging out across the street strapped with an AK-47, M1-Carbine, and a .25 semi automatic pistol.

We were just hanging out making light conversation. We were strapped just in case the 69's or 68's dare come through our hood looking to retaliate. About 4 of my homies got in a car to go get something to eat. Me, Baby Dee, and Nutty were left hanging out. We avoided talking about Scottie getting killed. What we didn't know is that a neighbor called the police on us. A few minutes after my homeboys left to go get something to eat, two crash unit vehicles hit the corner from San Pedro driving fast towards us. We all broke and ran through the backyard of the house whose driveway we were standing in. I heard the police cars doors open and the sound of footsteps running behind us. We were being chased on foot. When we ran we dropped the guns because they were too big to run with.

I hopped over this brick wall in the back yard and came out on 61st

Street. Baby Dee went left and Nutty went right. As I was running out the driveway on 61st Street a cop came out of nowhere, flashed a light in my face, and told me to freeze. I stopped on a dime, turned around and ran back through the yard I was in but I didn't hop back over the brick wall to 62nd Street, instead I went left and started jumping gates down 61st Street towards Avalon. I could hear multiple police radios as I was running. Each of us was individually being chased. I wondered how many cops were out there because it seemed like we were surrounded. I hopped up on one wooden fence and looked over and saw two cops with guns drawn, but they didn't see me because they were looking in the opposite direction. I jumped down and hopped over another fence coming out on 62nd Street three houses down from where I started.

I heard the helicopter coming quickly. I could hear the police still chasing Nutty and Baby Dee. I hid in this backyard squatted down by some bushes. The helicopter was circling and shining its light searching for us. I looked and saw that the police had me cornered in. One of them spotted me and I knew it was over. It was a group of 4 officers that captured me. After I was cuffed up they asked my name and I gave them an alias. Then this white male officer looked at me and reached into his wallet pulling out a photo. He put the photo up to my face and said your name is "Marlon Evans." He then spoke into his radio and said, "we got him! we got Baby Bam!" All of the officers then reached into their wallets or pockets and pulled out a wallet sized photo of me. They concurred that they had me. I was escorted to a police car and placed inside. I had looked into the back seat of another police car while being escorted and saw that Nutty had been caught. The police were still chasing Baby Dee. I waited in the police car and determined not to talk to the police because anything I said would only be used against me. I wasn't going to help the police build a case against me or anyone else. A few minutes later Baby Dee was gaffled up too and placed in a separate police car.

A dozen officers huddled up on the sidewalk and had a brief conversation then got in the cars. There were 4 police to a car and 3 cars total on 62nd Street not to mention the two police cars on 61st Street. When they got in the car I was nervous and filled with anxiety because I had a feeling that they were going to take a detour into an alley along the way and beat me senseless while I was handcuffed. I had a flashback of 1987, when the police beat me up and dislocated my shoulder for running from them. Or the time they dropped one of my homeboys off in Blood territory and let the Bloods know he was a Crip forcing him to find his way home while being chased down by rival gang members. Officers Lisa Crawford and Arcinega were my arresting officers and they were known for being dirty. One of the officers in the back seat with me must've read my mind because he said, "don't worry we're not going to beat your ass, we're going to let the court do it." I felt relieved.

Once we arrived at Newton Division Los Angeles Police Department they split us up by placing us in interrogation rooms by ourselves. Officer David Lott came into the room I was in and began yelling that he was going to beat my ass for trying to kill two of his fellow officers. Lott was a light skinned black cop with a bald head. He began punching at my groin area. However, my pants were sagging so he couldn't get a good hit in. I was still handcuffed. I began to scream and yell hoping someone came to get this dude. No one intervened. After a few minutes he left. I want to believe that my screaming prevented him from going further.

About an hour later I was escorted by two detectives named Biczo and Berdin to another room. In this room there were about six officers waiting around a small table. 3 were sitting in chairs and the rest were standing up. The room was small and we were bunched in. I was placed in a chair and unhandcuffed. I didn't know what to expect. The detectives sat down in two empty chairs. They questioned me without reading me my rights. They began questioning me about the police shooting and I asked for my lawyer. They continued to question me and I refused to talk to them. I braced myself for a beating because they became upset. One officer slid a paper with writing on it across the table and ordered me to sign it. I slid it back to him and said, "I ain't signing shit!" I was already laced to never sign anything a police puts in front of you because it could be a doctored up confession and that's hard as hell to overcome.

The detectives began telling me that they had 8 eyewitnesses who were going to testify that they saw me shoot at the police. I knew that was a lie so I replied, "if you got 8 witnesses then let's go to trial, why do you need a statement from me?" Two new detectives had entered the room moments prior and were listening to the interview. Their names were Peter Schunk and Gil Herrera. Herrera interjected by saying, "you wanna play hardball motherfucker? We'll put a murder on you!" I replied, "who I kill?" He responded, "that's for you to find out." I knew they didn't have any evidence of me killing anyone so I took Herrera's words as a bluff and scare tactic to get me to cooperate. Biczo told me that he knew that I didn't know the car I [allegedly] shot at was the police, but that I thought it was the Broadways. I just listened. He told me that I could get less time if I cooperated. I asked for my lawyer. Herrera was irate and said, "we'll give you 15 years to life!" I replied, "I'm young, I can do it." Herrera was a short pudgy Mexican with glasses in his early 50's in age at least he looked like it. They all got up and left the room, but not before they had me handcuffed again. I wondered why two sets of detectives were questioning me. I figured that they must all be working the same case. I was oblivious to the sinister plot that was brewing.

Approximately 45 minutes later detectives Schunk and Herrera came back into the room. Schunk was carrying a black beanie hat and Herrera had a camera in his hand. Schunk had me stand against the wall while handcuffed behind my back as Herrera took the first photo of me. Schunk then placed the beanie on my head and Herrera took a second photo. When Schunk put the beanie on my head I looked at him and asked him what is this for? That's why if you look closely at the six pack photo card, you can see that my eyes are looking at Schunk to my right and not Herrera who was in front of me taking the photo. Schunk replied, "you were wearing your beanie when you had your AK." I was puzzled by that statement because I knew that I was being charged with two attempted murders of police from Newton.

The weapon used in that crime was an M1-Carbine assault rifle. I knew that because the police raided my mother's apartment 3 1/2 weeks prior looking for the weapon. The AK-47 we got busted with was clean so something was up. They took me and cuffed me to the bench in the hallway. Moments later they fingerprinted me and cuffed me back up. About ten minutes later they told me my brother Pookie and my cousin Lil Pookie snitched on me about the police shooting. I just listened as they began to give details of what they said. Certain things they told me were false but some things they said were accurate and the only way they could know this is if my brother and cousin opened their mouths. I had to choke back tears when I heard what they said. But I stayed solid under pressure. My brother and cousin had both got picked up when the police raided along with my uncle Willie Blue. But out of the 3 of them only my brother and cousin came back talking about what the police knew.

I had my suspicions then but I gave them the benefit of the doubt. I assumed that it was probably the confidential informant who gave them my name in the first place and had the police raid my mother's apartment and Big Mama's house. My cousin was on probation and should have been violated if he wasn't cooperating with the police. Yet he came home the same day, now I knew why. An hour later these same detectives drove me to the Glasshouse downtown which was a substation for Newton and Rampart Divisions of the L.A.P.D. I saw Baby Dee when I got to the holding tank where they process you in. I asked where Nutty was and he said he didn't know. Come to find out, Nutty got released because the police just wanted me and Baby Dee. I asked him what the police were questioning him about. He said that they asked him about the AK-47 and the shooting at the gas station. I don't recall him mentioning the police shooting.

He had been to prison before so I didn't think twice about him making any incriminating statements against me. Baby Dee was on parole and he was being charged with possession of the AK-47. They charged me with the M1-Carbine because they assumed it was the weapon used in the police shooting. I told him what the police said about my brother and cousin. He was shocked by that. He mentioned that his girlfriend Tashevae (pronounced "Tasha-vay") was pregnant with his first child. That was cool. I was happy for him. I had love for Tashevae too. However, I drifted into deep thought. I was recalling the interrogation and what the detectves said about putting a murder on me. I recall Pookie telling me that they threatened to put a baby's murder on me which was killed in a drive-by in 52 BGC hood. I was in Oceanside, California when that shooting happened. I was still tripping off the statement the detective made about me wearing my beany when I had my AK.

Now that I knew for certain that Baby Dee was charged with the AK I really didn't understand what the hell he was talking about. Baby Dee mentioned again that his girlfriend was pregnant. I started to think about Scottie's murder, his funeral, the fact that I wouldn't be able to get at the cats responsible, my brother and cousin giving statements against me, I was facing a life sentence, Christmas was right aound the corner, I needed to contact my mother, Glynnis, Angie, and Sandy to let them know where I was at. Meanwhile, he continued to mention Tashevae being pregnant when he wasn't facing more than 3 years with half-time. After about the fifth time I snapped and said, "nigga fuck that fat bitch!" "These muthafuckas are about to try to give me life for some bullshit!" I didn't want to hear it because to me he was starting to sound weak. I felt like if he was that concerned then he would have been with her and not hanging out on 62nd Street. He got quiet. We spent the night in the

Glasshouse and two days later was transported to the L.A. County Jail.

CHAPTER SEVEN

Once we arrived at the county jail and got processed we were taken to the 9000 floor. As soon as we walked in the dorm it was chaotic. We saw our homeboys Slim-bad from 59EC and Baby Ed from 62EC. We greeted each other and then briefly conversed about what we got busted for. The 9000 floor was rugged and violent. Inmates had cash money on their persons and were able to wear their personal tennis shoes thus strong arm robberies were going down. A coward didn't stand a chance. You had to man up and be willing to get violent in order to survive. Whites were victimized and robbed by blacks and Mexicans. Bloods ("Damus") for the most part couldn't walk the mainline. There were a few damus who were riders and did walk the mainline. They earned their respect. However, there were some damus who wouldn't even bang their hoods for fear of a beat down. Crips dominated the county jail and dudes were really gang banging. The police were strictly no nonsense and would dare you to get out of line so that they could beat you half to death and then hide you from your visitors until your wounds healed up.

Lee Baca ran a cold system in those days. In the hallway there was a huge portrait of John Wayne which symbolized that the county jail was run by red-neck whites, many of whom were racist. The county jail could make you or break you. There was a saying in those days, "if you can make it in the county jail you can make it anywhere." Everywhere you went you were going to have dudes hitting you up asking where you were from. If you said the wrong thing dudes may rat pack you. It didn't happen all the time though. Wayside was notorious for this. You had to bang your hood no matter what. If you did something that was dishonorable, word spread through the county jail fast and dudes would be lying in wait to run into you so that they could beat you down and rob you. Some dudes' names went bad in the county jail due to fear.

Race riots between the blacks and Mexicans were ongoing and could pop off at any moment so you had to stay alert and keep your shoes on. Due to the riots many brothers were putting blackness over gang affiliation. It was hard to set-trip on your rivals when they stood by your side and didn't fold in the midst of warring with the Mexicans. Rats roamed the cells and hallways and the showers were filthy. If you didn't have any shower shoes then it was best to bird bath rather than go barefoot in the shower, it was that bad. You also had to watch out for informants seeking to learn about your case and get you to confess so that they could snitch on you in exchange for a lighter sentence.

I made collect calls to my mother and Glynnis to let them know what was going on with me. Glynnis was planning to visit me. I felt bad about being locked up for the holidays. My last Christmas on the streets was in 1987. A couple of days later I got arraigned on the police shooting case. I met my attorney, a middle aged black man wearing too much gold jewelry on his fingers and neck. His hair was slicked back. His name was Oran Franklin. I prejudged him on his appearance rather than his skills and that was wrong. I had heard many stories about dump truck public pretender attorneys who specialized in getting deals but if an inmate rejected the deal and went to trial the attorney wouldn't fight for him/her but instead would allow the District Attorney to introduce inadmissible evidence or fail to adequately investigate the case so that the client could get washed up.

I admit that hearing those types of stories distorted my mind towards all public defenders. I didn't trust Mr. Franklin. I was in the Municipal Court tank with about six other inmates when Mr. Franklin walked in and called my name. I stood up and told him I'm right here. He introduced himself and we greeted each other. He was holding a big yellow envelope full of photographs of the crime scene. He asked me if I wanted to look at the photos and I said yeah. He then explained how he had another case that he was preparing to go to trial on and thus he was going to ask the judge to give him a 60 day extension of time. I didn't have a problem with it. As I viewed the photos I realized that there were only pictures of the police car shot up and 62nd Street. There were 75 pictures total. After I viewed about 28 photographs I asked Franklin if I was on any of these pictures. He said no. I then replied, "Why do I need to look at these pictures then?" I was being an ass-hole. He became upset and said, "if you weren't running your big mouth telling everybody what you did your ass wouldn't be in jail now!" Mr. Franklin had a back bone and didn't hold any punches. His words sliced me like a knife because they were partially true.

I did tell my cousin Lil Pookie that my homeboys busted on the police, but I never told him I did it. I didn't brag about it either. He asked me what happened when me and Lil Mont saw him the next day and I told him. I became upset as well and cursed Mr. Franklin out. I told him he hasn't known me for 5 minutes and yet he's telling me what I supposedly told someone else. I called him a punk muthafucka and a bitch ass nigga. I was wrong for that. When we walked inside of the courtroom I tried my best to get him removed from my case. However, the judge kept him on. I was transported back to Wayside.

I ran across my homeboy Young Rob from 62EC. He was on trial for a kidnap murder robbery which occurred in the parking lot of Hollywood Park Racetrack. Allegedly he jacked a dude for $250,000.00 cash money and murdered him in broad daylight. He had 25 eyewitnesses to the shooting and he was facing the death penalty. I grew up with Rob and knew his whole family. His father Skip had • died in a fire at his workplace. His mother Mrs. Ross was a devout Christian and his sisters Sarah, Mamie, and Niecey were close friends with my mother. His older brother June was cool too. He was originally from 43 Hoover. We greeted each other and chopped it up about our cases. He said that it looked good. I myself didn't get that when there were supposedly 25 eyewitnesses to the crime. I did wish him the best though. I still needed the police reports to my case so that I could see what evidence the police had on me. Nevertheless it was good to see Rob. He used to frequent the bookie joints in the hood at a young age gambling on horses. The players respected him because he was a hustler. I loved him because he was a loyal friend and a rider for the neighborhood. We spent a few hours in the court tank conversing about the hood before we were separated and sent back to our housing facilities. I enjoyed the moment because due to the cases we were fighting there was no guarantee that we would ever see each other again.

Once back at Wayside I met a few cats that I became cool with such as: T-Stone from Blood Stone Villain ("BSV"), Fat-head and Lil Cee from Nutty Blocc Compton Crip ("NBCC"), Keystone from 30 Blood Stone Piru ("BSP"), Sasquatch, Blue, and Corkey from School Yard Crip ("SYC'), Baby Shady and Tank from 74 Hoover, Baby Huey from Marvin Gangster Crip, Fishbone and Lucky from 8 Tray Gangster Crip ("ETG"), Lil Tone-bone from 76EC, Peanut, G-Rat, and BK from 1st Street EC, Cat, Baby Tadpole, Gil-bone 1 and 2, Teaspoon and Baby Bam from Rolling 60's, G-Smurf and Sherm from Rolling 40's, Culpepper and Reese from Harlem 30's, Bogart from 87GC, Slim from 76EC, Lil Man from 59 EC, Snoop and Lil Doc from 69EC, C-Bone from 52BGC, One punch from Rolling 20 Bloods, Demon from 357 GC, my cousin Lil Set-trip from Bounty Hunter Bloods, Shag, Mac, A.D., Tone-tone and Cisco from Grape Street, Frosty and Pretty boy from 118 Carver Park Compton Crip, Dre, Lucky Fella, K9, and Dee from Avalon Gangster Crip, D-Dog, Lil Moon and Le-bow from Front hood Compton Crip, Pee-Wee from 118EC, and G-Spade from Swan.

I was in Wayside for about a month and a half when I heard my name being called out on the loudspeaker. They were telling me to report to the captain's office. It was around 7:30 p.m. I asked my unit officer where the captain's office was located. He told me where to go. I was nervous about this because normally if you are being called to the captain's or the chaplain's office for an unknown reason then it's most often that there has been a death in your family. I braced myself for the bad news. When I walked inside of the captain's office I saw detectives Schunk and Herrera. I asked them what's up. They replied, "we're charging you for the murders of Junebug and 3 other people!" I was stunned. Out of all the people I don't know how they came up with me killing Junebug. I said what 3 other people? They said the 3 people who died with him. That's the first time I knew how many victims died at the gas station. I was in disbelief. All I could think about is what they told me at the police station about putting a murder on me. For them to tell me that means that they've done it before to someone else.

This was pure retaliation for the two attempted murders on Newton officers. I wanted to kill both of them right on the spot. I didn't have a damn thing to do with the shooting at the gas station and me, Lil Owl, and Junebug all got along and had never had any discord between us.

Furthermore the 62's and 68's had never fought each other, not even at a house party where dudes often get drunk and start tripping. I was wondering who these bastards manipulated into identifying me. They asked me if I wanted to talk to them about it. I replied, " fuck you and suck my dick!" I didn't say anything to them. And why would I, when they knew I wasn't involved. Any witness they claimed to have against me was a coerced witness by them and that's fact. I knew my alibi and I wasn't about to expose my cards to them. They fingerprinted me to book me for the charges and I went back to my unit. When I got back Lil Gil-bone asked me what that was about and I told him, " cuz they just charged me with 4 murders!" I still couldn't believe it. I didn't know who the witness was against me but one thing was certain he or she was LYING!!!

I called my uncle Spark and Glynnis and broke the news to them. Neither of them could believe it. My world was being turned upside down by lies orchestrated by detectives Schunk and Herrera. That weekend Glynnis came to visit me. She had been coming to see me often and was making sure that I was financially straight as well as keeping money on the phone for me to call. We had a good visit. She kept my spirits up. When one is going through trials and tribulations it's good to know you have someone on your team who loves and believes in you. I needed all the love I could get. Glynnis and I went back to 1987. I had just come out of an accident and my face and left arm was badly scarred. Shavonda was going to Washington High School at the time and I was going to El Camino Real High School. I took a photo of myself in front of my house. Shavonda got a hold of the picture and took it to school. A few days later she rushed to tell me that she had someone for me. I said who? She said her homegirl name was Glynnis. That name was unique but strange. I played along. I said how is it that she likes me when she doesn't even know what I look like? That's when Shavonda told me about the picture I took and how she took it to school and Glynnis saw it and commented on it. I was shocked because that photo in my opinion was ugly. I was wondering if the girl had good sense. Shavonda gave me her phone number and I said that I would call.

At that time I was already in relationships with Chivetta and Creshinda not to mention other female fans in the neighborhood. I was 14 years old at the time so don't judge me. I called Glynnis to introduce myself and we spoke for about 30 minutes on the phone. I was trying to see what she was about, meaning is she immature and childlike as most 14 year olds are. If she was then I wasn't going to mess with her. We spoke on the phone a couple of more times and I decided to go pay her a visit. I had my homeboy Lil Quake take me over her house. When we got there I told him not to drive off but wait until I gave him the signal that it was cool. It was around 5:30 p.m. I walked to her front door and rang the doorbell. Her mother came to the door. Her name is Shirley. She looked at me with a frown and said, "Who are you here for?" I said, "Does Glynnis live here?" She replied, "Glynnis is on punishment and can't have company." I didn't let that deter me. I said, "ma'am can you have her come to the door just for 5 minutes, then." Shirley looked at me with a stern look and yelled out "Glynnis you have company at the door, some little boy." I heard Glynnis yell from upstairs "Who? What's his name?" Shirley asked me my name and I said "Marlon" which her mother repeated to her. Glynnis yelled back, "No, I'm not coming downstairs cause my hair ain't done!" Her mother and I looked at each other and I thanked her for her time. I went and got back in the car with Lil Quake. He said, "what happened?" I replied, "she wouldn't come downstairs." Glynnis and I wouldn't officially meet until September of 1991, after I got out of the California Youth Authority ("CYA").

In July of 1989, I was arrested for selling drugs/possession of crack cocaine and sentenced to two years in CYA. I was housed at Paso Robles in San Luis Obispo, California. I had some homeboys there such as: Lil Buzzie 89EC, Lil Ron-Ron 97 EC, Boo-Capone 1st Street EC, Lil Frog 62EC, Ken-dog 190 EC, Lil Wac 68EC, Lil Sandman 68 EC, Lil Bow-low 66EC, Shorty, Sons of Samoa ("SOS") EC, Lil Red-Devil 118EC, Lil Animal-Man 118EC, Slic-Ric 68EC, Lil Scrappy 43GC, and Lil Insane, Atlantic Drive Compton Crip. My bro Lil Fish from 62EC looked out for me while I was down and I paroled to his house when I got out in July of "91."

In September of '91, Shavonda brought Glynnis and her cousin Tammy over to Lil Fish's house to meet me but I was down the street with my bro Lil Ghost. We saw them when they came out of the yard. Shavonda saw us and began yelling my name. We went to go meet them. At the time I didn't know who these females were. I had forgotten about Glynnis because we hadn't spoken in years. When we met up I looked at both females and wondered which one it was that wanted to holler at me. Shavonda said, "Marlon this is Glynnis, Glynnis this is Marlon." I looked at Glynnis and she was attractive. She wore white Guess jeans, a white shirt with a slogan on it, and some white leather shoes which may have been loafers. She was 4'11 weighing 115 lbs and dark complexioned. Her natural hair was in a perm and it was long. I was really feeling her beauty. Her hands and nails were nice too. We shook hands and I said, " OK so you are Glynnis." She was timid in the beginning. We hung out for the rest of the day. Later that night we went to the Vermont Drive-In with my homie Baby La-La, Shavonda, and her home girl Renee in Baby La-La's Cadillac. We enjoyed each other's company.

I was single and fresh out of CYA and hustling to get up on my feet. I hadn't considered whether or not I wanted to be in a serious relationship. She left her pager in Baby Lala's car so the next day he brought it to me. Within a couple of hours the pager started buzzing. I ignored it because it wasn't my pager. The pager continued to go off non stop until I checked the number and saw that it was hers. I didn't call her back immediately because I was on the block grinding. But she continued paging so I went and called her from the phone booth on 61st Street and Avalon. She was excited to hear from me and we spoke for about ten minutes before I hung up. I had a gun and dope on me so I was watching out for the police and enemies driving down Avalon. During the conversation I told her that I'm going to get her pager to her but she told me to hold on to it. I was flattered that she wanted to keep tabs on me.

A couple days later I had to visit my parole officer. I was enrolled in a 12 step program at the parole office. My parole officer noticed the pager and asked me about it. I told him that it wasn't mine and that it belonged to a female friend of mine. Evidently he didn't believe me because when it was time to leave he told me to follow him into a back room. Once inside he had me sit down in a chair while another parole officer walked into the room and stood by the door. My parole officer then said, "I'm violating you for selling drugs." I lied and said I didn't sell drugs but he replied, "you got a pager so you must be selling drugs!" He gave me a 90-day violation.

I didn't blame Glynnis though because my parole officer was tripping. I was angry but it was out of my control. Once at the county jail I contacted Shavonda and told her what happened. She contacted Glynnis and told her what happened. Glynnis immediately rushed down to the county jail and called me out on a visit. I was happy to see her. She gave me the impression that she was cut from a different cloth than any other female I had been with. At the end of the visit she gave me a wet $40.00. It was called a wet $40.00 because the officer would dip the money in water prior to handing it to an inmate. I was appreciative of the money. About a week before I was about to get out I decided to call Glynnis just to see how she was doing because we hadn't spoken since I left the county jail. I called her from a park in Imperial, California while out on a work crew. I wasn't expecting anything from her.

When she answered the phone I was glad to hear her voice. She told me that she had been to my hood with Lil Ghost and she met some of my homies. They embraced her as my woman. I was surprised because we never discussed us being an item and I had gone to jail right after we met. For that reason I didn't think that she was even thinking along those lines. She surprised me even further by telling me that she bought me some clothes, shoes, and a leather jacket. I asked her how she knew what size I wore and she said that Lil Ghost told her. She was more than what I even imagined. I didn't know what to say. No other female had ever bought me any clothes before. It was always me doing for them. I was starting to really like Glynnis. She was claiming me as her man so I fell in line with it and we were inseparable from that moment. Eventually I fell in love with her and she inspired me to dream big. The things that stood out to me about her was that she was a go-getter, intelligent, street smart, she had a sense of humor, she dressed very well, she was hood but classy, and she didn't take crap from anyone. Glynnis became my backbone. She was my ride or die and she would do anything I asked of her. I wanted to do great things for her to show her how much she meant to me. Chivetta came around again once I was out and I was enthused to let her know that Glynnis was my woman. She acted as if she wasn't tripping but deep down I know that she felt some type of way seeing me with another female.

Unfortunately I received another 90-day violation two weeks after I was out for some more nonsense. My home girl Lil Quarter Pound allegedly borrowed her aunt's Hyundai for drugs before I even got out from my last violation. The aunt smoked the dope up and then reported the car stolen. I was at the Jack N the Box on Florence and Broadway in the Drive-Thru ordering food with my home girl Half-Pint in the passenger seat when a police car pulled behind us. Next thing I knew I heard Half-Pint say, "oooh!" I looked at her and asked her what's up. Then I heard the officer on his speaker telling us to step out of the car with our hands up. We got out of the car and I saw five police cars there with numerous officers standing out of the cars with guns drawn. They had me back up and lie face down on the ground. I followed their instructions. I was handcuffed and taken to 77th Street LAPD Substation where I was charged with carjacking. I asked the officer when the car was supposed to have been stolen and he said sometime towards the end of December. I was still serving my violation during that time so I was confident that the case would be dropped and I'd be going home. Half-Pint got released immediately. The next day a detective spoke to me about the robbery. When I told him my alibi he went and checked it.

Afterwards he came back and told me that the charge was dropped but that I had a parole hold which my parole officer could drop and I'd be released. My parole officer came to visit me a couple of hours later. He violated me for 90-Days again. I truly thought that my relationship with Glynnis would fail because I kept going to jail on her. However, she continued to stick around which was a testament to how dedicated she was to me. My feelings for her grew stronger. My mother didn't like her allegedly because she used to clash with her own mother periodically. But their bumping heads was just typical teenager drama. Personally I sensed that my mother may have been jealous of her. While in the county jail she visited me often and made sure that I was straight. I met an older cat named "Shitty." He was from Downtown and sounded like Redd Foxx when he spoke. Shitty used to crap his pants on occasions, that's how he got his name. He was around 5'6 and 160 lbs. If someone clowned him for crapping his pants he'd yell out, "Nigga I'll tear your head off and shit in your neck!" Everyone would fall out laughing. I used to tell Glynnis about him and make her laugh.

On April 28, 1992, I was released. That was the day before the riots. I took a cab home not knowing that Glynnis was on her way to pick me up with my brother Pookie in the car. She kept a rental car on deck. She also came from a good middle class family. Once out we were back in motion. We spent most of our time together and we both were horny as hell. We made love in a variety of places. The sex was great and all was right in the world. She introduced me to her home girls and grandparents and they liked me. I loved her but I learned that Glynnis was aggressive and would literally swing on me, try to kick me in the crotch, or pick up something to hit me with if we had a disagreement. I'd defend myself oftentimes just by simply restraining her.

Once she kicked me in the face while I was driving and almost made me wreck. She was out of control at times there were times I had to physically restrain her. Her mother once saw me with scratches on my face and neck and asked me how come I continue to allow Glynnis to assault me.

I replied, "Shirley, I don't want to hurt your daughter." I could've easily hurt Glynnis but that wasn't in my DNA. Glynnis used to enthusiastically tell me how her home girls used to fight their men and I began to believe that she thought that it was cool. Her parents weren't abusive towards each other so I sensed that she was picking up these behaviors from her girlfriends. Glynnis had a lot of qualities that I liked such as she was good with children, she had a kind heart, she was loyal, affectionate, unselfish, and she was business savvy. She knew a few ways on how to get money. She was knowledgeable in that way. However, the constant back and forth between us made it difficult at times to love her the way I wanted to.

One incident occurred on the day Big Sike got killed. One of my little homies saw her in my neighborhood dressed in some Daisy Duke shorts, a see through blouse with a bra, and some open toed pumps. He came and told me. A few minutes later I saw Glynnis and her home girl in some burgundy small car as I was coming from my home girl Niecey's apartment on 61st and Wall Street. I saw her and told her that it wasn't a good time to be in my neighborhood because Sike got killed plus she should go home and change. She copped an attitude and argued with me. I then said something slick to her friend like, "what's up with you can I have your number?" She didn't respond. I was actually only playing with her. I respected Glynnis enough to never dare holler at another female, especially someone she knew in her presence. I laughed as I got into Lil Ghost Cadillac and started the ignition. Glynnis got out of the car, walked up to me, and socked me in the eye with a ring on her finger. Pain ripped through my eye as I grabbed it and water ran down my face from my eye. I heard Glynnis run back to her girlfriend's car laughing, get in, and yell "go pull off!" I actually thought that she busted my eye until I looked at my hand and saw that the fluid wasn't blood.

I was angry as I drove to the corner of 62nd and San Pedro and pulled behind her girlfriend's car. I got out of the car and walked up to the passenger window and socked Glynnis in the forehead. I didn't hit her like I would hit a man but it was hard enough to let her know I wasn't playing. I told her again to get up out of my hood. She didn't listen. I drove to 61st Street and Avalon with Glynnis and her home girl following me. I hadn't even recognized Pookie in the back seat of their car. I parked and got out and stared at their car. I was frustrated that she was defiant and I said, "so you ain't going to leave?" Then I jumped on the hood of their car and ripped off the visor above the sunroof and threw it on the ground. Glynnis got upset and told her friend to get out as she hopped in the driver's seat. I was on the sidewalk when she backed the car up and drove up on the sidewalk trying to run me over. I immediately dived out of the way and pulled out a .357 Magnum and fired a shot at the car but I was actually trying to hit the tires, not her. She nearly wrecked.

That's when I noticed my brother in the back seat waving his hands for me not to shoot anymore. I looked around and saw about 25 people watching the spectacle. I began to feel embarrassed and ashamed. That's when I knew that we both were completely out of control.

Glynnis told her parents that I shot at her. When I saw her mother a few days later while looking for Glynnis at her parents home she asked me if I shot at Glynnis and I told her no I tried to shoot the tire out after she tried to run me over. Glynnis was scared of me for about a week until we made up. But I felt bad about the whole situation more than Glynnis knew or realized. She was the person I wanted to marry and have children with but here we were acting like fools in public. We was the talk of the town in my neighborhood for quite some time in a negative way which I didn't like. I blamed myself more because I knew better than that. I used to think to myself, "what if I'd shot her?" That was scary to even contemplate. I wouldn't have been able to explain that to her parents.

We made a beautiful couple and everyone loved us and thought we were crazy but It was then that I began thinking we needed to take a break until we learned to respect and love one another without the drama. The path we were on somebody was going to get hurt. Glynnis had gone and got my name tattooed on her three times. I knew that she loved me deeply and I loved her but we struggled with expressing love towards one another properly. I frowned on domestic violence but here I was indulging in it. In fairness we did have some good times together. We used to go out to breakfast, dinner, the movies, certain parties, and hood functions and have a good time with each other. I used to love holding her in my arms and waking up to her body snuggled against mine. We didn't squabble all the time but it was starting to become more frequent and more violent. This was the first relationship that I'd ever been in that was abusive and I didn't like it. Shortly thereafter we broke up for a few months.

Afterwards Angie and I got closer. However, Glynnis and I reunited and stayed together. My relationship with Angie slowed down but didn't end. I was wrong for that. My relationship with Glynnis was better though we did still argue from time to time. Glynnis was my heart and any female I dealt with when we separated knew about her including Angie. I was disappointed that I was back in jail. My family and Glynnis needed me free. I also knew that I needed a new career aside from a criminal lifestyle. I had enrolled into Maxine Waters trade school when I was out. I was taking up mechanical engineering and an electronics course on the weekends. But I was so distracted that I couldn't commit to anything that was going to better my future. I dropped out of school. I was also looking over my shoulder the entire time I was out because I never reported to my parole officer once released due to the two bogus violations he made me serve. I didn't feel like he was trying to help me succeed in life but only punishing me for the smallest infractions. For that reason I was reluctant to get a job fearing that my mailing address would be a means for the parole officer to locate me. I decided to start rapping. Although when I started rapping I wasn't any good. I was confident that I would eventually get better with continued practice and writing and I was right.

CHAPTER EIGHT

I went to court and got arraigned on the multiple murder charges. I plead not guilty and I met my attorney. He was a middle aged slender black man with a Jamaican accent. His name was Patrick Atkinson. I asked him for copies of the police reports which he agreed to send me. I was actually charged with 4 murders and one attempted murder. The attempted murder was on Lil Owl. The D.A was seeking the death penalty. All I was thinking was "how was I going to tell my mother this news?" A few days later I went back to court for the two attempted murders of Newton Division LAPD officers. I apologized to Mr. Franklin for disrespecting him and confessed to him that I prejudged him on his looks. I also admitted to having a fear that as a Public Defender he wouldn't represent me to the fullest which could lead to my being convicted for a crime I didn't commit. He listened to me without interrupting and when I finished he also apologized for the things he said. From that moment on we were good and he had my back. He also gave me all of the police reports in the case. While reading them my suspicions about Baby Dee were true. He had made an incriminating statement against me. In his statement he alleged that I told him about the shooting but I never admitted to being the shooter. He also stated that but by the way I was talking he could tell that I was the shooter. He further alleged that I use to call the M-1 Carbine "the Murder 1."

Actually, another one of my homeboys came up with that terminology. Baby Dee's statement was gut wrenching because he is someone I grew up with and embraced as a big brother. I couldn't believe that he made a statement on me all because he wanted to get released to see the birth of his first child. The sad part is that he still went to prison for possession of the AK-47. Now consider this, if I really was the shooter why wouldn't I just tell him I did it? He was somebody that I trusted for years up until that point. Next, I read my brother's statement. He lied to the police a few times during the interview. He was making up stories as he went along. Clearly he didn't understand that talking to the police was a no-no. His lies were so blatant that the detectives just started calling him on his lies. In the end they got him to agree that he heard that I was the shooter. One by one the people closest to me were crumbling under the pressure of interrogation by experienced detectives when all they should've done was remain silent which was their right to do. Lastly, I read my cousin Lil Pookie's statement. He stated that me and Lil Mont came over to Big Mama's house where he was living and spoke to him about the shooting. Truth is that we went over there just to kick it with him and he asked us what was all of that shooting he heard last night? He saw the news detailing a police shooting but wanted to know what happened. He had just left and went home approximately ten minutes prior. When he asked I told him the "homies got off on the police."

In his statement he alleged that I told him "we" busted on the cops. That's false. The evidence showed that there was only one shooter. So why would I say "we?" I never included myself. Also up until that point he and I were close like brothers and, like Baby Dee, I had no reason to believe he was a snitch. Thus why wouldn't I just tell him I did it? I had no reason to keep a secret from him or Baby Dee. I could've easily lied to both of them and said I don't know what happened or just refused to answer the question. The next statement I read was Tony Corley Jr.'s. That was Tone-Tone, Maggaleen's grandson. He alleged that he saw me the day after the shooting on the corner of 62nd and San Pedro early in the morning and I had a Tech-9. Also that I told him about the shooting. He assumed that a Tech-9 was used in the shooting. Truth is I didn't have a gun on me when I saw him out at around 7:00 a.m. by himself. I told him that he shouldn't be hanging out because the police got shot at last night and they are going to most likely come through the hood gaffling up anyone they think is from 62EC and take them down to the station for questioning. He had some bags of weed on him that he was trying to sell so I just gave him a heads up. I never told him that I shot at the police and evidently he didn't heed my admonition to get off the streets. I read the original police report from officer Derek Fellows. The police shooting occurred on November 22, 1992. He stated that when he and his partner pulled up they saw about 20 gang members with guns. Also that he didn't see the shooter. However, a few weeks later he made another report claiming that he recognized me as the suspect who kept popping his head up and down behind a truck that was parked in the driveway of the house we were hanging in front of. Fellows was lying. His original report is the truth.

He only made the second report after he saw me get brought in for the crime. This is an underhanded tactic police officers use to bolster their case and secure a conviction. Plus if he saw 20 gang members with guns then how in the world was he allegedly focused on me behind a truck? If he saw me, and I was the shooter, then why did he state in his first report that he never saw the shooter? Fellows wasn't credible. Him being a police officer doesn't make the things he said in his second report true. The detectives found a metal shroud that goes on top of an M1-Carbine in the driveway. Also for the record I wasn't hiding behind any truck nor was I popping my head up and down prior to the shooting. It was after 9:00 p.m. and the street light was out therefore Fellows couldn't have seen the shooter or me. Now what really happened in a nutshell is earlier that day the 52BGC's came through shooting on 3 occasions but only shot Tiny Rat in the leg (where was the police when my homies was being shot and shot at?). When the sun was going down me and more of my homies started pulling up. We got the rundown of what took place and cats were out there with a bunch of guns. We were posted up on the block for a few hours trying to see if the Broadways would come back through. When they didn't we decided to pile up in cars and head to the Crenshaw strip.

However, just when we were about to get in the cars one of my homies said to watch that car. I looked up and saw a car driving slowly with the high beams on. We all suspected it to be the Broadways. As the car got closer I stood back in the yard because I wasn't strapped. Someone yelled "that's the police" and I took off running through the backyard of the house we were standing in. As I ran I heard multiple gunshots. That's all I remember. Now how or why my name came up as the shooter I still don't know. However, there is an informant who was never disclosed in that case. He's not mentioned in the police reports but someone had the police raid my mother's and Big Mama's spots. My brother and cousin didn't run their mouths until they got caught up in the raids. For those of you who really lived the street life you know that some of your own homies will call the law on you with bogus information just to get you out of the way because they either are intimidated by you or they despise you. The police and prosecution don't factor these things in when they are talking to an informant.

After reading the paperwork I called the hood and gave the names of those who gave statements against me. They needed to be exposed. A week or two later Young Rob got acquitted on his kidnap murder robbery charge and went home. I was shocked but happy for him. I was hoping for the same result in my cases. I spoke to Nikki on the phone, she was Kemo's wife. She told me some disturbing news. She said that LaShawn told Scottie's mother that me and Kemo killed Scottie! I couldn't believe it. The whole hood knew what went down with Scottie's murder. Lashawn was delusional in my opinion. Plus Buckwheat was on the run for Scottie's murder. I was somewhat upset but the more I thought about it, Lashawn's allegation was so ridiculous that I pitied her. I didn't have any words for her. Shortly thereafter I went to court on the gas station shooting. I was fighting my case at the Criminal Court Building ("CCB") in downtown Los Angeles. My case no# was BA071499.

The police placed me in this cell that was small and jam packed with at least 35-40 people inside. There were people asleep on the floor waiting to be called for court. There was no room to sit down. I maneuvered my way against a wall. The place stank with musty body odors. As I looked around the room I noticed this dark skinned individual with a perm sitting in the opposite corner of the cell. It was Buckwheat! He had gotten arrested for Scottie's murder. The cell was too crowded for me to get to him. He saw me before I saw him. When we made eye contact he said, "I didn't do it, they are lying on me like they are lying on you." A minute later the police opened the door and called about six people for court, his name being one of them. My adrenaline was pumping. I knew that I had to do something to him. I couldn't let him slide. I didn't want to fight him, I wanted to stab him viciously for what he did to Scottie. However, if they placed us back in a cell together when I came out of court I was going to attack him with my fist. Now

Buckwheat could fight so it wasn't going to be easy. Win or lose I had to get at him. I contemplated assaulting him all that day. That was all I could think about. Now that I knew he was in the county jail it was only going to be a matter of time before we crossed paths again. I planned on being prepared. However, ironically we never ran into each other again. When I went to court I got some good news which I already anticipated.

The ballistics came back on the AK-47 and M1-Carbine neither weapon was used in the police or gas station shooting. The guns did not match. As far as I was concerned, the evidence proved that I wasn't the shooter in either crime. The shroud the cops found did not come from my M1-Carbine. Think about it for a moment. The police got shot at with an M1-Carbine. I owned an M1-Carbine. If I was the shooter would it not make sense for me to use my own gun? And if I was the shooter at the gas station then undoubtedly the AK-47 Baby Dee and I was busted with a day after the shooting would have been the weapon. The actual weapons used in either shooting were never found. Also, the shell casings at the gas station matched the ballistics to a double homicide on 35th and Arlington in November of '91, when I was serving my violation. That made me think that it was God who took me off the street when my parole officer violated me the first time.

If I wasn't the shooter in that previous double homicide then there was a reasonable probability that whoever committed that crime also committed the gas station shooting. I needed to know if this double homicide was a gang related shooting because if the Ak-47 traced back to a rival gang then it would exonerate me. What I didn't know at the time was that the detectives was lying to Lil Owl by telling him that I got caught with the murder weapon used to kill the people at the gas station. They were dirty. That lie kept the war going on strong.

CHAPTER NINE

I finally obtained my police reports from the gas station shooting. While reading through them I noticed a few strange things. There was a confidential informant who alleged a few things, none of which was true. 1: He stated that Lil Flux was the mastermind behind the shooting and I carried it out. 2: He alleged that the shooting was behind Junebug and Lil Owl giving drugs to this cat out of my hood named Kevin who wasn't a gang member but sold dope in my hood. Actually Kev grew up in the hood and sold dope on 60th between Main and Broadway. 3: He alleged that Big Fish got jealous and mad at Kev for selling dope in the hood and started a war with Kev. This war resulted in Ralph getting killed and allegedly I was the shooter. That was outrageously false. 4: Lil Flux, Lala, Fish, and Crumb jumped in a car together and went to the gas station. Also that me, Tiny Bubble, Worm, and my cousin Lil Pookie jumped in a red Cherokee Jeep with an AK-47 and went to go do the murders. 5: Allegedly I was bragging about committing the crime the next day.

Here's why none of this is true: a) Although Lil Flux and I were both from 62EC we didn't run the streets together. We may show up at the same party and have each other's backs as Six Deuces ("SD's") but that's as far as it went and he couldn't have ever gotten me to kill Junebug. If anything

I would have talked him out of it. I didn't condone homies killing homies. b) Junebug and Lil Owl sold PCP not cocaine. There was no clientele for PCP in 62EC hood. We had a rule that we could not smoke it and none of us sold it. To violate that rule got you a swift beat down. Kev sold cocaine and had been doing so on 60th Street for at least 8 years and my homies knew about it and never demanded that he stop. I certainly didn't. Also, I didn't even sell dope in my hood anymore. I went to Oceanside, California and started coming up selling cocaine. I caught a dope case out there as my proof. c) When Ralph got killed I was locked up for the dope case in Oceanside. d) Tiny Bubble was the person pulled over by the cops moments before the shooting occurred. In the midst of his traffic stop the gunshots rang out from the gas station. So I definitely didn't get into a jeep with him to go do nothing at no gas station. e) There was never any corroborating evidence to prove that I was seen in a red Cherokee Jeep or had access to one. Finally if all of the above people were truly involved with the shooting then why was I the only one charged for the crime? Lastly the CRI alleged that I was bragging about the shooting the next day.

That's false because I didn't have anything to do with the shooting. I had alibi witnesses who could verify that I was in Kemo's car which was parked behind Tiny Bubble's car ducking down hiding while the police conducted the traffic stop. I also heard the gunshots from where we were parked on 59th Place and Main Street across the street from Crip-Cal's parents house. I had no reason to brag about a crime I didn't commit when two of the victims were friends I grew up with and had love for. The problem with this investigation was that the detectives were making me the suspect as opposed to following the evidence. I saw a police report by a witness named Leroy Martin. The report was made only a few hours after the shooting. Martin stated that he didn't see the shooter or who had the gun in their hand but he saw a red and black car drive into the gas station and park by the air pumps next to the alley. There were no other cars in the gas station.

The driver of the red and black car was a black male in his late 20's to early 30's in age, 5'9 - 6'0 in height, clean shaven, and looked like he just got out of prison (meaning he was big or muscular). The guy wore a light blue jean shirt, blue pants, and a blue beanie hat. Martin saw this person get out of the red and black car and walk up to the cashier window and stand there without purchasing anything while he looked around. Martin paid attention to this individual because he was a new face at the gas station. He saw this person walk back to his red and black car and get inside. 5 minutes later the shooting began. Martin believed that the shots had to be coming from the red and black car because there were no other cars in the gas station. Martin's statement was not tape recorded. I also noticed that Martin's statement was given on December 14, 1992, at 3:00 a.m. However, the Confidential Informant's statement was given on December 16, 1992. I got arrested on December 14, 1992 at 10:45 p.m. The detectives placed a black beanie on my head and took a photo of me within a couple of hours after I was brought into the police station. Now I knew why the detectives told me, "you were wearing your beanie when you had your AK." They were making me a suspect in the shooting. Why do I say that? Because at the time of my arrest the only witness that gave a statement regarding the gas station shooting was Martin. Clearly I did not match Martin's description of the person who got out of the red and black car, so why were my photos placed in the six pack photo cards?

Furthermore, it now made sense why homicide detectives were speaking to me and taking my photos a full two days before they even spoke to their alleged informant. Schunk and Herrera didn't have anything to do with the police shooting case thus they should've never been speaking to me on the night of my arrest. They knew the suspect at the gas station wore a beany and that's the reason why they placed the beany on my head and took a photo. I was 19 years old at the time. I didn't look older than my age. In fact to many people I looked younger than my age. It became clear to me that the police alleging that a confidential informant pointed them in my direction was a lie. They already had me pegged to take the fall and the statements allegedly given by this informant was a made up story that the detectives helped to formulate so that they could frame me. The informant's alleged statement wasn't even signed by him. I just needed my attorney and investigator to unravel the web these detectives were weaving. I needed God's grace.

I found another police report again alleging that" Flux" whose real name is Willie Talos Jr. orchestrated the shooting at the gas station and I carried it out. I didn't know where they were getting this stuff from. The same report stated that "Flux" is short and stocky. Also I saw another police report where the detectives stated that "Chilli-Moe" from 66EC told them about a "smoker" (crack addict) who was an eyewitness to the gas station shooting. The smoker's moniker was "Clay-max." I then read another police report from a witness named Clarence Lavan. The report wasn't signed by the witness as Martin's was. Lavan was Clay-max. According to this report Lavan and his brother drove to the gas station in a red and black car. They arrived at 9:45 p.m. and parked by the air pumps and Lavan and his brother got out of the car. His brother James put air in the tire while Lavan walked up to the cashier window allegedly to get change for a $20.00 bill then walked back to his red and black car. That's when he saw a Burgundy Cherokee Jeep with 3 people parked on the side of the apartments on Grand Avenue.

A black male carrying an AK-47 ran into the gas station while shooting at the same time, ran up on Lil Owl's Cadillac and shot it up and then shot others in the gas station. The shooter wore all black and is from 62 and they call him Baby Bam. He also alleged to have purchased marijuana from me previously. This statement was fabricated by the detectives. Lavan's interview was tape-recorded. His statement was taken on January 4, 1993. However, Martin identified Lavan as the shooter! The detectives should've treated Lavan as a suspect and placed his photo in a six pack photo card for Martin to view. Instead on January 5, 1993, they showed Martin six pack photos of me. Lavan's photo was never placed in a six pack. Martin viewed my photographs and was unable to make a positive identification. He stated that he was, "75% sure that I came closest to the guy he saw that night standing by the cashier's window." These detectives were trying to convince Martin that he saw me instead of Clay-max.

Ask yourself this question: "why would the detectives show Martin six pack photos of me but not Lavan when Lavan admits to driving the red and black car and standing by the cashier's window just before the shooting? The evidence showed that the shooting occurred at 10:00 p.m. Which means Lavan was at the gas station 15 minutes before the shooting. Martin described an individual wearing a light blue shirt whereas Lavan described someone wearing all black. Lavan also never alleged to have seen me standing by the cashier's window 5 minutes before the shooting. Thus these witnesses saw two different people at the gas station.

However, the treachery of these detectives knew no bounds. I saw a report stating that Lavan identified me from a six pack photo card "F". My photo was the only photo out of 36 pictures that appeared twice in the photo spreads. Six pack photo card "A" showed a picture of my face without a beanie on my head. Six Pack photo card "F" showed a picture of me with a beanie on my head. When viewing the six pack photo card "A" Martin didn't recognize anyone and Lavan could not make a positive identification because the shooter had long hair and I didn't. Lavan stated that he was confused because although I look like the guy, his hair was longer. To that the detectives told him not to pay any attention to hairstyles because they are subject to change. The problem with that statement is anyone who knew me on the streets knew that I didn't wear my hair long. Lavan also stated that the shooter was muscular, stocky and in his mid- 20's in age.

After it was obvious that Lavan couldn't make a positive identification of me, one of the detectives asked his partner, "Do you have the picture with the beanie?" His partner said yes but it's not in a six pack though. Allegedly his partner left to go put the photo of me wearing a beanie in another six pack. While he was gone the other detective spoke with Lavan. He told Lavan how important his testimony was to the case. Lavan said repeatedly that he didn't want to come to court to testify. The detective told him that he couldn't guarantee that he wouldn't have to come to court. Lavan mentioned that Carlton T. Mosley ("Chilli-Moe") was a good friend of his. He told the detective that if word got out that he was talking to the police his life would be in danger.

The detective told him that he doesn't have to worry about me because I was already in custody. When Lavan heard that he began to further doubt that I was the shooter. He replied, "he is...man I could've sworn that was him." The detective told him yeah he came to jail shortly after the shooting. Lavan replied, "I don't see how he can be in jail when I seen him." The detective reiterated what he said about my coming to jail the day after the shooting and Lavan repeated what he just stated. Lavan was implying that the shooter at the gas station was still on the streets and that he had just seen him recently. Rather than the detective asking Lavan what he meant by his statement and trying to find out when was the last time he saw the shooter on the street, he instead switched the subject and started telling Lavan of all the benefits the witness protection program offered. Lavan admitted to having serious financial problems and at one time living out of his car with his wife and kids. Thus he was desperate enough to go along with the detectives plan to frame me even though he expressed doubts about whether or not I was the actual suspect who committed the murders.

Moments later the other detective came back with the photo of me wearing the beanie in a six pack card "F". Lavan then made a positive identification of me. However, he stated that seeing the photo of me wearing the beanie helped him out a lot in his identification of me because without the hat he couldn't identify me. He further stated that if the detectives guaranteed him that they would keep their end of the bargain then he would do it, he would sign the statement identifying me as the shooter at the gas station. The trickeration was in full effect. How is it that a guy who should have been the prime suspect was now the key witness against me? Explain that to me.

As I continued reading I found a police report signed by John Severin a.k.a. "Crook" from 62EC. He went to jail on a robbery in February of 1993, and in hopes of leniency he gave a statement against Lil Flux. Lil Flux also went by Tank. In Crook's statement to the police he stated that he lived one block away from the gas station. On the night of the shooting he was standing on his back porch smoking a cigarette when he heard about 17 gunshots. He said seconds later Tank came running through the alley carrying an AK-47. Tank saw him and asked if he could hide inside of Crook's house. Crook said he told him no and Tank murmured an expletive and then ran away through the alley. He described Tank as short, stocky, and dark skinned in his mid-20's. This was all the evidence against me. No other evidence tied me to the crime. The fact that I was young, broke, and black would play a major part in my outcome. Ironically, Tank's photo was not placed in any six pack photo cards for Lavan to view. Crook's statement implied that Tank/Lil Flux was the shooter at the gas station.

CHAPTER TEN

In Wayside I ran into Gil-bone from Rollin 60's. I knew of him through Angie because he was her brother. We introduced ourselves to one another and I asked about Angie. He asked me how I know her and I told him that she was my woman. He called her on the phone later that day and afterwards gave me a message that she was coming to visit me that weekend. I was excited. I missed her a lot. Angie was the opposite of Glynnis in attitude and personality. I could just chill with her all day. We never argued, fought, called each other out of our names, played games with each other, etc. She was mature. I enjoyed her company. I met her one day while I was in the Slauson Swap meet with a few of my homeboys. I was getting my hood stitched on a starter cap I bought in preparation for our Hood day when I saw this thick big booty sister walking down the aisle with caramel complexioned skin. By the way she was dressed I could tell that she just threw on some clothes to go shopping. She had her hair in a ponytail. She was 5'4 in height and approximately 145Ibs. I found her to be attractive.

Normally, I would ignore good looking females, so that they don't think they can get any man they want. But with her something just compelled me to approach her. I asked her name and she said Angie. She asked my name and I said Bam. I told her that my neighborhood was throwing a function that following weekend and it would be cool if she could come. I told her if she got some homegirls they're welcome to come too. She asked for the location of the event and I gave her the address and time to be there. I told her that she could be my guess. We both smiled at that. She gave a head nod and walked away. We didn't exchange phone numbers either, so if she didn't show then there was no way for me to contact her. I didn't trip off of it. My gut instinct told me we was going to cross paths again.

When the night of June 2, 1992, came She pulled up in her new red Nissan SX. We saw each other and I walked up to her driver's window. I smiled at her and said, "I see you made it." I was happy that she did. I noticed that she came alone which told me that she came for me. It also told me that she was feeling me. I had her park and get out of the car. When she got out of the car I saw her outfit. She was dressed nicely. She wore a white Skirt with a red blouse and a matching white blazer. She also wore some leather pumps. Angie smelled good and didn't wear a lot of makeup. I escorted her into the party. My homies charged at the door but she didn't have to pay. When we walked inside the party was already jumping. It was jam-packed and people were dancing and socializing, there was no drama.

My homeboy Big Deuce was Dee-jaying. Das-Efx's hit song was blaring from the concert speakers. Angie and I danced with each other till the song ended. We then found a spot to sit down and converse. She told me that she was single and she had a daughter. I didn't have any kids but I was in a relationship with Glynnis. I didn't tell her that because I wasn't sure where our friendship would lead. At that time we were friends so I kept it at that. About 20 minutes later Deuce asked me to get on the mic and perform a song I had recently written. I obliged and I guess it went well because the party continued and I wasn't booed off stage. When I was finished I went back to Angie. We was holding hands listening to MC Breed's "It ain't no future in your fronting" when Ruben came and told me what Denny had did to Larry. I saw Larry and his eye was bleeding all over his Royal blue silk suit. Larry was gay and some of my homies nicknamed him "Faggot Larry." Larry had been gay for as long as I could remember.

However, we had his back because he was family. I walked up to Denny and socked him in the face. I felt somebody push me out of the way. I looked back and saw that it was Lil Flux. He pushed me out the way and started beating up Denny. Within seconds there were six of us beating him down till he was unconscious. However, a riot and chaos ensued. Angie was unharmed. I met up with her outside. She pulled up on me and asked me if I wanted to leave with her and I declined her offer. Although I did give it some deep thought. At the time my homies were headed to 69EC hood to get at them about crashing our hood day party. About six weeks passed by when one morning I saw a dark colored super sport Monte Carlo with I-Roc rims on it speeding down 61st and San Pedro with the music bumping the Geto Boys song "Mind Playing Tricks On Me." I didn't see who was driving the car but my homie Lil T.C recognized her and told me that Angie was driving that car.

My homies had just had a meeting behind the apartments next to C-Bone's mother's house. Me and my homie Charlie Brown got down and I put hands on him. It was a real good fight though. A few minutes later she circled the block again and I flagged her down. She stopped the car and backed up. I walked up to the passenger window and stuck my head in the window. Angie was wearing a ponytail. I asked where she was on her way to and she gave a vague explanation I didn't buy for a second. I had actually remembered her from 66th Street Elementary School from back in the day. But she didn't go there long and I'd never officially met her back then. That's how Lil T.C knew her too. I perceived that she was driving around my hood looking for me. I asked her whose car she was driving and she said the car belonged to her brother Duke from Rollin 60's. I opened the passenger door and got inside to exchange information. By this time my relationship with Glynnis was close to the end due to all of the squabbles we were having. I was wrong for hollering at Angie but at 19 years old I didn't have all of the answers to solve me and Glynnis' problems. I held a strong feeling after our hood day that Angie and I would meet again. When I flagged her down in my hood that was the official beginning of our relationship. A few weeks later Glynnis and I broke up. Angie had a daughter by Boo from 107 Hoover. She told me about her family and I told her about mine. We started going out to eat and spending time together in between the times I wasn't in Oceanside hustling. She lived with her aunt on the west side near Imperial and Western.

I rarely went over there because that was Glynnis' stomping grounds. Angie provided me with peace of mind. I could just chill with her. She carried herself like she was older. We never fought or argued over anything and I loved that aspect about her. There was no tug of war between us. She was down to earth and I began to love her. The only problem is that I was still in love with Glynnis. For that reason I couldn't fully commit to her. Angie was in college at the time but I suspected that she was hustling because she had nice things, she wasn't broke, but she had no job. I never knew that she was trafficking drugs though. Her aunt was cordial and her daughter was well behaved which as a young single mother I had to give her props for. However, I did set boundaries with Angie. For example, I never took her to meet any of my family members but they all knew Glynnis. Although she did meet my brother and cousin Lil Pookie.

The first time I was intimate with her was at her aunt's house. I went to visit her sometime after 4 p.m. and about ten minutes after I arrived her aunt and daughter left to go shopping. I didn't know where they would be going or for how long. Angie invited me into her bedroom. Once inside she began looking for something as I sat on the bed looking around her bedroom. She had a king size bed with big pillows in white pillowcases along with a fluffy white comforter, the walls was either green or gray (I get those two colors mixed up), there were white curtains over the window, the floor was wood with a rug on it, and her closet had sliding doors. The room was neat and clean which told me that she was organized.

After she finished doing what she was doing she sat next to me on the bed and I grabbed her hand. We locked eyes and I leaned in to kiss her. She leaned in to kiss me back as we tongue kissed. Her lips and tongue were soft and wet. With my left hand I caressed her face and rubbed my fingers through her hair. With my right hand I fondled her breast. She wasn't wearing a bra and her nipples became erect. I kissed her neck and took her shirt off leaving her breasts exposed. She was wearing a pair of black stretch pants with no panties underneath. Her feet were pretty too. I became aroused as she unbuckled my Guess Jeans and pulled them down to my knees. Shortly thereafter we had sex. Afterwards she asked, "So now that you got what you wanted are you going to disappear?" I smiled because that's the typical thing for a young female to say. I assured her that she hadn't seen the last of me. Her attitude and personality was what I was looking for in a woman. At the time I decided to get involved with Angie I didn't know what to expect. Despite the fact that Glynnis had my heart I was starting to have real feelings for Angie which was unexpected. I used to joke with her too. One day I had her come and pick me and Lil Mont up from the Greyhound bus station when we came back from Oceanside. Selling crack was lucrative out there.

Angie never wore a weave because her hair was naturally long. She loved wearing a ponytail and I told her that Lil Mont said that her ponytail was fake. She became upset and shook her hair loose to prove that her hair was hers. She had a few choice words for him too. I laughed as she went off on him. He laughed too and told her that I was lying. She began to laugh while still noticeably irritated. I lied just to see if I could get a rise out of her. She showed me some spunk and I liked it. For these reasons I was excited about her upcoming visit. However, the weekend came and went without my hearing from her. Months passed by and yet still no word from Angie. I didn't know what happened to her.

CHAPTER ELEVEN

The drama just kept coming. I got into it with Lil Spooky-Slim from 190EC in Wayside Max over some nonsense. It lead to us squaring off about to fight. When I saw that he was hesitant about squabbling up with me I told him, "nigga you don't want to get down, I'll beat your ass!" As I turned to walk away he dope fiended me by hitting me from the back and giving me two black eyes. I wanted my run back but he had another homie from 190EC in the dorm name Crease. They got together and acted like they was going to jump me. So I laid in the cut and played it off like I let it go. Lil Spooky-Slim slept beneath me on the bottom bunk. I went to sleep and woke up at around 2:00 a.m. got off my bunk and beat the brakes off of him in his sleep. The whole right side of his face was swollen badly. I did him like that because he didn't give me a head up fight as EC's are suppose to do. If I had to walk around the county with black eyes then he was going to walk around with his lumps and bruises too.

The police heard the punches when I took off on him and flashed the light in my direction. I tried to cut to the bathroom but he stopped me and called me to the gate. He asked me if I was fighting just now and I said no. Then he shined the light in my face and asked me how I got the two black eyes? I told him that happened a few days ago when I got down with a dude who caught the chain ("went to the pen"). He didn't buy it. He said he heard fighting and now I had black eyes. He assumed that I was being victimized and moved me out of the dorm. That situation was one I finally learned from. For example, the same thing happened to me when I was in Paso Robles. I got into it with Lil Bolo from Swan and called him out to fight but he was intimidated and didn't want to fight. However, the next morning on the way to breakfast he crept up behind me in line and fired my jaw up! I hit the ground and bounced up. I was woozy. Seconds later my head cleared up and I turned to beat the hell out of him, but the staff had him handcuffed and placed him in a van to send him to the hole. I was fuming. He chipped my tooth so I had it removed. To make matters worse, that same day I was moved to a different cottage ("housing unit") So my opportunity to get my revenge was hampered.

However, Shorty from SOS EC got down with him when he came back to the cottage and gave him two black eyes. The lesson in these incidents was don't woff on anyone. If it's at the point where I feel like someone has crossed the line and disrespected me then I'm just going to get off on him right then and there. To hell with letting a dude plot on me and catch me by surprise. Ain't no rules in fighting when you're doing time. The motto is "get him before he gets me." Shortly after that incident I was involved in two seemingly back to back riots with the Mexicans. Back then they was receiving orders from prison to green light the blacks (meaning "attack the black inmate population!") Thus each time the Mexicans outnumbered the blacks in a dorm they kicked off riots. But if they were outnumbered then they acted like they were friendly. I didn't trust Mexicans. The sad part is that negroes always wanted to compromise whenever we had them outnumbered despite the fact that we saw how they treated and hated us. My mindset was,"let's smash them like they are trying to smash us." One thing about a race riot is that it will expose who's who.

I've witnessed some so-called reputable dudes in the streets run and hide in a race riot! On one occasion I peeped that a riot was about to jump and went and woke up a few brothers who were asleep. You always had to stay awake in dorm living or have someone watch your back while you slept, preferably not a coward. I could always tell when a riot was about to crack. When you're doing time you learn to monitor people's behavior the way scientists monitor wild animals. The Mexicans tell-tell sign back then was they would all keep their shoes on and play cards after breakfast. They would also try to obtain all of the dorm cleaning tools, (e.g. Push Brooms, Mops, and Mop Buckets) so they could use them as weapons against us. Brothers often had to set aside gang beef to unite against the Mexicans. Over the years I would learn to be respectful towards them as a whole but never get too close to them due to the racism that I've witnessed them display towards blacks. The thing about Mexicans is that they all come together in a situation even if some don't agree. When they attacked they went after whoever, especially the sick, disabled, and elderly. I had to check myself because I was becoming a racist myself and I didn't like it. Being subjected to so much violence, discrimination, and hatred, will change a person's mindset and disposition if one is not spiritually grounded.

Looking back I realize that for the majority of my life I was taught from home and the streets to strike back rather than display forgiveness towards those who wronged me. Forgiveness was seen as weakness and unfit for a rider. That indoctrination from an early age led me down some hard paths and dark roads. My insecurities would surface and cause me to react violently if I felt disrespected by someone, especially if I perceived that the dude was trying to punk me. My pride wouldn't let it slide. I had to show a dude that I wasn't no punk and the only way to do that was through violence rather I win, lose, or draw. I lived for my hood and I was taught that the only way rival gang members will respect my hood is if I was a rider for my set. Violence was all gang members respected. An individual received accolades in the hood for violence. What happens when you give a dog a treat each time he shows aggression? The dog will see that his aggression got him rewarded and will continue that behavior. The same with humans. I had to put hands on 30-30 from Harlem 30's brother named Red in Wayside Max for getting at me sideways. He ran from me after I got off on him.

CHAPTER TWELVE

Chapter Twelve

I went back down to the L.A. County Jail for a live lineup pursuant to the gas station shooting. I was number 5 in the lineup. I went into the room where the lineup was being conducted. They had me and 5 other inmates dressed in state blues place ropes around our neck with big numbers attached to them. The numbers were 1-6. During the lineup they had us stand side by side facing the window and then stand in line facing the back of each other's head for a side view. Leroy Martin was the only witness to attend my live lineup. Clarence Lavan didn't attend. The whole ordeal lasted about 20 minutes. Afterwards I was told I had an attorney visit and I walked to the attorney/client visiting room. When I walked in I was expecting to meet my lawyer Mr. Atkinson. Instead when the officer pointed me to where my visitor was waiting I saw a gray haired older white man wearing glasses. I sat down and he greeted me and told me that he was my investigator. He said he was a former cop. He also said that he had some good news for me Martin didn't pick me out of the lineup. He then said, "if you did this crime you need to tell me now so that it will result in you getting a lighter sentence." I looked at him like he was crazy! This dude wasn't working for me, he was working against me. I asked him where my attorney was and he said that Atkinson had a court appointment to attend and couldn't make it. I ended the visit because I had no words for this dude. I often wondered if he was really my investigator.

After I got back to my cell I questioned why Martin was at my live lineup when he originally identified Lavan as the guy he saw standing by the cashier's window. And Lavan admitted to driving the red and black car and walking up to the cashier's window just before the shooting began. I also wondered why Lavan wasn't brought to my live lineup when he was the only witness to identify me as the shooter (albeit with the unduly suggestive practices of the detectives). Is it possible that the real reason that Lavan didn't attend my lineup is because the detectives feared that Martin would recognize him and blow up their case against me?

I ran into J.D. from the Lench Mob. He came to jail for a murder. We used to hang out and share our raps. I was in CYA with his little brother. Ice Cube allegedly was paying for his attorney. We didn't spend a lot of time together. I also ran into Lil No-Good from Rollin 60's. He and I met on the streets and became cool with each other. We used to reminisce on the history between our neighborhoods. The Six Deuces were founders of the Neighborhood Crips. Lil No-Good was a solid individual who was well respected by his homies. His last name was Nelson and I used to wonder if our families were related. I also called my hood and found out that Lil Flux was wanted for a murder/ robbery. There was a Chinaman who owned a corner market called "Royalty Market" on 62nd and San Pedro. His name was Papason and he had been a staple in our community for over 30 years. The people in the neighborhood loved him.

During the '92 L.A. riots his market was the only Chinese market that wasn't burned down. Papason was kind hearted and compassionate. He would give you anything if you asked him, but he hated a thief. He would literally chase you out of his store if he caught you stealing. I was informed that when Scottie got killed Papason gave his wife LaShawn a few bags of groceries for free. I loved him because he was an upright man. He used to wear a jean money belt around his waist. He would keep at least $4,500 cash in his belt at all times along with a machine that dispenses quarters. This went on for years yet no one ever tried to rob him. I was told that Lil Flux allegedly sent Crybaby from 62EC into the store to steal something and ran out of the store expecting Papason to chase after him. When Papason chased him out of the store allegedly Flux was waiting on him and knocked Papason unconscious killing him. He then robbed him for his money he kept on him. The police arrested Crybaby who was 12 years old at the time and he told the police what Lil Flux put him up to. There was a reward for anyone who had information leading to Lil Flux's arrest. People in the community were upset by that situation. I got in contact with Sandy too. Sandy was a red-bone standing at 5'8 160lbs. She was my cousin Kemo's cousin.

Her and I met one night on 62nd and San Pedro. I walked up to Royalty Market looking for Kemo and saw him leaning inside of a car's driver's window. I walked around the front of the car and saw that there were 3 females inside. I was wearing a blue Georgetown jacket with the white sleeves, blue Guess jeans, a blue and white button down shirt, with some high top blue Chuck Taylors with blue strings. I had a fresh haircut too. I saw Sandy sitting in the passenger seat. She was watching me as I walked up to the passenger side of the car and asked her what her name was. She said Sandy. I told her my name was Marlon. We ended up conversing for about 15 minutes and I left with her information. She told me that she was Kemo's cousin on his father's side. She was single with no kids and had her own apartment. That was a plus to me. The only bad thing was that she lived on 52nd and Broadway in 52BGC hood. She was converting to the Nation of Islam. That piqued my interest. Not because I was curious about Islam, but because I saw it as a challenge to see if I could have sex with her. Sandy was a 6 looks wise but our personalities meshed together which enhanced her beauty. A few days later I spent a night at her apartment. I picked her brain to see what she was about. She kept a bunch of condoms in her apartment.

At first glance I was suspicious because I had never met a female who kept that many condoms. I didn't keep that many condoms! I asked her, "what's the deal with all of these condoms?" She told me that she contracted gonorrhea from an ex of hers name Lil Hoova-Jacc and the clinic gave them to her. I wanted to know how long ago she was cured. I've never contracted an STD and I planned on keeping it that way. She told me that she is cured now and that it was a few weeks prior to me meeting her. I appreciated her honesty but I definitely was going to use a condom if I had sex with her. She told me her religious beliefs which I didn't judge her for. I was a gang banger/drug dealer who believed in Jesus Christ as Lord and Savior. Picture the irony. I just didn't profess to be a Christian because I knew that I was a sinner who was not following God's commandments. She said that she used to be in downtown L.A. selling drugs and her mother was a drug addict. We had some things in common.

I was lying on her bed with my feet on the floor while she was sitting up looking down at me. It was late and out of the blue she said, "you know I'm not having sex with you." My thought bubble said, let the game begin. I sat up and grabbed her, pulling her close to me. I kissed her on her lips and she didn't resist. I kissed her some more for a few minutes. She took off her shirt. She was already barefoot. Her feet were OK, I could work with them. I've never sucked a female's toes but I do prefer a woman who takes care of her feet. My mother got me into checking out a female's feet. She used to say that the first part of your body that touches the bath water is the feet, if a woman's feet ain't right she ain't right. I kissed Sandy on the neck and licked her ear for about two minutes then I unbuckled her pants and she took them off. She was now lying on her back in panties and a bra. She told me that's as far as she was going to go. I laughed and she smiled. She asked me why I was laughing but I didn't give her an explanation. I kissed her on her lips as I caressed her body. Her skin was extra soft. I took off my shirt, pants and shoes. I saw that she watched me intently which filled me with enthusiasm. My penis was erect protruding through my boxers when I asked her, "so you really don't want to have sex with me?" I put her hand on my penis and looked her in her eyes. That's when she succumbed. She handed me a condom and I slid it on then I took off my boxers, her panties, and bra. I opened her legs wide as I examined her body. She was nice. I sucked on her breast until both nipples were wet and erect then I tongue kissed her as I slowly inserted my penis inside of her. I ain't going to lie, a part of me was thinking, "she bet not burn me!" (Laughter) She moaned and thrusted her hips into mine. She brought her legs up to my shoulders. With my right hand I lifted her butt slightly in the air for better penetration and we found our rhythm. The sex was cool. From that point on she and I became close. We never said that we were exclusive or that she was my girlfriend. I told her about Glynnis and I told Glynnis about her.

Although I omitted the fact that I was having sex with her to Glynnis. When I was on the run I used to stay at her apartment. I gave her money and looked out for her anytime I could. When I'm involved with a woman I have no problem with breaking bread because I expect the same in return. I got Sandy's phone number from Pookie. I called her collect and she was excited to hear from me. I was also happy to talk to her. We caught each other up on what had transpired in our lives since we last saw each other. She was struggling financially but still managing to keep a roof over her head and her bills paid. I told her about some of the things that I had been dealing with and she was upset. Sandy was of the mindset that all white people were blue eyed devils. So it was easy to get her to see my point of view. I didn't share the same view that white people were devils. For one not all white people had blond hair and blue eyes. I used to challenge her on an intellectual level even though I didn't consider myself intellectual. One day I asked her, "if white people are devils just because they are white then am I a saint for selling drugs and gang banging?" She couldn't answer my question. I was trying to help her see that racism and true spirituality doesn't mix. I was always taught that God was love and a person who didn't love and forgive his neighbor (no matter their race, beliefs, or lifestyle) would not enter into eternal life. Sandy used to ponder what I was telling her. I used to tell her to do the right things.

On another occasion before I was arrested, she told me how she had been out with a friend trying to rob some random white people. I questioned her behavior the way a parent would question a misguided child. Sandy's father wasn't in her life which made her susceptible to getting manipulated and steered in the wrong direction by a foolish man. I had enough love for her to not encourage her into committing crimes but instead to tell her to get a job and go to school. She loved me because I was different from the other dudes she was involved with. Sandy wasn't a bad person; she just sometimes made poor choices out of desperation in an effort to survive in the streets. And having one parent absent from your life and the other addicted to cocaine was a heavy burden to bear especially without a support system. I knew that all too well. Sandy and I would continue to converse for about the next two months until she couldn't afford to accept anymore collect calls. I had love for her and wanted to see her become successful in life. Her and I would cross paths again.

CHAPTER THIRTEEN

In April of '93, I had my preliminary hearing for the two attempted murders of LAPD officers. None of the prosecution witnesses came to court except officer Derek Fellows. During cross-examination he gave details of what he witnessed when he and his partner pulled up on 62nd Street. Fellows alleged that when they drove up he saw 15-20 gang members standing outside with guns. He saw an individual popping his head up and down from behind a truck that was parked in a residential driveway. Then he heard multiple gunshots coming from behind the truck which resulted in him and his partner returning fire. He alleged that I was the guy popping my head up and down from behind the truck. However, upon cross-examination he was impeached with his original statement that he gave to the detective that night. In his statement he said that he never saw the shooter. Fellows contended that he did see me because he had his flashlight on me from my waist up.

My attorney Mr. Franklin asked him, "what was he wearing?" Fellows said that he didn't recall. Fellows couldn't describe my hairstyle, facial hair, clothing, or state whether or not I was wearing a hat that night. Again his original statement was that he never saw the suspect. Bottom line is he was lying under oath because their case was weak. If he saw 15-20 gang members standing outside with guns why would he divert his attention to whoever was allegedly popping his head up and down from behind a truck? That question was never answered. The Municipal Court judge still bound the case over for trial rather than dismissing the case for insufficient evidence. I felt good about my chances of beating the case. The next day I called my mother to break the good news but instead I got hit with some bad news. She told me that Pookie called the police on her and alleged that she neglected my little sisters (all under 10 years old) to smoke crack. I asked her if she did what Pookie alleged and she adamantly denied it. I'd never known my mother to abandon her children despite her drug addiction. Pookie lived with my mother and one morning he came home to find my little sisters in the apartment alone with my mother nowhere in sight. So Pookie called the police on her. My mother's version is that she didn't have anyone to watch the kids and she had to urgently run an errand before my sisters awoke. The police came and found no evidence of Pookie's allegation so they left. Whether the allegation was true or not the news was disturbing. Pookie was out of pocket to call the police. I called my homie Young Rob and tried to get him to discipline Pookie for that but Rob wouldn't do it.

Seeing my mother on drugs was depressing because I remembered the person she was before crack got a hold of her. She used to work for the school board as a cook at 99th Street Elementary School for a number of years when I was a kid. There were also times where she temporarily had us on welfare which was shameful to my brothers and I but she did what she had to do to support us. But now she had no job and 5 daughters but was raising 4 of them while struggling. Her only source of income was her social security check and she received no support from the twins or my little sister Jasmine's fathers. Pookie wasn't a hustler, he was a gang banger. That's what he did best. He had shot this dude from 52 BGC in the face with a .357 Magnum and permanently disfigured him on 53rd and Main Street in broad daylight but nobody snitched on him for it. I believe that I knew the real reason why my brother called the police on my mother. It had to do with our childhood. As kids my mother was loving, affectionate, had a sense of humor, generous, but also a strict disciplinarian. She had moments where she was out of control. Her parenting style was yelling, cursing, threats, and beatings. She cooked, kept her house clean, and demanded that we do well in school. We all had chores to do and we better not leave home without doing them. We got beat with everything from belts to extension cords. My parents ran a tight ship and they didn't tolerate disobedience.

Unfortunately there were times when they were dead wrong but their pride wouldn't let them admit it which was frustrating. They provided for us but we didn't have a voice. It was their way or the highway. This filled us with resentment at times. My mother spent every dollar she got her hands on which led to her and Michael having arguments about money. When she had money she was in a good mood but when she was broke she started tripping on things out of the blue. My parents were abusive and didn't realize it. Society didn't frown on parents beating their children in those days. Talking back would get you slapped in the face inside of a grocery store and no one would say anything about it. Even teachers had permission to beat you. Pookie used to take his frustrations out on me. I recall one day my parents were gone and my brothers and I were at home. It was around 2:00 p.m. and I was asleep on the living room floor. I kept hearing a whooshing sound which woke me up. I felt some heat on my face. When I opened my eyes there was Pookie with a lit match and a deodorant spray can in his hands. He sprayed the match again causing a torch like flame towards my face. I immediately jumped back and screamed out of fear. He started laughing. I stood up and socked him in the face and we began fighting.

Deon would often turn a blind eye to us fighting which I hated. I felt alone and on my own growing up. One morning back in 1984 while my mother was six months pregnant with my little sister Micole I was in my bedroom and heard my mother yelling out of anger then hearing what sounded like fighting coming from the bathroom. I walked to the bathroom door and looked inside. I saw my mother beating up Pookie with her fists. He was balled up in the corner with his head down. My mother fractured her wrist. Despite the fact that my brother and I didn't get along, I felt compassion for him at that moment because my mother was out of control. I don't know what he said or did to cause her to react like that but she was wrong.

From that incident Pookie no longer considered her his mother. He would later strictly call her by her first name. His heart went cold towards her. He wouldn't talk crazy to her but he didn't feel the need to help her.

As I was reminiscing on my childhood I started to recall other things that I had in the subconscious of my mind. Just random thoughts that came out of nowhere. For example, I thought about the time when Michael caused me to have an outer body experience. We were at one of his friend's apartment buildings where they had a swimming pool. My brothers could swim but I couldn't. I was no older than 6 years old at the time. I was afraid to get in the water. Michael told me to get in and I refused. He then grabbed me and threw me in the middle of the pool on the deep end. I yelled in panic and fear. I saw myself sink to the bottom and my brother Deon jumped in to save me. When I came out of the pool I was crying, coughing, and shaking with a runny nose.

Michael called it "toughening me up." I thought about an incident that occurred with Felipe. When he and his family moved away he would periodically catch the bus to come visit us. One day I came home from around the corner to see Felipe, Pookie, and a few of Felipe's new Mexican friends in front of my house having a conversation. I walked up and greeted him and his friends. We hung out for about ten minutes and then started walking down 61st street towards Avalon (why I don't know). When we got a few houses from the corner Pookie started whispering to Felipe with a sly grin on his face. I didn't know what he was saying. I never liked to hang out with Pookie. All of a sudden Felipe walked up to this Mexican teenage boy who was taller and older than us. Felipe said something to the dude and hit him in the face. The dude hit Feleipe back and I jumped in to help Felipe. I felt like Pookie should've jumped in also because he was behind it. I was ten years old at the time. The fight switched from me and Felipe jumping this dude to me and the dude fighting head up. Long story short I got beat up and no one jumped in to help me. I walked off crying not because I had lost the fight but more so because I couldn't believe that my brother and so-called best friend would sit back and watch me get beat up by a dude over something they started. I was hurt.

Now where the dude went wrong is that when he saw me leave he didn't leave. I went to Carl Jr.'s record shop on the corner which was also an arcade/bookie joint. I found Deon and told him what happened. We then walked back down the street. I saw the dude in front of Raymond's house talking to Raymond who was also a Mexican. Pookie, Feleipe and his friends saw us and followed behind us. We walked up on the dude and Deon asked him if he put his hands on me. The dude looked at Raymond then back at Deon. Raymond interjected by exclaiming, "No

Deon your brother hit him first!" Deon replied, "Shut up punk before I beat your ass!" Raymond became upset but didn't say another word. Deon asked the dude the same question again. The dude was afraid to answer. Deon socked him in the eye and it immediately swelled and closed shut. The dude fell to his knees screaming while holding his eye. Deon turned on Pookie and threatened to beat him up if he ever allowed me to get jumped on again without helping me. That situation let me know that Deon had my back. I thought about the time when I first learned that my mother was smoking crack. I was 11 years old. Pookie caught Jeanette smoking a crack pipe and said, "ugh Jeanette you smoke crack?" Jeanette became upset and replied, "So what! Your mama does it too!" I didn't hear her say it but I was there when Pookie told my mother what took place. My mother became irate but didn't deny it.

That information turned my world upside down. A year prior I had learned that my father Edward was smoking crack. Now both of my biological parents was hooked. I lived in denial for years while refusing to accept the fact that my mother was a drug addict. I used to get into it with one of my homeboys for clowning that my mother smoked crack. I wanted to shoot him but didn't. At times I would come home and the house would be smelling like Primos. At first I didn't know what this strange smell was until one day I looked in the freezer to grab a microwave burrito and saw a Primo on the shelf wrapped in aluminum foil. Seeing that made me feel hopeless. Deon had previously told me what a Primo was, so I knew it was a marijuana joint mixed with crack cocaine. I couldn't escape the reality of the situation. I shook those thoughts because they were too painful and filled me with indignation. The sad part is that I called my mother to give her some good news and got bombarded with the bad news. Damn! I hated to call home. I could hear some dude down the tier loudly cursing out his woman on the phone. I heard someone else doing beats on his bunk with a toothbrush and an empty deodorant bottle. Another dude yelled out he got candy on the line for a dollar each.

The L.A. County Jail was active. You can find some of the rawest talent behind bars. Some of the best rappers, poets, singers, producers, comedians, and artists are incarcerated. If Record label A and R's were truly seeking to find great artists and songwriters they would be tapping into the prison oil well rather than constantly promoting average artists who can't write hit songs and haven't been through any real hardship in their lives. I couldn't wait to get out and get rich! My writing skills were slowly improving more and more. I wanted to change my little sister's future for the better and buy my mother a house. The thought of them struggling and moving from place to place didn't sit well with me. Ever since we lost our home we was living like nomads.

CHAPTER FOURTEEN

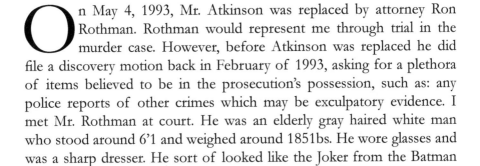

On May 4, 1993, Mr. Atkinson was replaced by attorney Ron Rothman. Rothman would represent me through trial in the murder case. However, before Atkinson was replaced he did file a discovery motion back in February of 1993, asking for a plethora of items believed to be in the prosecution's possession, such as: any police reports of other crimes which may be exculpatory evidence. I met Mr. Rothman at court. He was an elderly gray haired white man who stood around 6'1 and weighed around 185lbs. He wore glasses and was a sharp dresser. He sort of looked like the Joker from the Batman comic book. We spoke about my case for about 15 minutes in the court tank. I told him about my alibi and he said that he would check into it.

Specifically, he was going to request the L.A.P.D. log book to see if a traffic stop occurred during the date, time, and location that I alleged. He handed me his business card and told me to feel free to contact him if I have any suggestions. I accepted his card and when I got back to the county jail I wrote him a letter. I pointed out that from the police reports Mr. Martin identified Mr. Lavan as the person he saw standing by the cashier's window and he also assumed that Lavan was the shooter at the gas station. Weeks later Rothman found proof of the traffic stop and said that he would speak to my alibi witnesses.

On June 29, 1993, my preliminary hearing for the gas station murders was conducted. Leroy Martin, Clarence Lavan, and Donate Bavis ("Lil Owl") all testified under oath. Lil Owl showed up to court with Dog, Junebug's uncle. Dog was mean mugging me in court. To paraphrase what the witnesses said at court I'm going to start with Clarence Lavan. He stated that on December 13, 1992, he and his brother drove to the Mobile gas station on Gage and Grand Avenue in a red and black Charger. They arrived at the gas station at 9:45 p.m. When they drove into the gas station they parked by the air pumps next to the alley behind the gas station. Lavan and his brother James got out of the car. James went to put air in the car's tires while Lavan walked to the cashier's window to get change for a $20.00 bill. Lavan saw Lil Owl's Cadillac parked by the cashier's window and spoke to him. He also saw a lady in a blue van who was there then left. He saw Jamaica, a transient who pumped gas and washed windows at the gas station. He had a brief conversation with some people and walked back to his car. That's allegedly when he saw me running into the gas station from Grand Avenue and shooting an AK-47 at the same time. He stated that he watched me the whole time and got a good look at my face. Allegedly I ran up on Lil Owl's Cadillac and shot it up breaking out the car's windows. He saw Lil Owl drive off out of the gas station and turn left on Gage headed towards Broadway. He stated that I wore all black with a beanie on my head. His brother was scared and he had to keep his brother down.

He allegedly saw me shoot Jamaica then shoot at the other victims and come and shoot Jamaica some more. He alleged that I saw him and shot at him but he was never ducking down hiding. The lighting was good and he got a good look at me. He described me as muscular. He also stated that he saw a second suspect standing in the alley with a pistol who was short, stocky, and dark skinned. There was a Burgundy Cherokee jeep in the alley with a driver inside who he couldn't see. Allegedly after the shooting I ran to the Jeep in the alley and got in. He also stated that seeing the six pack of me wearing the beany helped him out a lot in his identification of me because without the hat he couldn't identify me. Lastly he alleged to have seen me once before in my neighborhood when he was buying weed from one of my homeboys.

My attorney declared him a hostile witness because he was refusing to answer my attorney's questions. When my attorney asked him didn't he say the suspect had long hair he denied it. Ask yourself this question, "who doesn't duck and hide when they are suddenly in the midst of a mass shooting where 4 people get murdered with an AK-47? Also, If Lavan truly got a good look at me and saw my face and recognized me from a time when he bought weed from my homeboy then why is it that he admits to not being able to identify me without the hat? When he viewed the six pack photo card "A" where I'm not wearing a beanie he can't identify me. He also said on his tape-recorded interview 4 times that the shooter had long hair. Why was he denying that fact in court? And if I fled the scene by running into the alley where a jeep was parked I would've had to have run past Lavan and his brother who was parked next to the alley. Thus why didn't I shoot him and his brother since I was allegedly trying to kill everyone in the vicinity? Lavan's testimony was false. What I didn't know at the time is that he told Lil Bow low and Chilli Moe from 66EC something completely different just two days after the shooting. I'll discuss that later.

Leroy Martin testified that he was at the gas station when he saw Lil Owl's Cadillac and the red and black Charger which Lavan and his brother were driving pull into the gas station. He saw a black male in his late 20's to early 30's get out of the red and black car and walk up to the cashier's window. He paid attention to this individual because he was a new face at the gas station. Martin never saw the dude with a gun. The dude didn't buy anything, instead he just observed the scenery with his hands behind his back. He didn't know which way the dude left or from where he came. He just saw the dude standing there and then disappeared. But then Martin contradicts himself by saying the dude walked back towards the red and black car. However, Martin wasn't sure if the dude got into the red and black car or walked back towards the alley. He alleged that five minutes later he heard shots coming from the direction the dude walked in. He never saw the shooter or who had the gun in their hand because he was ducking down hiding behind the gas pumps closest to Gage Avenue. When asked if he saw the individual in the courtroom who was standing by the cashier's window Martin looked at me and pointed in my direction. I was stunned and in disbelief. Clearly the evidence showed that Lavan was the person Martin saw standing by the cashier's window prior to the shooting. Furthermore no shell casings were ever found in the alley behind the gas station thus the suspect couldn't have been shooting from that location.

The detectives and prosecution were playing a dirty game of bait and switch. They knew Martin identified Lavan as the suspect but instead they only showed Martin six pack photos of me and none of Lavan. Martin never knew that he was identifying the wrong person but he did know that he wasn't sure that I was the actual person he saw. My attorney should've objected to the in-court identification because it was clearly mistaken. But being the dump truck attorney that he was he didn't object. Instead he asked Martin why he didn't pick me out of the live lineup? He stated that he didn't pick me out because he didn't see who was shooting and he wasn't a hundred percent sure. On the lineup card it says: Suspect in my case is number..... Martin wrote "NONE." In the remarks section he wrote "number 5 came the." He didn't finish the statement. Rothman asked him about his six pack photo identification where he stated that he was 75% sure that I "came the closest" to the guy he saw by the cashier's window. He admitted that he wasn't 100% sure that I was the guy he saw. Lavan never alleged to have seen me standing by the cashier's window prior to the shooting. Had I been in that location at that time then I would've been seen by Lavan because he testified that he walked up to the cashier's window. What I didn't know back then was that the district attorney Linda Reisz sent the detectives in my case a 3-page typed letter 3 weeks before my prelim. In the letter she explained to them that she did not believe that Clarence Lavan's testimony alone was going to be sufficient to obtain a conviction against me in light of the fact that Martin "assumed that Lavan and his brother were the shooters at the gas station." She told the detectives to go speak to a number of witnesses and explain how the crime occurred and eliminate Lavan and his brother as the shooters/suspects. That letter was kept hidden from the defense. There was no evidence presented in court which verifies that the detectives were able to "eliminate" Lavan and his brother as the suspects. Ms. Reisz was a petite white woman with black hair, attractive, mid 30's to early 40's in age and extremely ruthless.

Lil Owl testified that he drove to the gas station to buy some fuel injection cleaner. When he was getting back into his car he heard gunshots but didn't see the shooter. He started his car and drove out of the gas station. He stated that me, him, and Junebug were all friends and there had been no disputes or animosity between us prior to the shooting. He further stated that I had no reason to shoot them. He got shot in his shoulder and his back and was temporarily paralyzed. Now who gets shot in the back with an AK-47 and doesn't die or get paralyzed? I always wondered if there was another shooter and if Lil Owl truly got hit with an AK-47 like he alleged. Prior to my prelim he gave me the impression that he could care less if I got found guilty. I had called him and spoken to him on the phone. During the conversation we touched on a few things such as the D.A's bogus theory that our hoods went to war over drugs prior to the shooting, whether or not I got caught with the weapon used in the shooting, the streets was talking and he had heard that one of my homeboys was the actual shooter and wanted to know my opinion on it. We both knew that our hoods weren't at war prior to the shooting. If we were at war then he wouldn't have driven to any gas station in my hood. I sent my investigator to meet him and show him the evidence that I didn't get arrested with the murder weapon.

As for my home boy he mentioned I couldn't confirm or deny it because he wasn't with me when the shooting occurred. Towards the end of the conversation he said something that I'll never forget. He said, "Man, somebody got to pay for this." I asked him what he meant by that and was he implying that I'm the one who needs to take the fall for this case? He got quiet. I became upset and we hung up. That's when I knew that he was willing to sacrifice me as revenge for Junebug's murder. I then thought about doing something to him for real. I was hot. At the prelim he did help me to a degree but I felt like he could've done more. I was sent back to Wayside. On the ride there I was staring out the bus window looking at the traffic and observing the cities we passed by wondering if I was ever going to see the streets again. Out of anxiety and stress I had written Glynnis a messed up letter which was based on my insecurities. I wrongfully accused her of being unfaithful and slipping away. She was hurt by my letter and wrote me back. After reading her letter I was ashamed and felt horrible for getting at her the way I did. What I had to realize is that insecurities could jeopardize my relationship by pushing the person I loved the most away from me.

The 4th of July came and I started to reminisce on the worst year of my life. On the same date in 1986, I recall Deon wearing a black and yellow Pittsburgh Steelers sweater, black corduroys, and some black leather Adidas. His Jerry Curl was brushed back. We both were Steelers fans growing up. He was riding on Sakura's Riva Scooter. It had two 6x9 speakers on it. Sakura was Deon's girlfriend, Reka's sister. Reka had a brother named La Rue who was a millionaire and a baller. He had numerous dope spots in West L.A. Deon worked for him. Deon and Reka lived together. That day Deon and G-bone were riding around on the scooter. I was in the neighborhood purchasing fireworks from a Mexican family in the neighborhood. Me and a few of my homies were having a shoot out using Roman candles. Deon saw me with a bag of fireworks and asked to buy some from me because later that night he and Reka were going to have a fireworks display at their house on La Brea and Alsace in West L.A. He also wanted me to come. I said that I would and for him to have Reka pick me up. He said OK. Pookie was in juvenile camp at the time. My mother was pregnant with my sister Ebony. Reka came to pick me up at around 6:30 p.m. When we got to her house (her mother lived in the front house) there was a crowd of people outside lighting fireworks. Deon wasn't there yet, but he was on his way. I popped a few of my fireworks and hung out.

At around 7:45 p.m. people abruptly stopped what they were doing and started rushing to get into cars. I didn't know what was happening. I walked into Reka's mother's house and heard some females mention Deon's name. I asked her if she was talking about my brother and she said, "he ain't your brother." I replied, "Deon is my brother!" She then told me that he was in an accident. I didn't panic but I needed to go wherever he was at. I saw La Rue and I got in the car with him. He drove a convertible Navy blue Mercedes Benz. The accident occurred on Adams and Buckingham at the intersection. When we arrived Deon had already been transported to Brothman Memorial Hospital. This was the same hospital Michael Jackson went to when his hair caught on fire during the Coca-Cola commercial. I called my mother and told her what happened. She immediately jumped in our yellow Chevy Truck and drove to the hospital. I looked around the scene and the bike was totaled. La Rue sat in his car talking to someone on his car phone. Reka had driven to the hospital. I got out of the car and walked to the corner. I saw a white Lincoln in the street. This was the car that was involved in the accident. I saw this middle aged black man who was light skinned, slender, clean shaven, with short hair and wearing glasses. He was standing on the sidewalk looking out into the street. There were only about 4 or 5 people out there. No police were on the scene. I assumed that this dude was a bystander. I heard him say something about the accident which made me say that Deon was my brother. He looked at me and replied, "He's your brother? I'm sorry but if he dies he dies!" He let me know that he was the driver that hit Deon.

However, I wasn't listening anymore. That's the first time in my life I thought about killing someone. I wished at that moment that I had a gun so that I could shoot this insensitive, disrespectful bastard in the face. I was livid and what made matters worse is the fact that I felt helpless to do anything about it. I fought back the tears and walked to La Rue's car and got in. He ended his call and I told him what the dude said to me. He didn't respond the way I wanted him to. We drove to the hospital in silence. When we got there I saw my mother was there already. My homeboy Ray-dog was there also. About 20 minutes after we arrived a doctor called me, my mother, and Reka into a room and told us that Deon expired. We all burst into tears and I left the room. Ray-dog stopped me outside and asked me what happened. I mumbled, "he died." He looked at me in disbelief as tears filled his eyes. I found out what happened. Deon was riding down Adams and the light turned green. The driver of the Lincoln was in the turning lane on the other side of the street. Rather than waiting for Deon to pass by before making his turn he instead turned in front of Deon causing my brother to run into his passenger door at around 50 mph. Deon wasn't wearing a helmet as he was flipped in the air and came down head first. He crushed his chest when the handle bars on the bike broke off. An older lady who was a nurse was following behind my brother with her husband and saw the accident. She kept him alive till the ambulance arrived and she managed to get Reka's phone number from him. She called and relayed the message to Reka's family.

When we got home a lot of my family was there. My auntie Rosetta comforted me. Michael cried as he hugged me. Despite my parents flaws they loved us and were always there for us when it mattered most. A day or two later Reka showed up at our house and asked to speak to my mother. My mother went into the living room to speak to her. Michael took the day off from work. I was in my bedroom. Suddenly I heard my mother yelling in anger calling Reka a bunch of bitches. I went into the living room to find out what the commotion was about. I learned that Reka and her mother made all of the funeral arrangements without including my parents. She was dictating to my mother where the funeral was going to be held and where he was going to be buried. She meant well but went about it the wrong way. Reka was only Deon's girlfriend and soon to be baby mama. What she should have done was consult with my parents first and find out what their plans were and offer to help out in any way she can. La Rue found out what Reka did and offered to pay for the whole funeral. He also apologized for his mother and sister's indiscretion.

However, my parents rejected his offer. They didn't have the money to bury him but family members pitched in to help offset the cost. My mother asked my father Edward for some money to bury Deon and he replied, "Why? That ain't my son!" When I learned that I lost all respect for him. For most of Deon's life he had embraced Deon as his own son, but now that Deon was dead he had the audacity to disown him. I wanted to do something to him too. We drove up to Camp Miller in Malibu, California and broke the bad news to Pookie. He was sad. The Camp gave him a furlough so that he could attend the funeral service. The next month in August right before my mother's birthday my grandmother June passed away. They say death comes in 3's. In October on Michael's birthday which was the 14th he was driving home and got killed in a car accident. I still remember vividly what I experienced that night. I went to bed at 9:00 p.m. because it was a school night and I had to get up early to catch the school bus. I was going to Hale Jr. High School in Woodland Hills, California at the time. Michael was playing with Micole and kissing her. Micole was my parents' miracle baby. For years they had been trying to have a child but my mother kept having miscarriages. Michael became frustrated with the fact that my mother couldn't give him a child so he stepped outside of the marriage and had two kids by this lady name Connie. His children by Connie's names are Antoine and Tasha.

This situation caused a rift in my parents' marriage. My mother put him out of the house for at least a year. In life you reap what you sow. Connie turned around and gave both of Michael's children her boyfriend's last name. Michael was heart broken. My mother consoled him and they reunited. On the night of October 14, 1986, before I went to bed I also saw the nightly news and the main story was about the dude arrested for the Atlanta child murders. I went to bed. I was awakened from a deep sleep by loud screaming and crying. I lay in bed for about 4 minutes until I got my equilibrium. I got up and stepped outside of the bedroom. I looked down the hallway to my parents bedroom and their light on with my auntie Jeanette on her knees crying while rummaging through my parents closets. I walked into their bedroom to see what she was doing. I started to ask her what the hell she was doing but I didn't because she was grieving for some unknown reason. I walked through the kitchen and the light was on. I looked out our back door and saw that it was opened. I walked to the living room and the light was off.

My parents and sister were nowhere to be found. I went and opened up the front door and looked out. I saw my neighbor Roscoe crying in his front yard. I could hear his sobbing. I asked him why is everyone crying? He replied, "you haven't heard?" I said, "no, I just woke up." He said, "Tuda Ray died!" I heard him but it didn't register. I asked him where my mother was and he said she was at the hospital. I looked out the front door for another 5 minutes in silence. It was around 12:00 a.m. and dark outside. I went back through the kitchen and locked my back door. Jeanette was still searching for what I didn't know. 45 minutes later my mother came back home. I asked her if it was true about Michael and she said yeah. I got quiet as realization started to set in. I was only 13 years old yet dealing with so much and the trauma kept coming. I told my mother what Jeanette was doing and she thought about what I said and smirked.

I would later learn that Jeanette was rummaging through the closets because she was trying to steal the deeds to our house! Michael's mother was also in on the treachery. He wasn't dead for 24 hours before they were already making preparations to kick my family out on the streets. I forced myself to go to school that morning. I didn't want to be home with everyone grieving. On the bus ride I was silent. My homeboy Tarik noticed it and asked if I was OK and I told him no because my father died last night. He didn't know that but he felt my pain. He knew my whole family. The song "Stand By Me" played on the radio and I cried silently while listening to the lyrics. That was one of the hardest days to get through. My mother was doing everything she could to be strong. We went back up to Camp Miller to visit Pookie.

However, despite the fact he had 2 more months to serve they released him due to too many deaths in his family. I broke the news to him while my mother was with the counselor filling out the paperwork for his release. He thought we were just there for a visit. He was happy to see us. When I told him that Michael died and he was getting released his mood changed. He had a look on his face which to me represented sadness, pain, disbelief, and a partial smile like this has to be a joke. We buried Michael and a week later my mother gave birth to Ebony. Pookie and I were no longer fighting. We understood that we needed to grow up fast because we were all we had. Unfortunately we fell deeper into gang banging. I participated in 3 drive-by shootings on the Swans, Broadways, and Hoovers. Gang banging gave me an outlet to release my anger and frustrations but it couldn't take away my pain. There was an obvious void in the home due to both Michael and Deon being dead. Neither one of us wanted the responsibility of being the man of the house.

However, as fate would have it eventually I would be thrust into that role. The very next month on November 20, 1986, my mother sent me to Royalty Market to buy some groceries. It was around 8:30 p.m. I was walking home with a bag of groceries when Kemo called me from across the street on the corner of 62nd and San Pedro. I told him that I need to get home with my mother's groceries. He guilt tripped me into going back across the street to greet him. Moments after I was across the street talking to Kemo I saw a brown Monte Carlo drive up on us. There were about 7 of my homies hanging out on the corner. Kemo said, "Who is that?"

CHAPTER FIFTEEN

I looked into the car and heard a pop sound. Kemo immediately broke and ran. I tried to run but something was wrong with my takeoff. I heard another pop sound as the car drove off headed towards Avalon. Boxer shot the car up as it drove past him. I dropped the groceries and began checking my body to see if I was shot. I started from my head down. When I touched my left side I saw blood on my hand, I was hit! I laid on the ground on my right side. I started to feel sharp pain and burning. Boxer ran up, stopped, jumped in the air and screamed, "Cuz his guts is hanging out!" He began to cry. I looked down to my left side and saw my intestines partially hanging out. I immediately began to pray to God to save my life. My mother and family couldn't endure another loss. A crowd immediately formed around me. Females were crying loudly and my home boys were angry, shedding tears, and making preparations to retaliate. I heard my mother's voice as she screamed, "Noooo!" and burst into tears. I began to cry. Pookie walked up and looked at me lying on the ground. He didn't display his emotions as he just watched me. The ambulance showed up and drove me to Dr. Martin Luther King Jr. hospital ("Killa King") in Watts. The medical personnel kept me awake until I made it to the hospital.

They told the doctors I had a GSW to the abdomen. They cut off my clothes leaving me naked. I was immediately hooked up to an IV. A doctor told me that when she counts to 3 I will be asleep. She counted down and I went to sleep. I woke up in the middle of surgery and saw a pink room then went out again. When I awoke the second time I was in my room with a tube down my nose and my stomach bandaged up. The bullet only badly grazed me and there was no damage to my intestines. My uncle Spark, Pookie, and Baby Dee were standing at the foot of my bed watching me. I couldn't speak. Pookie asked me who did it but I didn't know. I assumed that it was some Swans by the direction they drove away. But I wasn't sure.

I learned that my brother and homies went and busted on the Swans, Brims, and Villains behind my getting shot. I went to sleep and the next morning I awoke to see my girlfriend Chivetta sitting by my bedside. I was pleasantly surprised because her mother Bobbi Jean didn't like me, so I was surprised that she let Chivetta miss school to let my mother bring her to the hospital to visit me. We held hands and just stared at each other. I smiled at her and she smiled and put her head down. Chivetta was shy and wholesome. We met one day when we were walking home from Bethune Jr. High School in January of 1986. I had on Deon's blue Jersey with a big white "62" on the back of it. I was shadow boxing and she was across the street behind me with her friend Venus watching me. They yelled out, "hey who are you about to fight" and started laughing. I felt embarrassed but I smiled and turned around to see who it was that spoke to me. I saw them and waited for them to come to me then I introduced myself to them. They told me their names and asked me where I was from. I told them that I'm from Six Deuce East Coast. They said, "for real what they call you?" I said, "Baby Bam." They said that they lived on 62nd Street between Main and Broadway.

I walked them home. They knew my homies Baby Sike, Lil Greedy, and Lil Stoney already. I got Chivetta's phone number and began to call her. She became my girlfriend. Shortly thereafter I met her brother Lamont and he joined Six Deuce too. He was nicknamed Lil Mont and we became best friends. His cousins were Rob-Dog and Robin from 62EC. His big sister Queenie became like a sister to me as well. She used to allow me to hang out with Chivetta whenever their mother was gone. Chivetta was beautiful and a few of my homies tried to holler at her but I had her on lock. Eventually my homies got the message and left her alone. I took her virginity. I didn't know what I was doing at the time but figuratively speaking we learned to ride that bike together. We were together for five years until I went to CYA. I did a lot for Chivetta in terms of looking out for her. I always envisioned us having children and getting married because she was with me through my hardest times and helped me get through it. Her kisses, hugs, affection, laughter, and softness was a bright spot in my darkness. I didn't just have sex with her I made love to her and treated her with respect.

Although I did have Creshinda on the side she never knew about it nor has she ever had to fight another female behind me. I wasn't perfect but I wasn't messy either. There was nothing she couldn't get from me. I began selling dope and having money. I just didn't know what to do with my money. It was hard for me to stack like I wanted to because if my mother found my money or drugs she'd take it. Often I'd have to start over. However, I stayed with fresh outfits and shoes on and kept money in my pocket to do whatever I wanted to do. I made sure that the things Chivetta's mother couldn't afford then I bought for her. I went to CYA in 1989, for selling drugs and got out in 1991. While I was locked up she ended up getting pregnant by Baby Swan from SYC. That's what broke us up and opened the door for Glynnis to come into my life. I'll touch on that in more detail later.

The next day after I got shot Pookie went to jail for having a shotgun. He was driving my mother's truck on his way to bust on the Swans when the police pulled him over and arrested him. He received a 6 months sentence in camp but ended up spending 5 years incarcerated and going to CYA because he wouldn't stop fighting and getting into trouble. None of us ever received therapy or counseling for the things we endured so we all coped with the overwhelming pain in our own way. For my mother it was crack cocaine, for Pookie it was gang banging, fighting, and misbehaving while incarcerated, for me it was gang banging, selling drugs, ditching school, and having sex with girls my age and grown women who sold their bodies for drugs ("Strawberries") when they didn't have any money. Some of these women were nice looking with amazing bodies. It never crossed my mind that this was child molestation. Crack didn't discriminate. Beautiful and successful people got hooked too. Once they were hooked oftentimes they'd lose their dignity for a blast. I was growing up fast in my early teen years.

Once I started selling drugs I was able to buy my own clothes, help my mother pay bills, buy groceries, and I sent Pookie a couple of packages.

I had to babysit my little sisters and change diapers too. I was the man of the house and my mother needed my help. At the time she was engaged in a bitter rivalry with Big Mama, Alfreida, and Jeanette over the house. They were envious and filled with anger towards my mother because she was receiving Michael's social security benefits for herself, me, Pookie, and my sisters Micole and Ebony. Big Mama was upset that my mother wouldn't give her $10,000.00. One day my mother and I were in the kitchen of our home when Big Mama barged in from the back door and started berating my mother and then called her a bitch. It took every ounce of humility I had to remain silent and not disrespect her by cursing her out. My mother responded with a few words but she was respectful. At that moment I saw Big Mama as a false Christian. She was someone who attended church services three times a week but as soon as she was angry her mouth poured out pure evil. She didn't show any love and compassion towards my mother. Instead her hatred towards my mother was so deeply rooted that she took it out on Micole and Ebony.

Every Christmas Big Mama would buy all of her grandchildren gifts except my little sisters. Big Mama and Jeanette used to call child protective services on my mother and allege that she was an unfit crack addict. Meanwhile Big Mama sold crack cocaine on the low and Jeanette and Alfreida were both crack addicts. They used to keep crack heads and drug dealers coming into our yard to visit them. Big Mama had a few church members (mostly men) who would come by to visit her. I found out that some of them were her clientele. I lost all respect for her as a Christian woman once I learned that. She was no different than the sinners she looked down on. I used to wonder how Michael would have reacted had he been alive to witness how his own mother and sisters treated not only his wife but his daughters after he died? I know that would've broken his heart. If the shoe was on the other foot he wouldn't have allowed his mother and siblings to mistreat or disown any of his nephews and nieces.

However, rather than trying to help and support my mother because she had suffered the loss of her mother, husband, and first born within a hundred days while being pregnant, I got shot in a drive-by a month after Michael's funeral, and Pookie went back to jail they instead saw it as an opportunity to attack and devour my mother. All of my life I was raised to see Michael's family as my family. Witnessing these things made me seriously rethink calling Big Mama, Jeanette, and Alfreida family. Although I still had a little love for them despite the fact that they were aggressively pursuing their goal to make us homeless. The scriptures say, "a man's foes shall be they of his own household" Matthew 10:36. I could've told my homeboys what was going on and watched more drama unfold as violence ensued but I didn't out of love and respect for Michael. My mother's father also began tripping on her about $700.00 that her mother gave her before she died. I came home one day and heard her crying while talking on the phone to someone. I listened from the other room to gather the details and became outraged. I saw their attacks on my mother as attacks on me and my little sisters.

As a result I disowned my grandfather till the day of his death and I didn't attend his funeral. It was hard to recognize family from the enemy during those times and as a result of the division I fell deeper into gang banging to escape my reality and give me an outlet for all of my anger. My family was supplanted by my homeboys and hood. If you weren't from 62 Neighborhood East Coast Crips you couldn't tell me anything. In hindsight I don't know how my mother made it through all of that and still manage to raise five children with an income below the poverty line and still keep a sane mind. My mother wasn't perfect and she had many flaws but despite her shortcomings she had love in her heart. She never abandoned her children nor did she ever allow any man to harm her children. Whenever my brothers and I got into trouble with the law she was there for us and always had our backs whether we were right or wrong. She suffered shame and humiliation on a scale that would've lead some to commit suicide and many others to lose faith in God but she continued to believe and trust God even in her weakness.

It seemed like God put her through the afflictions of Job. For that she was to be honored and praised in my opinion. I've never met anyone like her with the fortitude and perseverance she continuously displayed. She is and will always be my super woman. From my mother I learned to never give up and keep believing in God and myself no matter what the situation looks like. She was poor but she had love in her heart and that made her rich. Many people have judged, criticized, laughed at, gossiped and whispered about her in secret while smiling in her face but NONE OF THEM could walk ten yards in her shoes. I loved my mother whether she was addicted to crack, broke, doing bad and struggling. It didn't matter to me because I knew the real woman she was. To be against my mother was to be against me. In our darkest hour we supported each other.

As a result of the turmoil I witnessed between my so-called family

I had a lot of pain, anger, and fear bottled up inside of me because I was uncertain about my future. Good thing I had Lil Fish, T.C, G-Bone, and a few other homies to turn to. It was also around that time that I started hearing a voice in my head telling me that I was going to die in 1992. I thought that I was tripping at first. I assumed that I was telling myself that. But the reality is that I was hearing a voice and it wasn't coming from me. My first time hearing it was in 1987. I was coming home from Chivetta's house at around 8:30 p.m.

I was walking down 62nd Street and when I walked across Main Street it seemed like the street got darker and eerily quiet. Then I heard the voice. It spooked me so much that even though I had a gun on me I started walking in the middle of the street and looking around as if someone was out there with me. I eventually ran to San Pedro where I felt safer. I would hear that voice many more times over the years. I never told anyone because I didn't know how to tell someone about it. Plus I thought that if I acknowledged the voice in my head that it might come to pass. I was 14 years old at the time so what did I know? I lived in fear behind that for years.

CHAPTER SIXTEEN

I got word that Lil Flux got arrested for Papasan's murder and he was in Wayside. It wasn't long before we crossed paths. He was happy to see me. Mr. Low from 62EC was in the dorm with me. Flux saw him and told me to tell him that he's not from the set anymore and that he needs to roll it up ("leave out of fear for his safety') now or he would come in the dorm and make him roll it up. I looked at him and asked what was this about? He said La-La gave him the boot. I relayed the message to Mr. Low and he looked frustrated then rolled it up out of the dorm. I shook my head. Shortly after that I got word that Flux knocked out Hoova Lou from 94 Hoover. His name was ringing all throughout the county jail. Both of my attorneys told me that the D.A. was filing a motion to consolidate the charges against me. I was going back to court. I sensed that the prosecution was doing this to ensure that they got a conviction against me by painting a picture to the jury that I was some mad lunatic running around Los Angeles with assault rifles shooting at police and killing gang members. Rothman was also going to ask for the name of the confidential informant.

A week later I was in court. The prosecution moved to consolidate the charges against me and Rothman objected to it. However, the court sided with the prosecution. Rothman became my sole attorney. I was no longer fighting two separate cases but one case. I hated to lose Mr. Franklin as my attorney. A short while later my attorney asked me who Calvin Dixon was. I said, "Calvin Dixon?" He said, "yeah you know him?" I said, "yeah why?" He said, "that's the confidential informant!" I was in disbelief. Calvin Dixon was Crip-Cal! I was really tripping because he knew that Flux and I didn't run together on the streets and he was a witness to the traffic stop across the street from his house when the shooting at the gas station occurred. He saw me get out of Kemo's car after the police drove to the gas station. I started thinking about what I may have done to him to make him want to get me off the streets. I couldn't come up with anything. I'm the one who told him that a female he was dealing with had Herpes. I loved my homies like they were my family and I wasn't a bully. I was fair to my knowledge with everyone unless you did something cowardly or foul. I also wondered how long he had been an informant. I called the neighborhood and put the word out. Crip-Cal was still on the streets living on 59th Place and Main Street at his parents house.

I knew his whole family. His daddy's name was Boss. A shady mechanic in the hood who smoked crack cocaine. If you took your car to Boss and had him fix your carburetor he would fix it but a week later your brakes would go out. He was slick and he knew how to stay in someone's pocket. His mother's name was Cat. Cat used to boost meat from grocery stores and then sell it to people in the hood at a discount. He had an older brother named Nelson. He was from 87GC. They used to fight a lot. Once I saw Nelson chasing him down Main Street shooting at him with a .38 snub nose. His little brother's name was Jimmy Lee. Thus you know by his upbringing that Crip-Cal was scandalous and a liar. We nicknamed him "Shithouse Shorty" because he was full of it. But we loved him nonetheless.

However, now he was lying on a whole nother level and my life was in the balance. I wondered what the police had on him to make him cooperate. I didn't understand this. The same people who were family to me were the one's betraying me. I started to feel like I couldn't trust no one. Everybody was suspicious. That's a cold feeling to have especially when one is not too close with his own family and his woman is acting shady. I called Glynnis and she told me about a dude named Lewis who she met at her cousin's house. Allegedly he had been giving her oral sex but she never had intercourse with him nor did she give him any head. In fact she alleged that he didn't even want intercourse with her. I listened to her but I knew this story was false. She was getting at me like I grew up in Buffoon County on 35th- and Idiot Avenue. I expected this situation to come at some point. My thing was if you're going to tell.me a story about being involved with another- dude; tell the real one or don't tell me at all. Ironically right after she told me about Lewis her attitude changed. She went from being excited to hearing from me to now catching an attitude with me over the smallest things.

Visits slowed down too. I became anxious and suspicious and I wondered if her new attitude was connected to her new dude. I felt slighted. I felt like no other dude should come before me. I knew that I kept going to jail which also played a huge role in the choice she made. My love for her was still strong. Her actions were forgivable as long as she came clean. She wasn't good at lying to me. I could always see through it. I loved her family like they were my family. As months passed by and her attitude didn't change I assumed that Lewis was the reason behind it. I later learned that their relationship was serious. When you're incarcerated the mind can start to play tricks on you and cause you to stress over the facts, exaggerate the facts or imagine something that's not true altogether. I concluded that since she's doing her it's only right that I do me. The thought of her laying up with another man disgusted me. I didn't care about what I did when I was out. I was only concerned with the present which at that time the shoe was on the other foot. I'm not saying that I was right or that the way I was thinking was fair. But I am being real about the way I felt back then. I became financially desperate while at Medium North.

As a result me and a homeboy of mine I knew from my CYA days name Demon from 357 GC knocked this dude out and robbed him for $400.00. Demon used to be from PJ watts and was formerly known as Dre. We robbed the dude because he was a non-affiliate among bangers. He was flamboyant and felt too comfortable around dudes he didn't even know. In hindsight, I look back on that situation with regret. I spoke to Maya on the phone and Sherry was over at her apartment. I asked Maya to let me speak to her. Sherry and I had a summer fling in '92. She was a 7 on the beauty scale. She had a man at the time who she lived in Oceanside with by the name of Ricashay from 43 GC. She used to come on 61st and San Pedro with Maya and hangout from time to time. My uncle Willie Blue was her cousin. She grew up in the neighborhood but she was bougie. She dressed well and had a sense of humor. She was also petite. Something about her aroused me sexually. Glynnis and I weren't together so I felt like I was a free agent. I began flirting with her and she flirted back which surprised me because she was 4 years older, had known me for years, and I expected her to say something like her and I was like cousins. Instead she flirted back. I let her know that I just wanted to have sex with her because I knew she had a man and my heart still belonged to Glynnis. I wasn't looking for anything serious with her.

She gave me a proposition which was that I could have sex with her only on one condition "I had to give her oral sex!" I was like I'm good! I only did that with my woman, not random females. So for a couple of weeks we played that cat and mouse game until she got her request and I got the draws. But I was looking to pay her back for that. I was embarrassed with myself for not staying true to my principles. Not even Angie got oral sex from me and I had feelings for her. The good thing was Sherry wasn't a dirty female. She was fresh downstairs. I got my get back in dramatic fashion though. After about the third hookup between us she was hooked. One day I asked her to come to L.A so that we could kick it. Later that night she came and pulled up at Maya's apartment looking for me.

My mother lived upstairs from Maya and I had gone to visit her and my little sisters. My twin sisters Tyneka and Dyneka were 6 month old babies at the time. I ended up taking a nap with them after feeding them. I was in a deep sleep when I felt someone pulling on my pants leg. I woke up to see Maya at the foot of the bed. She was calling my name as I said, "what's up?" She told me that Sherry was downstairs waiting on me and I rolled my eyes and went back to sleep. Maya started laughing as she shook my pants leg and hit my foot. She told me to wake up and repeated what she said moments ago. She added, " she drove all of this way to kick it with you. I know you're not going to leave her hanging. "I was cold as I said, " tell that bitch I'm asleep!" Maya laughed but hoped I wasn't serious. She tried to wake me up but I wouldn't budge. I spent that night with my little sisters. Sherry drove 2 hours to L.A on a dry run. Within the next month and a half I hooked up with her a couple of more times but then abruptly ended it. Glynnis and I had been back together for a couple of weeks. She couldn't believe that I could just walk away from the sex but I did. I remember her telling me, "so you was serious when you said that you wasn't having sex with me anymore?" I replied, "Yep." Our relationship was purely physical with no strings attached. I just wanted to bust down that wall of bougieness she was displaying. But she was still a good person.

Her and I remained friends but I wasn't tripping off of her anymore.

During our conversation she told me that she had a miscarriage and there was a possibility that I was the father. I was surprised by that news and sorry to hear that she had a miscarriage even if the child wasn't mines. I knew how that event could traumatize a woman. I pondered the thought of "what if' for a moment and shook my head. That would've been crazy. We spoke about what was going on in the streets, in her life, and in my case. We laughed a few times and I enjoyed the conversation. After 15 minutes the call was over. Talking to Sherry lifted my mood for the time being.

About a week later I received a visit from Lily out of the blue. She was in the Job Corps downtown and heard that I was in the county jail so she decided to pay me a visit. Lily grew up down the street from me and was two years younger than me. I knew her sisters Linda, Lucy, and Caroline. As kids they were sheltered from the streets. Their parents kept them in Catholic school. They rarely came outside to play when we were little. However, they knew me and my brothers. When I got paroled from CYA in '91, I was walking past her house one day and felt someone staring at me. I looked to see who it was and I saw Lily looking at me. She was sitting on the porch. I called her to me and she walked up to the gate surrounding her yard. I asked her name because I used to get their names mixed up. She told me her name and I asked her age. She said that she was 16 years old. I was 18 at the time so to me her age wasn't a big deal. I was single but involved with Chivetta.

I hadn't met Glynnis in person yet. She and I conversed for 15-20 minutes and I left. A couple of days later Lucy and T.C pulled up on me in Lucy's Hyundai with Lily in the backseat. I don't know if Lucy and T.C was in a relationship, just friends, or sex buddies but they use to spend time together. They asked me if I wanted to go to the Santa Monica Pier with them. I was hustling on the block but I said yeah I wanted to go. We drove out to the pier and hung out for a couple of hours. Lily and I conversed about a few things such as her life at school, the things we remembered from our childhood, my having been to CYA, our relationship status, etc. I could tell that she was feeling me. She told me that she was a virgin and I smiled. That was good to hear. Afterwards they dropped me back off in the hood. We hung out a few more times but Lily couldn't leave home without Lucy as a chaperone which made it difficult for me to get serious with her although I did manage to take her virginity. Lucy and I used to hangout too. A lot of people used to think that we were together too. Truth is she and I were just friends. We never kissed or had sex. She was someone who was more like a big sister to me but she was crafty.

On a few occasions she talked me into buying her something to eat. The slick part is that she would get at me like she was about to treat me but in the end I'd be the one paying. Lucy had moves. In '92, I crept and got Lily pregnant but she didn't tell me. Instead she told Maya. Once Maya told me I approached her to confirm whether or not it was true. She seemed embarrassed to tell me but she confirmed that she was pregnant by me. I said a few words to comfort her. I didn't want her to feel like she was alone. I knew she was pregnant by me and if she decided to have our child then I was going to have to man up and be a father. Glynnis would be pissed but I wasn't going to deny or abandon my child. Lucy pulled up on me later that night yelling and cursing at me for getting Lily pregnant. She got at me sideways so I cursed her out. Although some of the things I said I didn't mean. My pride wouldn't let her talk to me in any kind of way. We eventually reconciled our differences and got back cool. Come to find out Lily was allegedly pregnant with twins. But by the time I found out it was too late because her mother had beat her and forced her to have an abortion.

She was devastated and truthfully I can't describe how I was feeling. It was seemingly unreal. Her mother was Catholic and abortion violated the Catholic tradition. I used to wonder if my skin color played a role in her mother's decision. While in the county jail facing the death penalty there was times when I thought about the twins and wished they was here to carry on my name. The flip side is that if I had children I wouldn't want them to grow up without me. I wanted to be a much better father than Edward was to me and Pookie. Nevertheless I was surprised by Lily's visit because it was unexpected. It was perfect timing though because at the time I was stressing and her visit put my mind at ease. She was happy to see me. She told me that she was single and doing well and I told her a little bit about what was going on with my case. She said that if I needed anything to let her know. Her and Glynnis hated each other. She knew Glynnis was my woman and that fact used to infuriate her. I didn't ask her for anything because I knew that she didn't have much financially to offer. She wasn't a hustler like Glynnis. I felt like the little money she was making at the time she needed it more.

Throughout my time in the county jail she would pop up periodically and visit me out of the blue. Fortunately she and Glynnis never ran across each other. She and I were also friends. I found out that she had been intimate with my homeboy Macaroni. I didn't trip off of it because I wasn't in love with her. Otherwise that would've been a serious problem. We weren't together so I couldn't say anything about what she was doing. I was cool with the fact that she still thought about me and came to check up on me from time to time.

A few weeks later I came back down to court from Wayside. I was on the 9000 floor and saw Crip-Cal. He had just left with a group of inmates who were moving to another unit. I heard his name when the officer announced it. I wanted to catch up with him badly and find out what the hell was going on. He had some explaining to do. I also wanted to put hands on him for working with the police. A few hours later they moved me to the 2000 floor. There were six man cells on the bottom tiers and four man cells on the top tiers. When it was crowded you'd often find two extra inmates sleeping on the floors of each cell. As I walked down the top tier to my cell I was bracing myself for a possible fight because you never knew who they were going to stick you in the cell with. You could be in a cell with your Arch enemy or a group of them. When I walked to the cell and looked inside I couldn't believe my eyes, this had to be a set up or a prank. Staring at me when I walked through the door was Crip-Cal!

I put my property and bed roll on top of my bunk. He tried to hug me but I cut him off and asked him was he a confidential informant against me? His eyes got big as he emphatically denied it. I asked him, "then how do my attorney know your name?" He looked confused. I told him that my attorney filed a motion to compel the prosecution to release the name of their informant and they gave my attorney his name. He denied that he was an informant but I didn't believe him. My thoughts raced as I quickly thought about what to do. One thing I had to rule out off the top was beating him down. I couldn't touch him because I could easily be traced to this cell. And I was leery about being in the cell with him. I felt like this might be a setup.

If I assaulted him then the prosecution would use it in court against me to convince the jury that the lies he was alleged to have told were actually the truth. I couldn't afford that. I told him about his alleged statements he made to the police. He continued to deny making those statements. I then asked him to recall the traffic stop in front of his house involving Tiny Bubble just before the shots at the gas station rang out. I asked him if Kemo was parked across the street from his house that night and he said yeah cause he remembered Kemo, Lil Greedy, and somebody else got out of the car when the police drove off. I told him to think about who that third person was that got out of the car with them. He thought about it for a moment and said that he didn't recall. I told him what he said and did that night at that moment and then told him, "You don't remember me getting out of the passenger side and saying that I dodged a bullet with the traffic stop because I was on the run?" He thought about it and got excited as he remembered and recalled everything that took place.

I told him I didn't know how my name came up as being the shooter when he knew that we all had love for Junebug and Lil Owl. I questioned him about Flux allegedly being behind the shooting and my being the shooter. He denied making that statement. He also knew that I never bragged about any dirt I have ever done. That's just not how I got down. He agreed and I told him that if you're truly not an informant then tell that to my attorney. He agreed to do so. The next day I called my attorney and told him to come visit Crip-Cal and get his statement from him. Rothman sent his investigator to take his statement and a few days later he transferred. I didn't even ask him why he was locked up.

CHAPTER SEVENTEEN

R ight after I ran into Crip-Cal my brother Pookie came to jail and was placed in my cell. He didn't have any money so I gave him some money and bought him canteen. He did some foul things to me over my lifetime but this was the worst. Yet I couldn't bring myself to do anything to him. Our immediate family had been through and lost so much. I loved him even if he didn't love me. I used to think about what Deon and Michael would say if they were here to witness it. He was on his way back to CYA for a violation. I didn't even speak to him about his statement because it hurt that bad. I couldn't understand how he let the police twist him up into agreeing with their theory. I knew that he was lying and the police did too. But none of that mattered anymore. All the police and prosecution was concerned about was that he eventually agreed with them that he heard that I was the shooter. To a white jury that was more than enough to get me found guilty. A week later I went to administrative segregation ("Ad-Seg"). That was the last time I saw my brother.

I ran into this dude named Demitrius Henson. He alleged to have witnessed the shooting at the gas station. He lived off Gage and Broadway. I asked him what he saw. He said that he was standing in front of his apartment building when he saw a Cherokee Jeep drive down Broadway and turn in the direction of the gas station. He said he turned his head for a second and heard a lot of loud gunshots coming from the direction the jeep drove in. He said that he looked and saw the jeep drive back to Broadway and turn right headed towards Florence. He said he only saw one dude in the jeep. I asked him if he could recognize him if he saw him again and he said yeah. Then I told him that the police arrested me for that shooting. He was surprised and said that the dude in the jeep was dark skinned. I asked him if he would be willing to come to court for me and he said that he would. I called Rothman and told him about Demitrius. Rothman sent his investigator to take Demitrius' statement.

A short while later I heard from Glynnis and she planned to come visit me. Momentarily things were OK between us. Plus I had gotten busted with having $300.00 cash on me which was against county jail policy so they froze my books. The most you could have on you at one time was $40.00. When they freeze your books it means that you cannot spend your money at the canteen and any other money you receive will be frozen too. The only way to get around it is to release all of the money to someone on the streets which will unfreeze your books. I had planned to release the money to Glynnis so that she could resend the money back to my books. In the meantime it was boring sitting in a cell all day.

At times I'd escape my reality by reminiscing on some of the happy times of my childhood. I'd come up with memories that were long forgotten such as the time when I spent a night at my grandmother Vergie's house and the next morning at around 7 a.m. my cousin Duane and I crept across the street to my aunt Hattie's house to visit her. Hattie and uncle George didn't have any children so anytime we came over she would welcome us with joy and cook us something to eat. She truly enjoyed our company as much as we enjoyed hers. Hattie was the most gentle, loving, gracious, and kindest woman I'd ever met in my life. We indulged in conversation while we ate and she kept a smile on her face whenever she saw us that could make your heart melt. Uncle George was a hater. He wouldn't even speak to us but you could hear him murmuring from their bedroom. Hattie didn't pay him no mind. She had an aura and spirit about her that was Godly and righteous.

Just being in her presence made me want to do right and be a better person so that I wouldn't disappoint her. After we finished hanging out with Hattie we walked back over to my grandmother's house. When we walked through the door there was my grandmother smoking a cigarette with a long ash hanging, standing up looking at us, with smoke coming out of her nostrils. She raised her voice and said "where you two little niggas coming from?" We both replied, "aunt Hattie's!" My grandmother stated, "why are you going over there for food when I cook for you here?" We explained that we didn't go over to Hattie's for the food, we went to visit her and she decided to make us something to eat. My grandmother just stared at us and thought about what we said. Clearly she had a bone to pick with Hattie for stealing her grandson's affection. It was a funny thing to see my grandmother get jealous behind that situation. My grandmother didn't want to be in competition with no one. But what she didn't realize at the time is that our love for Hattie didn't alter the love and affection we had for her. My grandmother was also loving, kind hearted, humble, and gentle. She awoke every morning at 4:30 a.m. and cooked breakfast for her family. She loved serving rabbit syrup with her pancakes. She would do anything for her family. She was fair if she had to discipline you and she didn't like us beating up the kids on her street. She'd occasionally yell out "you little Evans niggas is just like your grandfather!" I used to love to show her my report card and tell her how well I was doing in school.

During holidays she used to make her favorite peanut butter and chocolate cake, a jello mole which had marshmallows in it, and a German chocolate cake. Uncle Paul was her snitch. She had a loquat tree in her front yard. That's one of my favorite fruits till this day. Those were good times. I thought about Doc and Sassie at times too. On a couple of occasions I saw someone in traffic that made me turn my head because the person reminded me of Doc. He was such a cool dude, a good person, and a role model in our community. He was respected by everyone and he treated everyone the same; it didn't matter who you were. Everybody in the hood loved Doc. Men of character like him were rare to find. He didn't need to use his fist, a weapon, or talk tough for people to respect him. He showed me that it's better to be respected as a good person than to be respected because people fear you. After he passed away my neighborhood felt the loss.

As for Sassie I treated her like she was human. I used to feed her junk food and whatever else I was eating. She'd stare at me and I couldn't turn her down. She would always greet me with her tail wagging and leap up to lick my face. If she was chained up I'd unchain her and she ran all around the yard out of joy. I used to love wrestling with her or taunting her with a towel until she attacked it and ripped it up. I'd play pranks on her too. I put on a Halloween mask once and she became disturbed and started barking until I called her name out and she recognized my voice and calmed down. Sassie was a great guard dog. One time I had to call her off of my homie Mr. Lil Cee because he came into our back yard while no one was around and attempted to borrow a tool. Sassie bit him and he was hollering. She had a couple of litters of puppies too. Michael would sell the puppies for $50.00 each.

One of her puppies we named "Mama Rainy." She was dark brown with a black nose and a white patch between her eyes and on her stomach. She was muscular and had a smooth personality. She didn't bark much either. She and Sassie were close. She was 4 years old when she ran out into the streets and was hit by a motorist and died. Michael was pissed because the dude kept going and didn't pull over. Michael got his gun and pursued after him but couldn't catch up with him. I think he cried behind that. Sassie had Bopete too. He was all black and a scrapper. Michael gave him to our neighbor Andrew. Bopete won a few dogfights in the hood too. In those days people didn't let their dogs fight till death. I used to love watching a good dog fight. Unfortunately, both Doc and Sassie died in 1984. I was sad about that. I ain't never been close to a dog since.

On the corner of 61st and Avalon was Jaris' soul food joint. It was attached to a small club strictly for grownups. You had to be 21 years old to get in but you never saw a young crowd there. It was always people between the ages of 30 and up who went to the club. A black family owned it and the food was bomb. The only problem is that you would literally have to wait 45 minutes for your order to be ready. But it was worth the wait. There were times I dozed off and fell asleep waiting on my order and had the waitress wake me up when my order was ready. They sold the best French fries I'd ever tasted in my life. The club was always blaring some B.B. King, Al Green, Bobby Womack, Aretha Franklin, Marvin Gaye, Temptations, Barry White, or some other well known R&B or Blues artists of the day. As a kid I used to like looking into the club from the Cafe area and watching all of those thick hip sisters inside dancing. Jaris' closed in '88. That was a shame.

I also used to like watching the street races in my hood. The Gray Boys used to race their cars in the big alleys on 60th or 61st Streets. My father Edward beat the Gray Boys back in the day. They had love for me just based on the fact that Edward was my father. They were also good friends with Michael too. My neighborhood was popping as a kid growing up.

I called the hood and learned that Lil Ric-Roc from Q102 EC got killed at the gas station on Gage and Figueroa. My homies suspected the 68 PlayBoy Hustlers so they started warring with them. At the repast the 62's and 69's both showed up but were not intermingling with each other due to their ongoing beef. Allegedly Too-Cool from 69 EC told his homies that they were scared of the 62's in front of everyone that was out there that day which offended them. That night the neighbors found him shot dead behind the 69 apartments. His words cost him his life.

I heard my name being called for a visit. I assumed that it was Glynnis. I had plans on releasing the money off of my books to her because my account was frozen and talking to her about the issues in our relationship. I was tired of all the childish games she was playing. One minute we were cool then the next minute she had an attitude and I couldn't reach her. I felt like she was playing these games because I was locked up but if I was out she'd be singing a whole different tune. She was getting at me like I was a sucker and that was either going to end or we were going to have problems. When I got to the visiting room and sat down at the booth I was pleasantly surprised and confused when I saw Angie step to the window. She was smiling as she began by saying, "I know that you probably have other bitches coming to see you but your woman is back so tell them other hoes to back up!" I was skinning and grinning like a little kid but I couldn't let her off the hook though. I needed to know what happened to her. I asked her where she was and she told me that she recently bailed out of the feds. She had a drug trafficking case. She said that she went to jail before she could visit me. She then went full court press by telling me that she knew that I was facing a gang of time but she didn't care, she was going to be there for me, and she wanted to marry me.

I was speechless. Glynnis was my woman and she didn't say anything remotely close to what Angie had just said to me. On the contrary she was catching attitudes and being distant. Angie pulled out approximately $4,000.00 in hundreds, fifties, and twenty dollar bills. She then told me that she was coming to visit me Thursday through Sunday. She was going to give me $40 each day and send me a few hundred dollars to my books to make sure that I was straight. She was saying the things every dude locked up would love to hear. I loved her and she was a beautiful soul. But the only problem was Glynnis. They knew about each other but had never met. Glynnis was going to be coming to visit me within that time frame and I didn't want them bumping heads because she would try to fight Angie if she caught her visiting me. Glynnis still held animosity towards my ex girlfriends from elementary school.

I didn't want any drama between them at the county jail so I decided to keep it all the way real with Angie. I told her that I appreciated everything she said and I was grateful to have her in my life but I have a woman. Clearly I didn't think about how she would receive this information. Angie looked at me with an icy stare and after a brief moment to process what I just told her said "who?" I replied, "Glynnis!" She blew a gasket as she sarcastically replied, "that bitch is back?" I replied, "I haven't heard from you in 8 months since you told your brother that you were coming to visit me." She replied, "but baby I went to the Feds on this case." I then told her that I heard what she was saying but I didn't know that. For all of this time I thought you moved on. Nobody told me that you got locked up and Glynnis has been there for me. I felt like an idiot for keeping it real with her even though it was the noble thing to do. I can't lie, a huge part of me felt like I should've just kept my mouth shut and let her look out for me. Angie started crying and I felt bad. I tried to console her but she was upset with me. She couldn't believe I chose Glynnis. The way Glynnis was acting at the time I just hoped that I made the right choice.

I then did another bozo move. I trusted her enough to release the money off of my books to her and she reluctantly gave me a wet $40.00. That was the last time I saw Angie. She kept my money because she was hurt. At first I was upset but I eventually forgave her. She wasn't running off with my money, instead taking my money was the only way for her to make me suffer a small amount of what she was suffering. I played that whole situation wrong.

Chapter Eighteen

I was back in Wayside Medium North. I saw Joker from 69EC and my cousin Lil Set-Trip from Bounty Hunters. I got at Joker about a rumor I was hearing that he was supposed to be doing something to me behind my case cause Junebug was his cousin. He denied the rumor and we chopped it up for a minute. My homeboy Big Spike from 62EC had come down from prison for a child custody hearing. Spike had been down since 1981 for a murder in East L.A. Snowman from 69EC snitched on him. OG's from the neighborhood had been knowing this for years but kept it secret because they were playing favoritism. I saw my cousin through his unit's glass. He was in the "Damu" dorm. I saw him when he came to jail. I was surprised to learn that he had a murder case and that he was gang banging. He grew up in my neighborhood and knew a lot of people in the 62's but he never wanted to join a gang which was fine with me.

His mother Shirley was a good woman who was strong, wise, and independent. His little brother Coconut was quiet and a stick of dynamite waiting to be lit. Coconut joined 62EC and was nicknamed Tiny Casper. We went to 66th Street Elementary School together. My cousin named "Little" and sister "Bondie" also went there. I was a protector to them all. A few weeks after I got to Medium North, Lil Spooky-Slim and Mad

Boxer from 190 EC came to the dorm. Lil Boxer and Tiny Rat from 62EC were in the dorm also. I told them that me and Spooky-Slim had some unfinished business and we might be getting down. I called him to the back of the dorm and asked him if he was still upset by what I did to him in his sleep. Because if he was then we could get down right now and get it over with. He said that he was cool and that we were even. From that time forward we were cool. The beef was over.

I received two letters from a female claiming to be Junebug's sister. She was accusing me of killing her brother and threatening to have something done to my family. She never left a return address. I was bothered by it because she was oblivious to what was truly happening to me, the fact that I was being framed for this crime. On one hand I empathize with her because she, like so many others in society, tends to think that a person is guilty just because they are charged with a crime. That's definitely not true. On the other hand, her making threats to my family was going to get her hurt. Eventually, I saw that she was all mouth and didn't mean half of what she said. She was just grieving. I ended up going back to court about a month later and landing in the county jail. That's where I ran into my bro Cowboy from 42GC. We greeted each other with big hugs and smiles. Cowboy grew up in my neighborhood.

They used to live on 59th and Mettler Avenue. He and his brother Zach along with his cousin name Wino from 42GC were all like family. Cowboy was fighting a gang - related murder on some bloods. I was hoping he beat his case. We conversed about our cases, families, and neighborhood. I was glad to see someone I knew from childhood. One day I was summoned to the attorney/client visiting room. I expected to see my attorney but instead it was my parole officer. She was a black woman in her mid-30's. She was nice looking and curvy with big breasts. I was surprised because about 5 months prior I had a visit from someone at the parole office who asked me whether or not I wanted to serve my violation and I refused.

Now, this sister who I'd never met was coming to visit me. The attorney/client visiting room is different from the regular visiting room. In the attorney/client visiting room I was able to touch my attorney. She greeted me and introduced herself to me as my parole officer. She asked me whether or not I wanted to serve my violation and I told her no. I told her that I was facing the death penalty and wasn't thinking about no violation. She then began indulging in small talk by asking me about my family, relationship status, if I had kids, etc. I was trying to figure out what her angle was. She was asking me personal questions and I was starting to think that she was coming on to me. I started to say something slick to her just to see how she would react. Her reaction would either confirm or disprove my assumption.

However, I restrained myself. She was smiling a lot. I asked her about her relationship status and she was happy to tell me that she was single and lived alone. The more she spoke the more I believed my suspicion to be true. I looked over at the officer running the visiting room and he was staring directly at us. He was a redneck white man wearing bifocals with a thick mustache and no beard or sideburns. I told my parole officer it was time for me to leave. She gave me her business card to the parole office and said that I could call her anytime even if I just needed to talk. I accepted the card but never called her. The reason I was on parole was due to my selling drugs. Let me take it back to 1988. My mother was addicted to cocaine. She had gotten pregnant by this dude named Jeffrey who worked at Gage Liquor Store. But Jeffrey was married to Michael's friend Big Melvin's sister. He had children with her.

Shortly after he got my mother pregnant with my sister Jasmine he left her and went back to his wife. My mother was hurt by it because she had real feelings for Jeffrey. In my opinion it caused her more stress which led to her falling deeper into drug addiction. My mother and I both needed psychological and emotional help. When Jasmine was born my mother wasn't allowed to bring her home. Allegedly my sister had drugs in her system. This was all Big Mama and Jeanette was waiting for because it corroborated their position that my mother was unfit. The social worker started doing pop up visits. She was a big boned Black woman probably in her mid 30's. One day she pulled up unannounced and Jeanette ran up to her car with dope in hand thinking she was a person looking to buy drugs and asking her what she needed. All of these things lead to my little sisters being placed into foster care. I wondered if I'd see them again. My mother and I were devastated. I could sense that she was starting to lose her will to keep fighting because every time we turned around there was another loss. I tried to support her as much as I could but at 15 years of age and in the streets there was little that I could do.

I was gang banging, selling drugs, and chasing girls. In October of '88, I sold some dope to an undercover cop and went to jail when the police raided my house and found dope and guns. I received 9 months in Juvenile Camp and was sent to Camp Munz. Back then the "WAR

ON DRUGS AND GANGS" was in full effect thus I received the maximum penalty for a person who'd never been to camp. I broke my hand rat packing Pokey from the Jungles in East Lake Juvenile Hall. Gang banging was real and I was participating in all of the activities. I felt like I had to build my reputation by fighting my enemies. Being a buster was disgraceful and I couldn't go back to my hood with smut on my name. My mother was left alone and our family was officially torn apart. When I first got to camp it was rough. I was frail with a broken hand and my enemies saw that as an opportunity to test me.

These dudes had been in camp for at least six months and was physically fit from lifting weights and eating good. They was some cowards though because they waited for my homies Lil Sandman 68 EC and Lil Crip Dog Q102 EC to go home to start tripping. My hand was still in a cast but Q-Bone from West Side 104 th Street Hard Time Hustlers had my back. I met Day-Day from 92 Hoover. At that time he was Glynnis' boyfriend. I knew about him but I didn't tell him that I use to talk to her too. He was cool. He received six months for manslaughter when he accidently killed his homeboy J-Dog while playing with a gun. But I got nine for a dope case. That was crazy. While in camp I started back going to school which was mandatory. I got my groove back and started liking school again. I even made plans to enroll in summer school when I got out. I wanted to do right (at least for awhile) when I got out. The teachers really were trying to help us. I even ran into a counselor I recognized from Bethune Jr. High.

Every time we saw each other back then it was a foot race because I was ditching and he was trying to stop me but he could never catch me. He and I became cool. In camp we used to go hiking in the mountains. I used to like that a lot. While in camp I was being introduced to a different way of living that was free from gunshots, drugs, addicts, dysfunctional families, police harassment, and having to watch moving cars or look over my shoulder. I still had a lot of emotions bottled up inside of me because I didn't trust anyone to talk about the things I'd been through. I used to take offense to adults who didn't know anything about me, never took the time to get to know me, but felt confident enough to tell me what type of person I was based solely on the fact that I was gang banging, selling drugs, and grew up in the hood. People like that didn't command my respect because they were judgmental. I needed help not to be judged.

My homie Lil Bam from 118 EC arrived at camp. We knew each other from the streets and Juvenile Hall. It felt good having a homeboy from my hood come to camp cause dudes were acting hella funny but I held my own and pretty much stayed to myself before he came. I was doing well so the director of the camp told me that he was going to release me two months early. I was happy. He told me that he just needed to contact my mother and she could come pick me up. It was May 6, 1989, the day before my 16th birthday. A few hours later I was informed that I couldn't go home because the police raided my house and took my mother to jail. I tried to hold it all together but I went outside, found a spot by myself, and broke down and cried for about 20 minutes. I hadn't cried in a couple of years up to that point. The thought of my mother doing time and me having to remain locked up tore me up. I felt like we were cursed. On May 8th at around 7 p.m. my mother came to pick me up with G-Bone and my aunt Paula. I was happy to go home but not as excited as I was before I got the bad news.

On the way home everyone was silent as we drove through the mountains. Then my mother told me that we lost our house and we were homeless. I was stunned and in disbelief. It took me a minute to process that information. I asked her how that happened and she couldn't explain it. The thought of being homeless was numbing. At that moment I literally stopped giving a damn. The thing only left to take was our lives which I felt was next. My mother asked me what I was going to do and where I would go. I told her that I'm going to the hood. I wasn't about to go live with my aunt Paula because she already had too much going on at my grandmother's house. My plans of going to school died. I had to get on my grind. When we got to the hood I went to my godfather Burbank's dope spot and he fronted me an ounce of cocaine. My mother and I then went on 61st and I saw the windows on our house boarded up. Big Mama rushed to change the locks on the doors too. Had my mother and I known anything about the law we could've sued Big Mama because she had no authority to change the locks or board up the windows while all of our property was still inside. Only U.S. Marshals have the power to evict.

We also would have sued to get our house back because there's no way that we should've been homeless. I crept into our house from my bedroom window and unlocked the door to let my mother in. The house was ransacked. Things were everywhere. We stayed inside for about 30 minutes while looking around and gathering a few things then left. While coming out of the front door we saw Big Mama standing outside waiting on us. She threatened to call the police on us. I became enraged and had to catch myself from doing something to her. She was fouler than dog shit on a newborn baby's blanket! I literally contemplated beating her up and then getting into it with my uncle Spark behind it. But out of respect for Michael and Spark I restrained myself. My mother went to stay at a friend's house on 49th and Avalon. I had no choice but to get out there in the streets and hustle. By 8 a.m. the next morning I had $900 and a few rocks left. My entire hood was a booming dope spot. The funny thing about being homeless is you find out quickly who's really there for you. When you're poor and struggling doors close on you. All of the hardships made me ruthless and rebellious.

My uncle Clydell and my aunt Niecey was the only ones out of the neighborhood who was there for my mother and I. To them I am forever grateful. I was moving fast hustling but it was hard to stack the way I wanted to because I was homeless. Continuously I had to spend money for food, clothes, hygiene, and motel rooms for my mother and I to stay in. One thing about it I made sure that we was dressed nicely everyday. I gave my mother the money to put down on an apartment for us but allegedly she got robbed for it at the gas station on Slauson and Broadway a couple of hours after I gave it to her. That was another loss which had me hustling backwards. I went through the hood looking for the culprit so that I could gun him down but I couldn't find him. My mother knew all of my homies so it wasn't one of them. I got shot in my right hand by the Broadways two weeks after I got out while grinding late at night. My other hand was now in a cast. I had a gun in my right hand when they shot me. They shot this female smoker named Lodi Dodi a few times. I thought she was dead but she survived.

Days later I was going through busting on the Broadways. I had shootouts with them when they drove through my hood. It was on sight whenever I saw one of their cars. I was pulling up dumping on them no matter what time of day. It was on with the Swans and Hoovers too. Chivetta was by my side most of the time and I made sure that she was straight. I really thought that we would be together forever. Young love will fool you. I used to creep and sneak her out of the house so she could spend nights with me in my motel room. Her mother still didn't like me.

My cousin Lil Pookie and homie Lil Wooder were my road dogs and like little brothers to me. Lil Wooder was still learning how to talk to females. One night he came to my motel room at the Regal Inn while I was with Chivetta and asked me to come kick it with him in his room when I get some time. About an hour later I went to his room and he was there alone. I asked him who he was in the room with. He said that he was with my homegirl Eva but she wasn't messing with him and left. He was watching porn with the covers up to his neck. I sat on the bed and started chopping it up with him. I didn't trip off of him being under the covers until about five minutes later when I looked at him and saw his face contorted while his hand was rapidly moving back and forth under the covers. That's when I jumped up and yelled, "aw nigga you nasty!" He was masturbating to the porn. I hurried up and left while laughing. It was too funny for me to put my hands on him. My homie Lil C-Bone brought some new young dudes (about 5 of them) to the hood to get initiated on the set. Me and Baby Sike beat all of them up and told them they still weren't from the hood. Niecey's girlfriend FreDonna took a liking to me and used to call me her son. She was nice looking and hella cool. I had a lot of love for her. I caught another dope case for possession less than 3 months after I was out and was sent to CYA for two years. I was waiting for Lil Ghost to get out. Ironically he got out a few days after my arrest.

While inside I learned that Lil Wooder snitched on a double murder and Chivetta got pregnant by Baby Swan from SYC. To make matters worse my bro Lil Fish told me to be silent as he called her on the 3 way. He began asking about her pregnancy and what she was going to do when I came home. She then began speaking negative of me and then said that she was stupid for listening to me when I was out. I was furious and couldn't wait to get released, which was a few months away.

She was ungrateful and treacherous. I never introduced her to drugs or crime, I wasn't abusive to her, I looked out for her without asking for anything in return. I provided for her even when I was homeless but she had never looked out for me. She didn't look out for me while I was locked up and she didn't have the decency to break up with me before she moved on. I felt like I should've cheated on her with her friends and cousins. Our relationship would never be the same. When I got out she immediately came around crying, apologizing, and retracting her statements. Females love to talk high power when a dude is locked up but it's a completely different story when they see him free. Nevertheless I hit Chivetta a few times to satisfy my desires but she and I were nothing more than friends.

While I was in CYA my mother did clean up her act and get my little sisters Micole, Ebony, and Jasmine back from foster care. That to me showed the love she has for her children. I was proud of her for that and I give her props because many mothers don't do what's necessary to obtain their children back from the system. My mother would always do whatever she needed to (short of committing crime) in order to provide for us and she always had me and my brothers backs as kids growing up. She was hard on us and wouldn't hesitate to speak her mind but she would give her last dime to ensure our happiness. All she asked for in return is that we get an education, stay out of trouble, do our chores, and graduate from high school.

I missed and remembered so many things from my childhood. Because we had the first big screen T.V. in my neighborhood along with On and Select T.V. which were the original cable boxes back in the days, Michael used to invite all of his friends and people from the neighborhood over to our house to watch the boxing matches. We saw the Sugar Ray Leonard v. Tommy "Hitman" Hearns, Muhammad Ali v. Leon Spinks, and Hearns v. Marvin Hagler fights all of which were classics. Each time our living room was crowded with people yelling and screaming along with the smell of mother's enchiladas or tacos filling up the house. Kids and adults' eyes were all glued to the T.V. My mother would feed everyone too. Those were good times.

I also remembered this dude out of the neighborhood named Chicken who used to be in front of the lawnmower shop on 62nd Street and San Pedro. Chicken never joined a gang. He was dark skinned and approximately 6'5 250 lbs. He was quiet, humble, and respectful. Nobody messed with him and he didn't bother anyone. He was a big Cornfed brother. His little brother Buck was from 62 NHC. However, he died by drowning somewhere in the south while visiting family. I saw him get out of character once and it was memorable. I was walking down San Pedro in the daytime. I couldn't have been no older than ten years old when I heard what sounded like a car tire blowing out as a car was driving. I immediately turned to see what it was and that's when I heard the sound again. However, it wasn't a car tire blowing out, it was Chicken kicking a dude in the chest twice. The man was on the ground looking up at Chicken while scared to death. That was crazy.

Then there were the local alcoholics like Moose and Hobo who always hung out on the side of Royalty Market while sitting on milk crates. Moose didn't have any teeth in his mouth but he was always smiling and playing his guitar. Back in those days kids were taught to be respectful to all elders no matter their conditions. My aunt Willie Mae owned a cleaners on 62nd Street and San Pedro. We used to send our clothes there to get cleaned and pressed from time to time. Later on Deon stopped going to her cleaners when he learned that she was conspiring with Big Mama against my mother. So me and Pookie followed suit. Willie Mae was upset when she saw us walk past her cleaners with our clothes and head to the cleaners one block away on Gage. Mr. Evans had the bike repair shop on San Pedro next to Gage Liquor Store. Kids from the neighborhood went there on occasion to get their flat tires fixed. But once we learned how to fix our own bikes and patch up our inner tubes Mr. Evans went out of business with us. He was a good man and another pillar in the community.

Lil Ghost grandfather Ike was a family man and a hustler. He use to shoot dice at night in front of the liquor store from time to time. Ike had a shot on him. He broke the dice game up a few times. He wasn't no punk either. He'd fight a dude over his money. He drove a white van. I liked Ike and he was someone I respected. I remember the cotton hair rollers females use to wear in their hair. They went from cotton to plastic. Dudes who wore perms kept rollers in their hair too. That was considered fly back then.

I used to be addicted to Ms. Pac-man arcade games. Ms. Pac-man made me a criminal. I got beat a few times for stealing quarters from my parents to play that game. Michael was so cold he'd remember exactly how much change he had when he came home from work and went to sleep. He slept with his eyes open so it used to be tricky stealing money from him because at times I wouldn't know if he was awake or truly sleeping. When he woke up and found out his change was gone he'd go on a rampage doling out whippings. In the end I gave up stealing and Ms. Pac-man.

As a kid I was a huge fan of the Cosby Show. Claire was beautiful and the finest mother on T.V. She was loving, intelligent, kind hearted, and graceful. She didn't parent by using profanity, yelling, or threatening to beat her children for getting on her nerves. Dr. Huxtable was a role model and a hands-on father. He wasn't a strict disciplinarian. He talked to his children and listened to them. He didn't expose them to crime and drugs. His children had college funds and didn't have to look outside the home for role models. The Huxtables didn't have any financial struggles either. All of the children genuinely got along too. Watching the Cosby's was a way for me to escape my reality. I wished that my family was similar to the Cosby's. They were the perfect example of what a family should be like. Too bad it was just a T.V. show.

In the county jail I continued writing raps because it was therapeutic and gave me something worthwhile to do with my time. I was working towards making my dream of being a rap star come true. There were many artists that I was a fan of back then. Ice Cube dropped the song "Tadow," Snoop Dogg dropped "Murder was the case," Biggie dropped "Big Poppa and Warning," E40 dropped " Sprinkle me and Captain save a hoe," DJ Quik dropped "Dollarz + Sense," and Dr. Dre dropped "Keep ya head ringing." The West Coast was popping and I longed for my opportunity to break into the Hip-Hop industry.

When I was a kid I didn't know what my gifts and talents were. I didn't see anything special about me. I played Pop Warner football from the age of 10-12 for the Hawthorne Packers. I played defensive back and my strengths were hitting and tackling. I could catch it too. Coach Sands used to try to get me to learn the offensive playbook but I didn't have any interest in playing on offense because I saw the favoritism being displayed towards the coaches sons. Truth be told I didn't like their sons and I used to try to punish them in one on one contact drills. We used to practice at Hawthorne High School and at Jesse Owens Park. My first season went well. We finished 7-5 as a new team. My brother Pookie played for the Vikings and my cousin Duane played for the Bears. My mother showed up at every game and always brought enough food to feed the whole team after the games but the powers that be were ungrateful. At the end of the season we had a team banquet at the Airport Park Hotel. During the event certain parents were honored for their contributions to the team. My mother was disappointed when she was overlooked. Playing football allowed me to meet new people, get a closeup look at new communities, and see a different way of life. We used to play teams from upper middle class neighborhoods such as Gardena, Torrence, Redondo Beach, Carson, Banning, Inglewood, and Pacific Palisades. Through Pop Warner football I was able to see how people outside of the hood lived which caused me to dream of something more than what the hood had to offer. The downside of playing football was when my parents forgot to pick us up from practice and we'd be waiting outside hungry till at least 45 minutes to an hour after practice was over. I met Michael McGowan while playing for the Packers. He and I both were claiming 62 EC but neither of us had ever met.

Once we started naming the 62's we knew it became clear that we both were from the neighborhood. Lil Sad was his older cousin. We became friends. I stopped playing football when my parents couldn't afford to pay the enrollment fee for me to get my uniform and officially be a member of the team. I was disappointed because playing football gave me an incentive to do well in school and it occupied my time to where I wasn't thinking about the streets or our financial hardship. But once I was no longer playing football I got caught up in the streets. Michael McGowan was nicknamed Baby Sad. He and I fought when I got officially initiated into 62 EC. Back then I thought he was down. He hung out with Lil Stoney, Lil Greedy, Baby Sike, Lil Roscoe, Lil Asmo, and Tiny Bubble. But there were signs of weakness within him. He was getting passes because of Lil Sad's reputation. Years later his cowardice would reveal itself. In hindsight there were a number of things which made me want to join a gang. For example, my OG homies used to hang out next door to my house and I knew them and had love for them.

My parents used to take us to various concerts in parks which were hosted by radio stations such as K-ACE, 1580 Kday, 1230 KAT, or KUTE 102. No matter where we went the 62's showed up and showed out. Within a short time of the 62's arriving at the park there would be a commotion. Then I'd see people screaming and crowds scattering because my big homies were beating up people and robbing them. I used to trip off of that as a kid. At that time I didn't want to be a gang member. I used to tell my homie Wooder that I wasn't going to be from 62. However, when I saw the 1979 movie "The Warriors" it planted a seed within me. That was my favorite movie as a kid. I grew fond of the characters, especially AJax and Swan. The movie depicted gang banging as dangerous but exciting and the members were loyal to one another even to the point of risking their lives. The Warriors were some unpretentious bad asses. They were forced to fight every gang they came across until they made it back to Coney Island due to them being falsely accused of killing Cyrus. Although only ten Warriors attended the gang meeting and they lost 3 members on the way home they stood tall and put hands on every rival gang they fought against. They were truly some underdogs but they came out on top. That movie gave me a different perspective about what gang banging was about and it lit a flame inside of me.

I went to school the next day and tried to emulate them while only in the first grade. I can now see that from early on I wanted to be a part of something greater than myself but Satan deceived me into thinking that gang banging was the answer when it wasn't. A couple of years later in 1981, Lil Oscar from 62 EC got killed at the age of 16. His girlfriend was my neighbor Cookie. I remember that it was one night when a lot of kids were still outside playing after the street lights came on. I was in my yard because my brothers and I had to be home by the time the street lights came on. If we weren't my mother would whistle down the street for us and we better come home shortly thereafter or there would be consequences. Someone came from around the corner and told everyone that Lil Oscar got shot.

Instantly the whole crowd broke and ran around the corner to 59th Place and San Pedro where Lil Oscar was lying on the ground. I also ran around the corner to see what was going on. I saw Lil Oscar on the ground gasping for air. He had been shot in the neck. He was walking with Lil Sike and Lil Sad when a car drove up and started shooting. Only Lil Oscar got hit. The ambulance took forever it seemed to come to get him. When they arrived they drove him to General Hospital but they didn't appear to have any urgency in getting him to the hospital as they casually drove him away. Later that night word spread that Lil Oscar died and the Swans killed him. Cookie, Candy, Evette, and a few other home girls from 62 EC were crying hysterically on our front lawn. Back then the home girls were called lettes (pronounced "lets") which was short for Criplettes. The 62's allegedly retaliated and murdered Chuckie from Swans and another individual. Now the Swans are alleged to have come up with their gang name from Vertis Swan. Vertis was buff and had hands back in the day. He was originally from Castle Crips which was a small gang that existed in the 70's but died out in the early 80's. Vertis became a member of the East Coast Crips. He had a crew of dudes who looked up to him and ran behind him. They called themselves the "Swanny Boys."

They eventually became Damus and became instant rivals to the East Coast Crips. They used to wear white rags the color of a Swan. When Lil Oscar got killed the neighborhood took it hard. After the ambulance drove away I recall this older black woman admonishing the 62's to stop gang banging so that they don't end up like Lil Oscar. But Big Quake said, "Crips don't die, we multiply and we ain't gonna ever stop Cripping, can't stop won't stop!" I went to school with his nephew Jack and I knew his sister Evette. Also Deon and Lil Oscar were friends. Deon looked up to him. Next was Crazy Larry. He got killed trying to rob a liquor store. Then a month or two later Termite got killed by the 52 BGC's. He was only 14 years old and the youngest 62 to die from gang violence. I felt the pain of their deaths because I personally knew them. A few years later Syco from SYC was killed in 1984. He died on

April Fool's day. Syco's family moved into my neighborhood in 1982 or '83. He was Deon's age and they were close friends. I knew his whole family. His mother's name was Ella Ruth. His older brothers' names were Tony and Robbie. And he had a little sister named Debbie. They were related to Romeo from 62EC. Syco's real name was Edmund but he hated for anyone to call him that. He couldn't stand cats either. He would kick them in the air anytime he got near one. On the night of March 31, 1984 he and Robbie were coming home from work and were mistaken as being members of 62EC and ambushed by the 59 Hoovers.

They shot Syco multiple times, killing him. Robbie didn't get hit. Earlier that same day Marvin Gaye's father had killed him. My brother Deon asked me if I heard the gunshots when Syco got shot and I said no. Syco died the next morning. I remember coming home from school and seeing my mother sitting at the kitchen table. I greeted her and poured myself something to drink. Then she calmly said, "Marlon you know your friend died today." I said, "who Syco?" She said yeah. I drank my kool aid in silence as the thought of Syco dying registered with me. That was the first time that I actually thought about shooting someone. Syco was murdered as retaliation for when the 62EC's murdered Smiley from 59 Hoover at 61st Street Elementary School the year before on April Fool's day. Another incident occurred around that same time. I was at Carl's Arcade/Bookie joint playing the "Dig Dug" arcade game when I heard commotion right outside the door. I didn't know what it was and I didn't check at the time because I was preoccupied with trying to win and extend my game. A few minutes later my game was over.

I had a pipe with a handle bar grip on it I found and was walking around with. When I stepped outside the door I saw a group of my homeboys on top of this big dude beating, kicking, and stomping him. He was on the ground but fighting back. Pookie was also hitting him. That's when I hit him in the head twice with the pipe. My homeboy Sugar Bear pulled us up off of him and escorted him to safety. He was from 52BGC and had gotten caught slipping in my hood. Getting caught slipping could get you killed. In 1982, a lot of kids from the neighborhood joined 62EC (my brothers included).

Overnight it seemed that the 62's gained at least 35 new members. I followed in my brother's footsteps. Back then everyone was close like family. We all hung out with each other and played football together at U.S. Motors off of Slauson and Los Angeles Street. We used to ride bikes from the hood to Venice beach and we used to go to the movies together downtown or Huntington Park. My parents were good to our friends. But my mother didn't like Gangster John because he used to curse out his mother. She used to threaten to beat me if I got caught hanging with him. My parents didn't mind if Deon and Pookie hung out with him. They sent mixed messages to us. My parents didn't seem to have a problem with my brother's gang banging. They alleged that they wanted to do everything they could to prevent me from following them down the wrong path. I recall Michael telling me, " we might have lost your brothers but we ain't going to lose you!" That didn't make sense to me. I felt like there should have been one set of rules for all of us.

One morning my mother came into our bedroom and noticed that Deon didn't want to move from this certain spot on his bed. She asked him to get up. When he got up she saw a lump under his mattress and called Michael to our bedroom. When he came in she pointed to the mattress and he lifted it up and found a sawed off shotgun. It was Deon's. I just knew he was going to get a beating but they surprised us all by taking the gun and not punishing him. That sent the wrong message to us. I knew a lot of 66's, 68's, and 69's too. Thus most of our childhood friends joined East Coast Crips. Banging didn't seem so bad. It was like having a second family. Gang members seemed to have an independence which I found to be appealing. I never knew that it would become addictive as any hard drug.

CHAPTER NINETEEN

There was a combination of things which made me want to sell dope. For example, my neighbor Andrew was the first dude I saw go from rags to riches in the dope game. I remember it was around 1982 when he came home with a brand new two tone colored Cadillac Seville and parked it in his mother's front yard. All of the neighbors came outside to admire his new car. Back in those days the Seville was considered the top luxury car. I saw Andrew's dress code change. He started wearing suits and alligator skin shoes ("Gators") with fat gold chains and gold rings and watches. He was having money and it made a difference. He was now being looked up too and envied in the neighborhood. There was also Blackjack, Burbanks, and Spud who were having money from selling cocaine. There was also C-Bone, Lil Man, T-Dog, and Casper who were all having money as well.

Deon started selling cocaine in 1983. He started carrying between $500-700 on him daily. His wardrobe was upgraded and he no longer needed to ask my parents for money. In those days the type of money he was holding was a lot because the cost of living was cheaper. I envied that lifestyle because you could be independent and not have to worry about whether or not your parents had some extra money for you to be able to do what you wanted to do. Deon started bringing home more money than my parents. Although my parents knew he was doing wrong they were reluctant to hinder a third income from coming into our home. This sent a message to me that I should do the same. I used to get beat for stealing. Cocaine brought enough money to where one didn't need to steal. There were also a few embarrassing moments which occurred that made me determined to sell dope.

One day my mother and Michael had been feuding over what I don't know. She asked me to walk with her around the corner to U.N. Market which was owned by some Asians. I went with her and once inside I saw my girlfriend Lajuana Pittman and her mother walking down the aisle shopping for some grocery items. I waved at Lajuana and she acknowledged me. Our parents knew that we were boyfriend and girlfriend. I didn't have any money on me. My mother was planning to cook some Spaghetti for dinner. She also grabbed a few items she needed to cook dinner. When we got in line Lajuana and her mother were directly behind us. As we got to the counter and placed our items up there for the cashier to ring them up I was looking at Lajuana and smiling at her. Then I heard the cashier say the cost of the items was $15.70. I waited for my mother to pay the cashier. She counted her money and she was $3.35 short. It seemed like time just slowed down dramatically and the place got quiet as all the people who were in line just stared at us. Black people ain't got no shame. I saw my mother put her head down in shame as she told me to go around the corner and ask Michael to give me the rest of the money. I did as she told me but when I got to the corner I saw Michael in the car with his friend driving off somewhere. I went back to the store to break the news to my mother. It was embarrassing having to put back items especially in the presence of my girlfriend. I also felt bad that I didn't have $3.35 to my name to cover the cost. I was 10 years old at the time.

It was May of 1986 when I began selling cocaine. Tim-Loc gave me five $20 rocks and told me to bring him back $90. I was naive to how much I was supposed to be getting and Tim-Loc was scandalous. I was on 62nd and San Pedro hanging with Gangster John when a customer pulled up asking for $20 of rock cocaine. I leaned in the car to make the sale oblivious to the fact that my mother was driving past at the same time. Gangster John didn't even say anything. When I came out of the car with the money my mother saw me out of her side mirror and immediately yelled, "Marlon! Come here and get your ass in this truck."

I was embarrassed as I did as I was told. She drove me home and grilled me. She took the dope from me. I told her that Tim-Loc gave me the dope. She was irate and threatened to call the police on him. She instead told Deon expecting him to reprimand me but he was about to give me my own sack because he didn't want me working for anyone else. Jeanette was eavesdropping and went to tell my mother. She cursed Deon out and told me I couldn't hang with him either. I would eventually start selling cocaine anyway. I can't fault my parents for my selling drugs because they both were against it and tried to prevent it, but I was just determined. I was sent to the module in January of 1994, a week before the big earthquake in North ridge that knocked down part of the freeway. When the earthquake hit all of the lights in the county jail went out and the entire building started rattling hard. It felt like I was on a ship in the midst of the sea caught in the middle of a tumultuous storm. The bunks were shaking so badly it felt like the screws were going to come unloose. The tremors lasted for about fifteen minutes. That was scary. In the module dudes were getting robbed, beat up, tied up, whipped with shower shoes, and ran up out of there. It was a zoo. It was loud there throughout the day from dudes talking over each other on the tier or beating on the bunks making music. It was hard to get some sleep in that environment. After a while I adapted to it. Lil Bow-Low came to the module and I asked him if he knew a smoker name Clay-max (i.e. Clarence Lavan) and he said yes. I told him that Clay-max came to my prelim and identified me as the shooter at the gas station. He looked surprised then he told me that Clay-max came up to him and a few other homies from 66 EC (including Chilly Moe) two days after the shooting and told them that he was a witness to the shooting. However, he described the shooter as short, stocky, dark skinned, with long reddish hair (braids), and wearing a red shirt. He stated that Clarence alleged that the dude was a "Blood" who he recognized from when he was visiting his girlfriend who lived in a Blood neighborhood. Lil Bow-Low sounded credible as he recited what Clarence told him. Clarence had said similar things during his tape recorded statement and at the prelim. On tape Clarence was sure that the shooter had long hair but he switched up his statement by saying the shooter was light skinned rather than dark skinned. I asked Lil Bow-Low if he'd be willing to come to court and testify to what Clarence told him. He said that he would, so I called my attorney and told him to come visit Lil Bow-Low and get his statement because he didn't have much time to serve. Rothman sent his investigator Moore to visit Lil Bow-Low. Lil Bow-Low's name is Ashawnto Ross. We went to Bethune Jr. High School together along with Junebug and Lil Owl. We all were little homies from the Six Pack and we all got along. Lil Bow-Low said that Clarence approached them with the information about him witnessing the shooting. Clarence testified at prelim that he was afraid for his safety because the Crips was coming to his house "being friendly" and asking him if it was the Bloods who did the shooting.

If my homies came to his house asking him if some Bloods did the shooting, then it's because that's what he originally told them and they were trying to confirm it. Also why would he be in fear for his safety when he testified that my homies were being friendly? If they wanted to harm him to prevent him from testifying they could easily have done so. But they didn't touch him because they never knew that he was lying on me in court. Clarence alleged that he had a brother in law from 68 EC. I found out that Scrappy was the person he was talking about. Clarence fled the crime scene on the night Junebug and Lil Owl got hit up at the gas station. It was 3 weeks later when Clarence spoke to the detectives for the first time. Had Chilly Moe not told the police about him they wouldn't have known anything about him. Within the 3 weeks between the time the shooting occurred till when Clarence spoke to the detectives the Six Pack erupted in war. The 62's, 68's, and 69's all went to war behind Junebug and Ice getting murdered.

Personally I believe that the Six Pack going to war behind the shooting at the gas station is what caused Clarence to switch up his statement and his theory about who committed the murders at the gas station. The hard part was proving it. During his tape recorded interview with detectives Clarence wondered how the shooter could be in jail when he'd recently seen him on the street. The detective told him that I came to jail after the shooting but Clarence was in disbelief because he was certain that the shooter was still on the streets. Clarence stated, "I don't see how he could be in jail when I saw him." To me this was further proof that I was being framed. The detectives knew the actual shooter was still on the streets during the date of their interview with Clarence. But I was the guy on their radar who they became fixated on. The truth didn't matter to them. Operation "Destroy Baby Bam" was in full effect and there was no turning back. Only God could deliver me from their diabolical plans.

What society fail to realize about police and their investigations is that they can gather credible information/evidence which undermines their theory of the case and point to someone completely different as the suspect but they will ignore, disregard, or hide that evidence from the defense and still seek to send the wrong person to prison solely because they want that certain individual to be the suspect even if he's not. The District Attorney's Office are co-conspirators in this injustice. They victimize the poor minorities because society has sent a message that they don't care about what happens to them. Therefore the injustice is rampant and ongoing. While in the module I passed my time writing new raps, exercising, hanging with my homies, and socializing with dudes in there from various hoods.

CHAPTER TWENTY

y attorney informed me that he had spoken to my alibi witnesses. He said that they all corroborate my innocence and confirmed that I was with them on 59th Place when the traffic stop and shooting at the gas station occurred. However, a jury may not find them credible because they are my homeboys. I told him that the prosecution was charging me with shooting at the police because my homeboys and family (i.e. gang members) made statements against me. I also asked him why is it that gang members testimony is credible when he/she is testifying for the prosecution but unreliable when testifying for the defense? Rothman couldn't answer that question. I told him I was a gang member so quite naturally that's who I was hanging out with. Contrary to the propaganda fostered by District Attorneys offices nation wide the vast majority of gang members are reluctant to come testify for the defense in a murder trial out of fear of being retaliated against in some way by the police and prosecution. Especially dudes on parole they don't even want to see the inside of a courtroom if they don't have to.

When gang members willingly put their freedom and safety on the line to testify on the behalf of a defendant in a murder trial then 9 times out of 10 their testimony is credible. If gang members know that their homeboy is guilty then they will not come to court and testify for him. No one wants to come to court and say that they was with an individual during the time of a murder when there's a possibility that the prosecution may turn around and charge them with murder too. This is how most criminals think. So-called gang experts may disagree due to ulterior motives but answer me this question: "How can a person be an expert in something that they themselves have no first hand knowledge or experience in?" In other words how can a non gang member be an expert on gangs? To me that's like saying because I watched a hundred episodes of ER five times now I'm an expert in treating gunshot wounds and heart disease. Absolutely ridiculous.

I made it clear to Rothman that I wanted my witnesses called to court. I knew that without my defense witnesses no jury would believe that I was innocent. It would just be my word against the prosecution witnesses testimony. Plus I was a gang member. That in and of itself was two strikes against me before a white jury. Back in the county jail I was involved in another race riot with the Mexicans. This time we took off first. I got sliced across my left elbow but it was friendly fire. As a result of my injury I was taken off of the mainline and thrown into the "CRIP" module which is a housing unit strictly for Crips from various neighborhoods. They placed me on Baker row and into a six man cell with Lil Old-man 118EC, Pie 97EC, Q.Twin Q102 EC, and Baby T.C. 62EC.

The module was filled with active and many reputable gang members. Many dudes passed through the module during my 18 month stay there. Dudes such as: Mad-Bone, Lil Crazy-Dee, Baby Casper, Tiny Evil, Lil Opie, Lil Chilli Mike, and Baby Gangster from ETG, Blacc Dog and Baby Sleep from 111 NHC, Lil Tookie from PJ Watts, Bang, Sleep, Mousie, and C-Money from Rollin 40's, Pookie Twin 1and 2 from Rollin 90's, Roscoe, Peanut, F-Bone 2 and 3, Lil No-Good, Head, Lil P.J, Lil Cousin Carrie, Sinbad, Lil Devil, Baby Duke, Loco Coop, Crazy Coop, Lil Hog, Shoes, Lil Bam, Baby Bone, Keater-Roc, Dollar, Baby Tadpole, Tiny Wino, Tiny P.J, Tiny Crip-Cal, and Baby Earl-Dog from Rollin 60's, Lil Mike and Lee-Lee 97 EC, X-Ray 89 EC, Lil Bonehead, Lil Butch, Cornbread, Concrete, Lil Spooky-Slim, Low-Down, and Meco from 190 EC, Lil Q.Twin, Smiley, Rat-Capone, and Lil Johnny Ray from Q102 EC, Lil Ducc-Down, Lil Papa, Lil Joker, Baby Buckwheat, Tee Loc, and Lil Lumberjack from 69EC, Lil Bow-Low, Lil Brotherhood, and Baby Roc from 66EC, Baby Wolf from 68EC, Lil Spike, Lil Flux, Young Rob,

Worm, Lil Ed, C-Rag, Baby Pookie, Lil Crumb, Baby Boo, Bill Blast, Bunchy, Tiny Bubble, Hamburger, Tiny Mont, and Lil Frog from 62EC, Clown from 1st EC, Lil T-Dog, Slim-Bad 1and 2, and Bear from 59EC, Skin, Lil Bean, Baby Blue, and Cyco from 76EC, Outlaw and Maniac from 118 EC, Cowboy, Teaspoon, BK, John John, G-Moe, Fee-Dog, and Wino from 42GC, East Side Blue, Bohanna, Lil Scrap, Boxer, G-Slim, Lil Snipe, and Fat-Dog from 43GC, Ant-Capone and G-Tee from 87GC, Blue Devil 1 and 2 from 55NHC, Black and Devil from 107 Hoover, Baby Ed, Baby Boxer, and Lil Spoon from 83 Hoover, Lil Tank from 74 Hoover, Lil Day-Day from 92 Hoover, Baby Worm and Weasel from 59 Hoover, T-Dog, Joker, Nay Nay, Baby Vern, and Duck from Insane, Baby Boy, Frog, Foe-Head, and Tiny Ric Roc from Harlem 30's, Nugget, Lil Bang, and Raymond Dee from Raymond Crips, Arsenial, G-Moe, and Baby Lee-Dog from Avalon Gangsters, Lil Cee from Kitchen, Woody and Vamp from 357 GC, Scrap 1and 2 from Main Street, G-Roc, Spider, and Country from 52BGC, Dee-Loc from West Boulevard, Baby Snap from SYC, Greg from NHCC G-Mac and G-Dog from Watts Baby Locs, Boniac, Zen-Dog, Tay Dog, Short Dog, and C-Looney from Venice Shoreline. And quite a few others came through the Crip module. C-Rag, Baby Pookie, and Hamburger was all crimeys on a murder case.

It was the summer of '92, when those 3 along with my homegirl Boogie got together and decided to go do a drive by on the 52 BGC's. C-Rag and Hamburger were in one car with a 9mm. Baby Pookie and Boogie were in another car with no gun following behind C-Rag and Hamburger. They drove to 53rd Street between Main and Broadway and Hamburger busted on the Broadways killing Dizzy from 52 uncle who weren't gang members. During the shooting a witness at the crime scene identified Boogie as the person hanging out of the car window yelling, "bust on them niggas cuz!" The 52's jumped in a car and chased after them to retaliate. C-Rag and Hamburger got away by hitting a corner in the hood. That night the 66EC's were giving a party on 66th Street between Main and Broadway. Baby Pookie and Boogie didn't hit a corner in the hood like C-Rag and Hamburger did. Instead they allowed themselves to get chased up Main Street from 53rd to 116th Street. Boogie was pregnant by Baby Pookie at the time. The Broadways shot the car up with a .44 Magnum. Boogie got hit in the stomach and almost died. She lost her baby and was in a wheelchair. When they got to 116th Street they were saved by officers from the 108th Street Division L.A.P.D. The police drew their weapons to arrest the Broadways but they told the police that Baby Pookie and Boogie were responsible for a drive-by shooting on 53rd Street and Main.

The officers arrested the Broadways and then checked out their story. Once they confirmed that what the Broadways told them was true they arrested Baby Pookie for murder. Boogie was rushed to the hospital where she eventually lived. However, she was also charged with murder. Ironically the Broadways who shot her and killed her unborn child were released and never charged. Now that was crazy! A few days later the police arrested C-Rag for murder. Hamburger was still on the run. When C-Rag got caught he ended up confessing to the shooting which implicated everyone involved. Hamburger got arrested about 8 or 9 months later. When he got caught he confessed too. The question in my mind was who snitched on C-Rag and Hamburger because they both got away. I was looking at Baby Pookie with suspicion because he was the one who went to jail first. Boogie was in the hospital at the time fighting for her life so she couldn't have said anything. Baby Pookie was accusing C-Rag of snitching. But no one accused Baby Pookie of snitching on C-Rag and Hamburger.

Come to find out there was a confidential informant in their case who snitched on C-Rag and Hamburger. They also had people at the 53rd Street crime scene snitching on them. I told Baby Pookie that he and Boogie got caught dead bang for the shooting so they were going to jail regardless. Boogie later started snitching too. I saw her on my way to court one day in the hallway as I was being escorted to the court holding tank. She told me, "Marlon I know that you are going to be mad at me but I'm going to tell too since everybody else is telling." I just looked at her and didn't say anything.

Technically C-Rag did snitch but I must admit that the facts of their case was unusual and convoluted compared to the typical case of somebody who got snitched on. I was upset from the very moment I learned some of the details of their case while I was still on the streets. Specifically I couldn't understand why Baby Pookie and Boogie would go on a mission with no gun just to watch a drive by shooting! Or why Baby Pookie would drive past the hood when he knew that there was a party on 66th Street and there were at least 200 gang members out there with hella guns? Truthfully I felt like he put himself in a trick bag. Had he not did a bozo move from the jump and gotten caught none of them would be in jail. I also believed that C-Rag confessed when the police interrogated him because he assumed that he was going to somehow take the murder charge off of Baby Pookie and Boogie. A rookie mistake he can't undo.

They was all going to prison regardless even if C-Rag didn't say anything. Baby Pookie kept pressing the issue so Lil Flux knocked C-Rag out in the cell. And Lil Ed tied up Hamburger and whipped him. Baby Pookie and Hamburger were related to each other. Hamburger's older brothers were E-Roc and Lil T.C from 62EC and Easy from 66EC. E-Roc was quiet but a rider who got killed in 1986. Lil T.C and Easy were both down homies although Lil T.C was more rugged than Easy. Hamburger was from the hood but wouldn't hang out in the hood so it was a surprise to me that he went and put in some work. While in the module the 60's didn't like the fact that the 42GC and 43GC were on the same tier with the EC's and West Side Neighborhood Crips. They wanted to smash the 42's and 43's but me and my homies from 62EC would always intervene. Back in 1984, some of the 43GC's used to claim EC.

They were thinking about turning EC for good. Also it's been alleged that Pitbull from 43GC started the Delamo Blocc Crips a.k.a. 190 EC. We also shared some of the same enemies such as the Broadways. Whereas the 60's were allies with the 52's. Also Cowboy and Wino from 42GC were like family because they grew up in my neighborhood. Me and Lil Scrap from 43GC went back to 1987 with each other when his mother and sister moved into my neighborhood and we were CYA babies together in Paso Robles. I was taught to be loyal to my true friends. Bottom line we weren't about to let the 60's or anyone else smash the 42's and 43's. Lil Hog from the 60's and Fat-Dog from 43GC got down with each other head up and that was it.

I heard from Jameka. She was a female who I met one day in traffic while driving to my hood one morning. I learned that her father managed some apartments on the corner of 60th Street and San Pedro. We hooked up a few times and she got pregnant. She already had a one year old daughter and her mother had just passed away a couple of months prior to me meeting her. She was enrolled at Locke High School at the time. I wasn't in love with her and I felt like she had too much on her plate to be raising two children at 16 years old so I suggested that it might be best if she had an abortion. I made it clear that the decision was hers to make. If she did decide to have the child then I wasn't going to neglect my child even if it cost me my relationship with Glynnis.

She had the abortion but years later I felt guilty about telling her to have an abortion. I looked out for her on a few occasions when I was out but I was irresponsible when it came to sex. I'm just grateful that I never contracted an STD. She and I became friends but she still had feelings for me. She was doing well for herself. She had her own apartment, a job, and was raising her daughter. I encouraged her to continue doing what she was doing. She bought me a pair of British Knights ("BK") shoes but the county jail wouldn't let me receive them. We conversed for about 4 months.

CHAPTER TWENTY ONE

I spoke with Rothman and he said that he had been in contact with my defense witnesses. He said that they were cooperating with him. That was good news. We learned that Newton destroyed all of the physical evidence in my case which was highly unusual in a death penalty case that was a year away from trial. Something didn't add up. I wondered whether or not the other double homicide that the same AK-47 was used in was also gang related. If so then which gang was responsible because that could point to my innocence? Especially if the gun traced back to a rival gang. We went to court and had a hearing on the destruction of the evidence but the trial judge denied our motion claiming that we failed to show bad faith on the part of the police and prosecution. I found that ridiculous. My trial judge was Robert J Perry. A white man in his mid 50's in age with a reputation for washing dudes up. He had about a 99.5% conviction rate for murders. That alone should raise eyebrows because it's a clear indication that he was corrupt.

People in society don't get an accurate depiction of what really takes place behind closed doors in a murder trial when there are no cameras and media in the courtroom to document the events. Trial judges fix the outcome of many trials in prosecutors favor by granting most, if not all, of their motions while denying many defense motions which makes it hard to receive a fair trial. During the hearing the officer in charge of the evidence room testified that he didn't give the authorization to destroy the evidence in my case. This should've raised red flags but it didn't. My trial was to proceed like nothing ever happened. Right after this I was hit with some devastating news. Baby Pookie and C-Rag came back from court alleging that they met some dude named Skillet from Grape Street while in the court tank who had Glynnis' name in his mouth. He alleged that Glynnis was his woman and that she lived with him. He used to let her hold his money. Upon hearing that news I immediately called her and grilled her about Skillet. She admitted to having sex with him and holding his money but denied that she was in a relationship with him. I couldn't understand her logic. She sounded like she was in denial when she gave me her version of the story.

Now I knew about Lewis but I never knew anything about Skillet. This caused me to question how many more dudes was she out there messing with that I didn't know anything about. I felt like I couldn't trust her, she was sneaky, messy and she was no different than any other scandalous female. I also felt like a fool because everybody in the Crip module knew that she was my woman. But now it was revealed that she was in at least two more relationships with other dudes. I thought about how I rejected Angie's proposal for Glynnis about a year prior to this and I felt like an idiot. My heart was hurt and I wanted my revenge. I was feeling salty while contemplating what to do. As fate would have it about a month later I received a letter from Angie. She had received her time and was in the Feds. She apologized for taking my money and said that she was hurt that I chose Glynnis over her. She still loved me and wished me the best in my case. I was excited to hear from her because at the time I was frustrated and angry with Glynnis. I wrote her back and told her the situation with Glynnis and how I regretted choosing Glynnis over her because I had since found out that she was unfaithful and thus unworthy. I told her that I loved her and although I hurt her by choosing Glynnis, I did it because Glynnis was the one holding me down and had been there for me. Thus I did what I believed was the right thing to do. I told her the truth rather than leading her on with lies or keeping secrets from her. She wrote me back a few weeks later telling me that the Feds allowed her to read my letter but they wouldn't give it to her because I wasn't on her correspondence list.

However, she was going to seek to change that. She also wanted to rebuild our relationship which I was willing to do. I felt like Glynnis stepped outside of the relationship so I didn't owe her my loyalty any longer. I wrote Angie a second letter telling her that I was on the same page with her and I updated her on my case. I didn't receive any mail from her again. I just assumed that the Feds prevented us from communicating. I wrote to her once more but I didn't receive a response so I didn't write to her anymore. While in the module I was confined to my cell. I was on Baker Row in a six man cell with Baby Pookie, East Side Blue, Cowboy, Fee-Dog, Pie, and Lil Flux.

Oftentimes I'd go into deep thought thinking about a multitude of things. I was constantly thinking about my future and reflecting on my past. I thought about my family on my mother's side. My uncles Ledell, Peter, Robert, Sammy, and Ernest. Ledell at the time had a few children. However, I only knew the name of his daughter Kisha. I believe that I had met her only once at the time. I had love for Ledell because he had our backs. He was my mother's baby brother. I hadn't spoken to any of my uncles since I had been locked up. Peter raised pigeons and was a good man. He gave Pookie a place to lay his head when he got out of CYA and he took my sister Jasmine in when my mother struggled to raise her. Sammy just disappeared off the face of the earth. He was here one day and gone the next. Even his wife and children never heard from him again.

Personally I believed that he was killed and we just never knew. He has two children Sammy Jr. and Selena. I've never met them in person. Robert had a wife, a son, and a daughter. He lived behind Mona Park in Watts. He was a cool dude with a good personality and soft spoken. Ernest was married with two daughters Rene and Tammy. They lived right around the corner from my grandmother Vergie. I'd often go visit them whenever I spent the night at my grandmother's house. Tammy was only a year or so older than Deon. We were close. Their family was a quiet and meek one with a lot of love. Tammy was beautiful too. I used to wonder if she had a boyfriend and if so was he a good dude. I didn't want to have to hurt anybody behind her. I really never saw or knew Rene because she left home at a young age. They had a weenie dog that used to stand on two feet and get excited when I came over. They were always welcoming to my brothers and I. I also used to think about my aunts Lena and Rosetta. They both were younger than my mother. Lena had two children Tyrone and Tanisha. Tyrone's father died when he was a child. My brothers and I were like brothers to him. Lena used to live in the Imperial Courts when we were kids. I used to love to spend nights at her place. We had fun over there. Tyrone would spend nights at our house too. We were close growing up. As we got older he also started selling dope but wouldn't gang bang. That was fine by me. I admit that I tried to get him to turn 62EC. I had his back though if he ever got into some trouble. I took a gun case for him back in 1987.

The police pulled us over in my homeboy Lil Fox's car. He was in the backseat with a .25 semi automatic pistol I let him hold. I was in the passenger seat. When the police pulled us over he stuck the gun under my seat. I took the case and got probation. I didn't want Lena to know that he was envying the street life. After I got shot in "86" I often kept a gun on me. Tanisha was just a sweet little girl. Rosetta had three kids. Darion, Boogie, and Kennisha. Darion was like a little brother to me. I used to be rough with him and Tyrone because as kids they weren't rugged. I didn't want them to be scary or soft. Boogie and Kennisha were younger. I still remember hearing the sound of the train passing by early in the morning whenever I spent the night at my grandmother June's house.

I often wondered what happened to my mother because her attitude and personality was different from her parents and siblings. My uncles Alvin and O'Dell both died when I was a kid. I didn't know much about them and if they had children I'd never have met them. In hindsight I thought about my family often because I longed to have them in my life. None of my mother's siblings were crack addicts to my knowledge. On the flip side my father, my aunt Jessica, and uncle Paul all fell victim to crack addiction. Also Big Daddy, Alfreida, Jeanette, Willie Blue, and my cousin Bucky were all addicted to crack as well. Not to mention multiple members of the Taylor family. Witnessing all of these people get snared and trapped by cocaine as well as transform them from people progressing to declining affected me in a number of ways. It was hard for me to see myself being a success when I was surrounded by failure and people making poor choices. On one hand there were my brothers following the path of being gang members and criminals. On the other hand I was witnessing the decline of my family and community through drugs, not to mention the division in the family due to my mother's-in-law despising her.

I was the baby boy so quite naturally I was going to follow someone's example. I chose to follow in the footsteps of Deon and Pookie. I realized that cocaine made people lose their dignity and self respect when I began hearing stories from Deon about how some of the finest women in the neighborhood were now selling their bodies for crack. My next door neighbor Candy was a prime example. Candy was fine with a big round booty and big breast. She had a daughter by my homeboy Wooder. I recall the day Deon came home talking about when Candy went down to the 62 dope spot and was offering oral sex in exchange for cocaine. He said that dudes lined up to give her some dope. Allegedly Wooder was livid. Most of my homeboys didn't think they had a chance with Candy until they found out she smoked crack. There were other females in the hood who did the same thing. Once I learned that my mother was smoking crack I dreaded the day that I'd find out that she sold her body to my homeboys for sex.

By the grace of God I've never heard of my mother stooping that low. I probably would've tried to kill whoever she sold her body to had she done something like that. When you're locked in a cell you begin to reminisce on a variety of things: painful and happy. For example I found myself thinking about Ms. Jeffrey. Back in the day kids could walk through the hood and see hella fruit trees in peoples yards. We had an avocado tree in our backyard. The Mexican family across the street had a Tangerine tree in their yard. Ms. Jeffrey had a Pomegranate tree in her back yard. Maggaleen had a lemon tree and my neighbors to the other side of us were growing bananas. On occasion we would walk around the corner and then creep into Ms. Jeffrey's back yard to pick the Pomegranates. They were juicy. Ms. Jeffrey was a no nonsense old lady. She didn't want anybody touching her tree. She shot at my homeboy for stealing her fruit. After that we all left her tree alone. In those days people supported corporeal punishment. My parents used to give all of their friends permission to beat me and my brothers if they caught us misbehaving. Children were taught to stay in a child's place.

Education was emphasized with the threat of a beating if we didn't do well. I did well in Elementary. My report card was full of A's and B's but let my mother tell it I was still bad as hell. My first grade teacher I don't remember much. My second grade teacher was Mrs. Breuer, a slender white woman with short hair. She was nice. My third grade teacher was Mrs. Jacobs. I use to imitate Butch on the Little Rascals in class by using my right hand to hit my left hand with a frown on my face. Mrs. Jacobs told my mother about it. I got good grades though so I was focused. It was in Mrs. Jacobs class that I met Lil Wolf from 68EC. He wasn't a gang member back then. He was going with my bro Lil Ghost cousin Keisha. I was going with Lajuana at the time. We would hang out together and I would always catch Keisha staring at me especially whenever Lajuana and I were kissing. Keisha and I would become friends with benefits as teenagers. I was in love with Lajuana. She was pretty, skinny, and bowlegged. Over time we just grew apart. The embarrassing moment which occurred at U.N. Market didn't help matters. Her brother Chim-Chim was like a big brother to me. She had older sisters who were beautiful too. My fourth grade teacher was Ms. Harris. She was a gorgeous young black woman. I can't ever forget her. She had a good personality too. She was good with kids.

My fifth grade teacher was Mr. Johnson. I hated him. He was a gay and arrogant middle aged chubby black man. He would swat me in the hand with two rulers taped together for the smallest infractions. A couple of times I flinched at him like I was going to sock him. He would become furious. Ironically I got A's and B's in his class. He told me that I wasn't going to be anything in life. I wanted to curse him out so bad but that would've been the death penalty in my household. Creshinda and Shavonda were in the class with me. My favorite subjects in school were reading and mathematics. I could've won the school spelling bee but I was doubting my abilities. I always had a good memory too. But I lacked confidence at the last minute. Every word that was given to spell I knew it. I studied all of the hard words first like hors d'oeuvre and Ouija. The word that the last two standing couldn't spell was enthusiastic. That was an easy word to spell for me. I regretted backing out of the spelling bee.

My sixth grade teacher was Ms. Robinson. She was a short black woman with a loud voice. She wore big hair and big sunglasses. I liked her a lot. She laughed and smiled a lot and knew how to bring out a child's best. I had a lot of friends in Elementary. My road dog was Jermaine. I used to call him Pitbull because he was short, stocky, and looked like a bull terrier in the face. Jermaine and I used to do a lot together. We listened to Eddie Murphy's "Raw" comedy tape when it came out and were dying laughing. He used to like to wear red and he had an uncle named Willie who he idolized as a Damu. I knew that Jermaine would eventually be a Damu when he grew up but I didn't let that interfere with our friendship. One time this fat bear looking kid was bullying Jermaine. Jermaine was intimidated when the dude pushed him. I stepped in and socked the dude in his face twice. He looked at me and bear hugged me then threw me to the ground and kicked me twice. We were at school and a teacher saw us and took us to the principal's office. Jermaine didn't even help, he just watched. I forgave him but that incident showed me that he didn't have my back like

I had his. All in all I had a good time at 66th Street Elementary School.

When I graduated I was uncertain about Jr. High School because Deon and Pookie used to have exciting gang related stories to tell from their Jr. High School experiences. They glamorized the stories about ditching school, fighting rival gang members, and having girlfriends to the point that subconsciously I was longing for the same experiences. I remember that they were both going to Horace Mann Jr. High School. One day they came home from school alleging that they had witnessed Opie from ETG get murdered at a bus stop near the school. They said that Ken-Bone from Rolling 60's rode up, I believe, on a bike with a shotgun and called out Opie's name and when he turned to look Ken-Bone shot him in the face. I was in a trance listening to that story trying to visualize what that must have looked like. That was crazy for sure. Shortly thereafter Ken-Bone was murdered in retaliation for Opie's murder. For these reasons my mindset was tainted in regards to what Jr. High School was supposed to be about. It's no coincidence that I didn't do well.

I was ditching a lot for no apparent reason in the 7th grade. I felt like it was my right of passage. My reasoning was irrational. After a while I didn't even know which classes I had anymore. I knew not to let my parents or any of their friends catch me ditching because it would have gotten ugly for me. My parents did teach us to do the right things even if they themselves didn't always follow their own advice.

CHAPTER TWENTY TWO

When my homie Lil Frog came to the module he was placed in the cell with me and a few more of my homies. While he was on the streets we used to converse from time to time and he would always be excited to hear from me. At that time he was living with Chivetta's mother Bobby Jean which was mind boggling to me because it seemed like Bobby Jean was cool with all of my homies except me. When Lil Frog came to the module he was placed in my cell. At the time it was me, Boxer and G-Slim from 43 GC, along with my homies Worm and Lil Frog. Frog greeted everyone but me. I found that to be weird. For 3 days we didn't speak until I got fed up with his antics and flashed on him. Afterwards he got his act together and put an end to the childish games. I had love for him though. He was someone that homies from my generation didn't know growing up because he didn't run with us or hang out on San Pedro where everything was going down. His sister Rochelle used to be my girlfriend in elementary school and I never knew that she had a brother. I heard about him in juvenile hall. At that time he was calling himself Lil Bunchy. I embraced him because I didn't hear any smut on his name. We also were in Paso Robles CYA together. He stayed on the mainline for about a year then went to fire camp. Lil Frog wasn't necessarily the violent type. He was more about getting money. He actually lit a spark under me to take my education seriously and stop goofing off.

One day while walking back from school he and I had a debate about who was the smartest among the two of us. I was adamant that I was smarter until he killed the whole argument by saying, "If you are so smart then why are you in that Special Ed class?" I replied, "Special Ed!" "Nigga what Special Ed class you talking about?" He said, "The classroom you go to in the morning!" I thought about it and immediately it hit me that all we did in that class was go to sleep, play board games, cards, and watch "Roseanne" on T.V. The teacher didn't mind. I laughed but I also felt like an idiot for not recognizing this on my own. Soon after I did my work and got out of that class in a month's time. Within the next year and a half I raised all of my test scores dramatically. I went from an 8th grade reading and comprehension level to 11th grade. My math scores went from 7th grade to 12th grade. My science grade jumped from 7th to 11th grade. I also won a Spelling Bee. I vowed to never let my education slip again. Being a dummy wasn't a good look on me. I got paroled before I could graduate.

I remember one day Glynnis handed me a piece of mail and asked me to read it. I silently read it until she asked me to read it out loud. That's when I realized that she wanted to see if I could read. I passed that test. Once I educated myself my views on a lot of things changed. I was able to see that some of the things some of my older homeboys use to preach was flawed and pure nonsense. I was also able to recognize those who talked the talk but didn't walk the walk. For example, back in the 80's it was common to witness OG's kicking it in the hood while drinking Gin or Hennessey while a homeboy's low rider or a coupe was parked bumping oldies and hear them glamorizing homies walking prison yards such as Folsom, San Quentin, Soledad, and Tracy. They spoke of these prisons and the homies doing time inside of them with the honor and enthusiasm educated people spoke of attending prestigious college universities. The message was that if any homie could walk those yards, hold his own, and remain solid then he was a down homie (or a rider) worthy of the utmost respect.

As little homies listening to this rhetoric we began to envision ourselves going to prison, staying down for the hood, getting swoll (buff}, and coming home to homeboys and homegirls showering us with love and respect. We didn't necessarily fear receiving a life sentence for the set (hood). Catching a life sentence for killing an enemy earned us stripes and boosted up our reputation in the hood if we didn't snitch. This type of corruption entering our minds made us wild and rebellious. We were too blind to see that this false indoctrination was designed to rob us of our future and the potential that we had as young talented Black males. As kids we were also too blind to see that some of those preaching this poison didn't practice what they preached.

Once I started educating myself I began to see some of the flaws in the rhetoric that was passed down. I credit Lil Frog for waking me up. Lil Frog was short timing. He ended up getting released after a short period of incarceration and started having money. Young Rob came back to jail for another kidnap robbery case. We discussed his acquittal on his previous case. He told me that he knew he was going home when he woke up one night and saw a huge angel with long wings standing in his cell and looking down on him. He said that he was terrified and speechless as the angel told him that he was going home. I listened intently as he described what he saw. I believed in God as well as the existence of angels, demons, and Satan. Thus what he was telling me wasn't hard to fathom. I knew that his mother Mrs. Ross was a devout Christian woman who possessed the gift of healing.

Back in '86, about a month after I got shot in the stomach I was in excruciating pain so much that I was bent over and couldn't stand up straight. My mother sent me to Mrs. Ross so that she could pray over me. Once she did the pain immediately went away. I then knew God was real. Also one day in '88, Baby Dee and I was on 59th Street at the corner of Inskeep Avenue when we saw this religious woman walking towards us with a Bible in her hand. I assumed she was a Jehovah's witness. We both thought about walking away from her but instead we listened to her for 15 minutes as she spoke to us about God. She prayed for us and invited us to attend her church which was Baptist. Later that night me, T.C, and Baby Dee were in a car with this white girl from Woodland Hills, California name heather who T.C was in a relationship with and this light skinned black female name Keisha I was talking to who also was from Woodland Hills. We met them on 60th Street and San Pedro while they were visiting my home girl Tiffany at her parents house.

At the time I was actually attending El Camino Real High School with them although I spent my time ditching school. Tiffany had a younger sister named Robbie. They didn't gang bang. They were squares but good people. Back to the story. Me, T.C, Baby Dee, Keisha, and Heather were in Heather's brand new Lincoln Mark VII as we drove down the Crenshaw strip. T.C,

Baby Dee, and I were G'd up. We all had on blue sweatshirts, brown Khaki pants, with blue Colorado boots with fat blue strings. We looked like Crips.

As we passed by 77th and Crenshaw we saw Young Rob parked and looking under the hood of his car. His car wouldn't start because the engine overheated. He was dressed in a two tone blue and gray silk suit with matching gators on his feet. We pulled over and T.C and Baby Dee got out of the car to check on Rob. I stayed in the car. None of us had a gun and we were in Inglewood Family Blood hood. It was around 8:30 p.m. Heather asked me if I was going to go with my homeboys. I then got out of the car to ride with them. The females drove off leaving us which I hadn't anticipated. I immediately looked around and saw two black dudes standing on this porch whose house we were in front of. One of them wore a red Jersey with a red 49er hat. They were Damus. Rob asked the dude with the red Jersey could he use his water hose and the dude said, "Naw Blood!" I said let's get out of here cuz. T.C and Baby Dee agreed. Young Rob saw this gorgeous light skinned big booty sister standing on the sidewalk and approached her to get her phone number. She had just pulled up in her Suzuki Jeep, parked, got out, and stood there not saying anything to anyone. Keep in mind that we were in an area of Crenshaw that no one hung out at.

There were no other people around. I couldn't believe that at a time like this he was thinking about females. We all told him to come on at least 3 times but he ignored us. Then I saw a black Chevy drive past us slowly with about 5 dudes inside. The car turned on 77th Street and went down the street. I perceived these dudes to be Damus. I yelled for all of them to come on. I wasn't trying to get shot or killed because my homeboy was thinking with his penis. I could care less about any female at that moment. Rob was still talking to this female trying to get at her. I told them to come on once more then I said to hell with it and started walking heading towards Florence to Rollin 60's hood. I was pissed off with all of them.

I was walking looking down at the ground when T.C yelled, "Marlon!" I looked up and saw this short dark skinned dude holding a chrome magnum in his hand at the corner about 20 feet in front of me. The gun was big. I was spooked. I hurried up and went back to where my homeboys were. The dude with the gun yelled out, "what's up Blood!" Now everybody sees the urgency. T.C asked the female to give us a ride to Manchester and she said, "no, I don't know y'all." I said, "Cuz knock the bitch out and take her Jeep!" Baby Dee and T.C agreed. Just when we were about to carry out our plan she changed her mind and drove us all the way to our neighborhood. For some reason the Damu boy didn't shoot when he could have for sure killed me. Baby Dee and I later reflected on when the lady from church came and spoke to us earlier that day. We concluded that talking to her and letting her pray for us saved our lives. I stopped messing with Keisha and that white girl.

Another situation occurred in "92" when I was out. Glynnis put me up on a lick. One of her people was involved with a drug dealer. The dude lived alone in L.A. in a neighborhood watch community on the west side. She told me that he was going out of town for the weekend and he had money inside. I was also informed about the type of car he drove. If the car was gone he wasn't home. I was down for it. I told my cousin Lil Pookie about the lick and we went to check it out for ourselves.

When we got to the location the dude wasn't there. We walked around the house and I noticed an alarm box on the side of the house. We walked to the back yard looking for an entry point. The back door had a sliding glass door which was open but there was a thick bar gate outside of it and it was locked. We needed some big bow cutters to cut through these bars on the gate and we were skinny enough to slip inside and burglarize the house. The hard part was finding some bow cutters because during the riots every major store got broken into. We were also racing against time. We drove back to the hood and asked around for some bow cutters but nobody had any big enough to cut through the bar gate. I was frustrated. Unbeknownst to me is the fact that my mother went to church on a Wednesday which was unusual for her.

Two days later I went on 61st Street and San Pedro and Big Mama saw me and called me into her house. I went inside and she told me that my mother called her and told her to tell me that while she was in church the Pastor lady asked everyone in the church 3 times who has a son named Marlon. After the third time it dawned on my mother to raise her hand. When she did, the Pastor told her that God had a message for me. The message was that I was planning on doing a robbery involving large quantities of dope. However, God told me not to do it because it's not going to go the way I planned it and God wants me to read Psalms chapter 91 seven times a day. I was stunned. My mother was living in Compton at the time and I hadn't been to see her in a few days. Plus I wasn't the type to tell my mother the dirt I was doing in the streets.

My mother witnessed me shoot up a Mexican dude car back in "88" but she just so happened to be pulling up when I started shooting. Other than that she may have imagined or assumed what I was doing in the streets but I wouldn't tell her. Thus I believed the message that Big Mama gave me. But I did want to be sure. When I saw my cousin I jammed him up about it. I asked him if he open his mouth and tell my mother or Big Mama about the lick. He said, "Naw I didn't why?" I told him about the conversation I had with Big Mama. He said that he didn't say anything. I made him put it on the set. He said, "Cuz that's on 62EC I ain't told nobody shit!" Looking at him I knew he was telling the truth. I made the decision to take heed to the warning I received. I didn't do that lick. It wasn't worth my life no matter how much money and dope was involved. I also started reading Psalms chapter 91 everyday.

Each day I did I was kept safe from harm. I escaped going to jail, 1 car accident, 2 near car accidents, a drive-by shooting, and a few other bad situations. Glynnis later asked me why I didn't do the lick. I told her the message I received from Big Mama and she mocked it by calling me scary. I was offended by that. I then told her that I didn't care about how she felt about it and I would rather be scary and alive than ignorant and dead. Playing with God was just not something I was willing to do. Glynnis was feisty with a sharp tongue. She was trying to put some money in my pocket which I appreciated about her but I wasn't about to let her pump me up for failure. I thought about the risk and rewards and weighed the pros and cons but decided not to do it. Some things one has to be smart enough to walk away from.

About a month later my mother and I went to meet the Pastor lady. Her name was Peggy. She was in her early sixties, light skinned, short, petite, and nice looking. She had an attitude and personality that was graceful. She lived in Compton off the corner of Rosecrans and Butler. We took my twin sisters with us. When we got there Peggy invited us into the den. Her home was tranquil. I had my little sisters in my arms while sitting on the couch. In a short time me and the twins were fast asleep. I awoke a short time later when I felt hands on my head and heard someone praying over me while speaking in tongues. I opened my eyes to see that it was Peggy and a dark skinned lady. I sat silently until they finished. Afterwards they said that they saw stars around my head. Peggy then prophesied to me that God had great plans for me and that he was going to separate me from gang banging and that he would break the bond between me and my homies. I just listened without responding. I didn't doubt what was said to me, I just kept it in mind. A couple of months later I wrecked my Cadillac while racing on the freeway with Lil Greedy coming back from World on Wheels skating rink. Kemo and Pookie were in the car with me. My Cadillac was clean, stocked, with an engine in it.

On the freeway it felt like we were floating. The freeway was clear for miles ahead. I was doing around 150 mph and had passed Lil Greedy up by at least two off ramps. I softly pumped on my brakes a few times to slow down but they weren't working properly. I then took my foot off the breaks and gas and allowed the car to cruise. The car began to slow down to about 80 mph. I saw a big rig ahead about 2 1/2 miles in front of me so I started pumping the brakes again continuously but the car still wouldn't slow down. We were getting closer and closer to this diesel and I became anxious because at the speed I was driving it seemed like it was going to be extremely hard for me to avoid a collision. I switched lanes to drive around the diesel but the car started swerving and then hit the center divider as we passed up the diesel and did a 360° turn landing in the path of the big rig which at that point was about half a mile behind us. I lost control of the wheel when I hit the wall but Kemo grabbed the wheel and steered us out of traffic. We stopped and got out of the car to observe the damage. The whole quarter panel and A-frame was smashed in. To fix it was going to cost some real money. I felt that I'd do better just buying another car. I got off the freeway and drove to my mother's apartment and I parked my car behind there. Kemo, Pookie, and I parted ways.

I went into my mother's apartment around 1 a.m. She was sitting in the living room with a frown on her face watching T.V. I felt negative vibes in the air. I had just wrecked my car and I wasn't in the mood for no attitude or argument. I made a phone call which lasted for about 20 minutes and then hung up. Immediately after she started questioning me in a sarcastic tone. "What are you gonna do with your life?" she asked. I started to be a jerk and asked her the same question but I didn't. Instead I said, "huh! what are you talking about?" She began criticizing the life I was living and telling me that I needed to change and do the right things in life. She was telling me something real but I wasn't receptive to it because clearly she wasn't following her own advice. I started to criticize her for using drugs and messing with dead beat bums but I held my tongue. I was offended by her lecture which I felt was self-righteous. I felt like her being in the financial situation she was in with no job and no child support from Jasmine and the twins' fathers was one of the main reasons that compelled me to get in the streets and hustle because I couldn't sit back and just focus on myself while her and my sisters struggled.

I hated the fact that I had to sell dope to support us. I wished that she wasn't on drugs but had a good job. I wanted to be able to go to school and get a job and get up on my feet the right way without having a mother on drugs and struggling. I felt like I couldn't truly focus on myself because I was too concerned about them. But again I held my tongue out of respect because had I said what was on my mind it wouldn't have come out right. She continued with her criticism and told me to get a job. That was hypocritical to me because she wouldn't go get one. I told her that I don't live with her Pookie does, so she needed to tell him what she was telling me. I also added that he won't hustle or get a job but yet she criticizes me for my lifestyle. I told her she doesn't say these things when I'm putting money in her pocket. She stated that Pookie ain't trying to go back to jail. That further offended me for two reasons: 1. I didn't want to go back to jail either but I was willing to take penitentiary chances to provide for my family. 2. Pookie could've got a job if he wasn't trying to go back to jail. She was allowing him to live for free. I looked at her like she was crazy because she didn't know Pookie. He was constantly doing dumb things which I had to reprimand him for.

For example, my homies stole a brand new Acura Legend and did some dirt out of it. The back window was shot out yet my brother was driving around in the car like it was his until I checked him. My mother and I didn't see eye to eye so I left her apartment in anger. I went and sat on the top of the steps of the apartment and thought about my life. Tears came to my eyes as I determined to truly get up on my feet and never look back. I heard a gentle voice speak to me and say that I was going to go to Oceanside and go to jail. I thought I was tripping but I knew that I heard a voice. Moments later the same voice said that I was going to go to jail for something real serious and it's going to be extremely hard for me to get out but I'm going to eventually get out. I still thought I was tripping until I caught the Greyhound to Oceanside and got arrested for drug possession an hour after I arrived. While I was in the county jail facing the death penalty on this case it was absolutely clear to me that those messages were prophesies from God. God is real.

Drama and war broke out in the Crip Module between the EC's and Hoovers behind dudes rapping over the tier. The Hoovers dissed EC and it was on. The next morning about 7 EC's went down to the court tank and smashed Big Devil from 107 Hoover and another dude from Hoover. In those days the police would open the cell doors and just let out anybody to the court tank even if you didn't have a court date. Devil was rushed to the hospital and came back to the Crip module later that night in a wheelchair. The Hoovers were enraged behind it because Devil was a reputable from his hood. The war lasted for 4 months with the EC's coming out on top. Every time we met up in the court tank with the Hoovers we were taking off on sight. Pie from 97 EC got disciplined because he allowed Lil Slim bad from 59 EC to get down with a Hoover head up and Lil Slim bad came back with a black eye. Lil Flux knocked Pie out on his feet because he complained about having to do 200 burpees straight.

Afterwards me and Baby Pookie tied him up and whipped him with shower shoes then slid him under the bed for about an hour. The lesson in his discipline was that ain't nobody bigger than EC. Pie was an OG but that didn't matter to us. Shortly after that me and Lil Devil from Rollin 60's got down behind him and Lil Brotherhood from 66 EC getting into it. I lost that fight but it didn't break my confidence. He learned that he couldn't get at nobody from EC disrespectfully. You win some, you lose some. Some of my homies wanted to trip but it was my call. I squashed it because the whole situation was behind some nonsense and wasn't worth my homies and the 60's warring over.

Many of their homies felt the same way. The Hoovers rat packed Baby Snap from SYC in the cell which led to them and the 83 GC's getting into it. Then you had Big Scrap and Lil Scrap from Main Street both in the module for murders. Big Scrap had a triple murder at a car shop and was facing the death penalty. He used to clown around a lot and would often yell out over the tier "suck my entire dick!" to no one in particular. It was hilarious. Black Dog from 111 NHC was the only dude in the county jail with some black and white Stacy Adams. Lil Smokey from 69 EC came to the module. He was out of there within 48 hours once he saw me and Lil Flux. We were locked down and couldn't get to him. Elbow from Rollin 60's got beat down and dragged out on the tier because he allegedly had smut on his name. Sleepy from Rollin 40's and another individual took off on the police in the chow hall because the cop was arrogant and disrespectful.

They stopped allowing the Crips to walk to chow after that. Lil Flux went to court and came back with a gang of canteen after he knocked out Hitman from 53 AGC and robbed him. We squared off with the 60's again behind them tripping on the 42 and 43 GC's. They were our allies, we weren't about to let nothing happen to them. The 60's wanted to roll them up off of our tier but me and my homies weren't having it. The 40's, 90's, and Blue Devil from 55 NHC backed the 60's. The Harlems and Raymonds stayed out of it. Black Dog was in the cell by himself with four 42 and 43 GC's so he didn't let his position be known. Again the situation got squashed because dudes knew that had we blown up in the module it definitely would have spilled out into the streets just based on there was a gang of reputable gang members from both sides in there and we had a gang of knives. People were going to get hurt. The end result was the 60's stopped tripping on the 42 and 43 GC's. The module was real savage life. I received a letter from Lily. She was now living and working in Cincinnati, Ohio. She also gave me her phone number and asked me to call her collect which I did.

During our conversations we'd talk about many things. She used to tell me about life in Cincinnati, her goals, and her new relationship. From our conversations I knew that she was still in love with me and she was willing to do anything I asked. But I chose not to exploit her feelings for me because I still had Glynnis in my heart. Although I did indulge in phone sex with her on a few occasions. I was at a point in my life where I didn't want to play games with her. I instead encouraged her to save her money, further her education, and succeed in life. I felt like she just needed someone to believe in her. I gave her that. Her moving to Cincinnati was a bold move. I noticed that every time I turned around there she was. I appreciated that about her but I didn't act on it. I kept our relationship on a friend level. On another note Lil No-Good from the 60's beat his kidnapping case but came right back to jail 4 months later on a new beef and Young Rob ended up beating his second kidnap robbery case. I didn't know the facts of his case and I didn't ask but some people have 9 lives.

CHAPTER TWENTY THREE

My attorneys spoke to my defense witnesses and obtained exculpatory statements from them. However, my investigator was afraid to go to my neighborhood and speak to Chilli Moe. I didn't understand that. I asked him why he was afraid to go in my neighborhood and he said that my neighborhood was a violent area. I tried to convince him that nothing was going to happen to him but he didn't buy it.

I spoke to my cousin Darnell Garner. He was like a big brother to me and my brothers. Back in the days I used to love it when he came over our house to hang out with us. Darnell was a player and a sharp dresser. He drove a school bus by day and hustled on the side. He was excited to hear from me. His sister Charlene and brothers Darren and Bucky were some of my favorite cousins. My cousin Little and her family lived across the street from Darnell when we were kids. His road dog was Nate Ness. Nate grew up on 62nd Street and Avalon. Neither of them ever chose to gang bang even though they grew up in the hood and knew all of my homeboys. Darnell told me that Nate was asking about me and I told him to tell Nate I sent my love. It was good talking to him. At first I didn't know which Nate he was talking about because there was another Nate in the hood who was a dopefiend.

On another note Cowboy from 42GC lost his mother to cancer while he was fighting his case. I was one of many to comfort him in his time of grief. He took it hard. Losing family members while incarcerated is hard. It's also something very few of us consider when we are out on the streets breaking the law. We assume that our family members will outlive us when that's not always the case.

I called Kemo and checked up on him. He was doing his usual which was being a player and loving the night life. He told me something that messed me up. He said, "I got some bad news to tell you." I replied, "what you talking about?" He said, " you know your girl died!" I didn't know who he was talking about. I said, "who are you talking about?" He said, "Angie!" I thought to myself he doesn't know what he's talking about. I told him, "No she's not because Angie is in the Feds." He said, " I know she was in the Feds that's where she died at!" I was stunned!!! But I couldn't accept what he was saying. To my knowledge Kemo didn't even know Angie. I asked him was he sure and then he told me, "Cuz I mess with her cousin in 111 NHC hood and we went to her funeral." I was speechless. Angie's aunt lived in that same area. Now I know why she didn't write to me anymore. I managed to ask him how she died. He said that she got into it with some females and they jumped her. Angie allegedly requested medical attention but the officers ignored her request and the next morning they found her dead. That news left me in disbelief and denial. Denying her death was the only way for me to cope with it. I just stopped thinking about her altogether or at least I tried to. But when you have real love for someone you can't help but think about that person. My life was something you couldn't make up.

During the war with the Hoovers, Bear from 59 EC got stabbed by some Hoovers coming back from court in the court tank. Lil Scrap from 43GC came to his aid and got stabbed too. Their injuries weren't life threatening though. I was cellmates with Lil Flux. I spoke to him about my case and his case. I let him know what Crip-Cal and Crook told the police about him. He just got quiet. I couldn't understand why they would both implicate him in Junebug's murder. He and I both knew Crip-Cal was lying about the things he told the police. But I was wondering why Crook would tell the police that Lil Flux showed up at his backdoor with an AK-47 seconds after the shooting trying to hide in his house.

Flux never gave me an explanation but I gave him a heads up that my attorney spoke with both witnesses and was planning on calling them to court to testify. I believed that the prosecution was actually planning on calling Crip-Cal because he was their informant. Flux never mentioned the police ever speaking to him about this case. I also asked him did he do what people in the hood said he did to Papason. He denied it and said that he was outside the store drinking a beer when he felt someone bump into him causing him to drop his beer and his natural reflexes caused him to swing on the dude not knowing who he was swinging on. He said that Papason's death was a pure accident. He also denied robbing Papason. After that we didn't talk about our cases with each other anymore.

I spoke with Baby Biscuit from 68EC on the phone. He also grew up in my hood. Our families knew each other. His uncles Clarence Price and Piggy were friends with Michael. Clarence's nickname was "S.B." He used to be buff. For years we never knew "S.B" stood for "Stay Broke." People gave him that nickname allegedly because each time they went to a shindig Clarence would show up dressed sharp but wouldn't have any money to get in. Someone else always had to pay his way inside. We spoke about my case. I told him what Lil Owl said about somebody needing to pay for the shooting. He said that everyone knew I didn't have anything to do with it. I told him to talk to his boy because he sounded like he wanted me to take the fall for this. I felt like Lil Owl could really help me if he wanted to.

I went to court in January of '95, because we had a discovery hearing. My attorney was asking for the police reports to the double homicide that the shell casings from the AK-47 at the gas station matched. We wanted to know if that shooting was gang related because all we knew at the time is that two people got killed on 35th and Arlington in November of '91, when I was serving a CYA violation. During the hearing the court asked the D.A. whether or not the assault rifles Baby Dee and I got busted with were the actual weapons used in the police and gas station shootings. The D.A. told the judge that the guns didn't match.

The D.A. agreed to give us the police reports and the court agreed to give us a hearing at a later date so that we could find out if that double homicide was gang related. I also had a "Due Diligence" hearing because Clarence Lavan allegedly couldn't be found by the police and prosecution despite the fact that he was placed in a witness protection program. The prosecutor was new to my case. Her name was Eleanor Hunt. She was a petite white woman in her 30's. She was arrogant, ambitious, and headstrong. During the hearing the D.A's investigator took the stand and swore under oath that Lavan was unavailable as a witness for trial. He then began describing all of his efforts he exercised in trying to find Lavan. He alleged that he checked DMV records, his mother's residence, and other last known places where he may have lived. He threatened to serve Lavan's mother with a subpoena if she didn't have him come to court. Lavan called the investigator and allegedly threatened to never come to court if the D.A. harassed his mother again. Allegedly Lavan was afraid of the Crips and they knew where he was. Also the detectives were contacted by Lavan a few times during that time. Allegedly Lavan was upset with the prosecution because he felt like they reneged on his deal. He expected more than what he was receiving from the prosecution which to me suggested his testimony against me was based solely on the benefits/gifts he assumed he'd get in return.

Further, the D.A admitted to not contacting Lavan for at least 6 months once she took over the case from Linda Reisz. Lavan had expressed multiple times in his tape-recorded interview that he didn't want to come to court. That was part of the reason why Ms. Reisz placed him in the witness protection program. She wanted to make sure he came to court. Reisz testified that when she was on my case she was in constant contact with Lavan and never had any problems with him. He was cooperative with the prosecution. In the end the court found that the D.A. exercised due diligence in trying to locate Lavan and for that reason he was declared unavailable. This meant that now the prosecution could use Lavan's preliminary hearing transcripts at my trial rather than having him testify at my trial and subject him to cross-examination. Personally I had my own theory of what happened. I didn't buy that the detectives didn't know how to find Lavan. They even said that one of the detectives was contacted by Lavan more than once. If Lavan didn't want to be found by the prosecution then he definitely wouldn't have called the detectives on the case when they were looking for him. That's common sense. The real truth is that the prosecution felt like they had a better chance at conviction if Lavan didn't come to court. Thus they duped the court into believing that he was unavailable as a witness.

Now, his preliminary hearing transcripts could be read to the jury without my attorney being allowed to cross-examine it or point out the flaws and inconsistencies. Prosecutors throughout the state will deny that they do this on purpose but the truth is that they sometimes use this tactic when prosecuting a weak case where identity is an issue and they really want to seal a conviction. I don't put anything past anyone in law enforcement.

Shortly thereafter I learned that Crip-Cal was found murdered somewhere on the westside of Los Angeles. He had been dead for some time when I found out. I didn't even know that he had got out. That was unfortunate. I was looking forward to him coming to court and refuting his alleged statements and attesting to my whereabouts when the gas station shooting occurred.

My attorney approached me with a deal. The prosecution was offering me a 22 year deal for two manslaughters. I didn't understand what he was saying. I was charged with 4 murders, 3 attempted murders, and possession of an assault rifle so when he said 22 years for two manslaughters I wanted to know if the D.A. was going to drop the murders. Rothman was vague with me and I didn't receive straight answers to my questions. Therefore I immediately assumed that this was some trickeration. I thought that they might be trying to get me to take a deal for the police shooting and then turn around and recharge me for the murders. It sounded too good to be true. I did seriously consider taking the deal even though I was innocent because I've seen and heard about dudes getting offered deals and rejecting them only to go to trial and lose. The end result is they get life sentences. One person in particular is my homeboy Big Wolf from 68EC. He caught a murder case on a Swan and the D.A. offered him 12 years joint suspension and he rejected it thinking that he could beat the case. He went to trial, lost, and ended up with 25 years to life. He spent 30 plus years in prison. I didn't want to end up like that. I told Rothman to let me think about the deal. I was willing to take 17 years right then. I felt like I wasn't going to beat all of these charges with a state appointed attorney.

As long as I could see some light at the end of the tunnel then I had to consider the deal. I spoke to a few cats about the deal that was offered to me. One of which was Big La-La. He was at my uncle Spark house when I called. They all told me to take the deal. They said forget about the fact that I'm innocent. He said, 'You rather take 22 years with half time than go to trial and get the death penalty if you lose." That was some real talk. Juries and prosecutors don't care that young black gang members are sometimes innocent. They view finding us guilty as another opportunity to take a criminal off the streets. I was ready to jump on the deal but then I received a letter in the mail from Rothman telling me the deal was now 15 years to life. I changed my mind about taking the deal. Anything with a life sentence was not an option for me. I told Rothman that I wasn't taking the deal.

If I was going to receive a life sentence then they were going to have to give it to me at trial because I definitely wasn't going to willingly take a life sentence for crimes I didn't commit. Rothman tried to convince me that taking the deal may be my best option because he believed that I had only a 50-50 chance of beating the case. I still wasn't thinking about taking no "L (life sentence)." Back in the county jail I was contemplating my whole case weighing the pros and cons.

East Side Blue, Cowboy, Baby Pookie, Fee-Dog, and Pie were my cellmates. We all got along well and formed bonds. Lil Flux had been sent to High Power. Before he left I heard him talking to Reka on the phone. When he got off the phone I asked him was that La Rue sister he was talking to and he said yeah. I told him that she was Deon's baby mother. He was surprised. He called her back and put me on the phone. Reka got quiet when I told her who I was. I asked about my nephew and she said that he was doing OK but she wouldn't put him on the phone. When I was out in '92, Pookie ran into her somehow and she allowed him to pick up my nephew Lil Deon. Pookie alleged that he bought him some new shoes and took him to the movies. Afterwards Reka allegedly called Big Mama and left a message with her that if Pookie didn't return my nephew by 9:00 p.m. she was going to call the police on him and report a kidnapping. Pookie took my nephew home. When I found out about it I was upset. I told him don't go and pick my nephew up again because Reka was playing a dangerous game. If she would've falsely reported a kidnapping to the police after she gave my brother permission to take my nephew I would've done something to her. Reka and I hung up. She was keeping my nephew from seeing our side of the family due to a grudge she held towards my mother. Women can divide an entire family with their grudges and vindictiveness.

From my mother's standpoint, Reka was disrespectful towards our family. My mother alleged that when Deon died her and Michael went to go see the casket that Reka and her mother bought my brother. According to my mother the casket was cheap ($500) and wooden. She felt like if they were truly willing to pay for my brother's funeral then they should've asked for my parents' input and chose a decent casket to bury my brother in. I couldn't fault my mother for her feelings. Reka and I didn't speak again. One thing that I became aware of even back then is all of Reka's baby daddies ended up dead! After my brother she had children by Maniac from Marvin Gangster Crip. Her little sister Sakura also had a child with Maniac.

In 1989, when I was on my way to CYA I saw Sakura in juvenile hall. I asked her why was she incarcerated and she said that she was being charged with Maniac's murder. Come to find out Sakura and her other baby daddy name Norvell from Grape Street was both charged for the murder. Norvell got convicted for it. Also a year after Deon was killed their brother La Rue was murdered inside of Harold and Bells soul food restaurant by two hitmen. Their family was never the same.

I saw Lil Hog from Rollin 60's in the module. We knew each other from Sylmar Juvenile hall in 1988. Back then Sylmar was considered a juvenile hall for Damus. Me, Lil Hog, Lil Boo from Rollin 60's, and Baby Donut from 111NHC was all in a unit filled with Damus. We held our own. In those days juvenile halls had weights. I saw some of the biggest dudes in juvenile hall. Ironically most of them was enemies. I'd be lying if I said it wasn't intimidating. Dudes like T-Bone from 52 Pueblos and J. Lok from Crenshaw Mafia was huge. They looked like grown men not teenagers and they was set tripping. I was skinny and small, barely 5'7 140lbs with no muscles. I always banged my hood though no matter how big a dude was. And I was willing to fight for my hood. I broke my hand fighting in juvenile hall. Lil Hog was also a big dude for a youngster. The Damus didn't want to fight him head up. I saw Lil Hog on the streets too. He was Lil F-Bone's road dog. He and I was close.

I remember that East Side Blue used to always talk about getting money. I had love for him. Listening to him reminisce on his upbringing made me like him more because I was able to relate to him. The 43GC's respected him. Lil Flux used to be jealous of our relationship. He couldn't understand why I gravitated to East Side Blue and had Cowboy's back like I did. He didn't understand that they were riders who didn't throw their weight around to try to intimidate their homies. They embraced their homies and weeded out the busters. Whereas Lil Flux threw his weight around and did try to intimidate his homies. That made him a bully in my opinion. The trip part is that once you got to know Flux he really wasn't a bad dude. I had love for him and respected him. He knew that he had hands and that used to go to his head. His ego was huge. Cats from every hood knew of him and many were afraid of him. I wasn't though. A few times me and Baby Pookie had to stand our ground against him. He used to bully Pie and disrespect him. Pie was scared of him. I was raised under Bubble, Limes, T-Dog, C-Bone, Sike, C.L, Quake 1 and 2, Bam, Lil Fish, Ray-dog, Darcy, G-Bone;

Casper, Greedy, Tim-Loc, Boxer, Wooder, J.C, Big Ed, Nutty, Insane Wang, and T-Capone. I learned different things from all of them. But one thing they all had in common is that they all embraced real homies and weeded out busters. They didn't try to bully or intimidate homies.

To me that's what my neighborhood was all about. We were riders who didn't have to do unnecessary things to gain respect and when it was time to get active we performed. We had a saying: "Liked by few, hated by many, but respected by all." That was our motto. We carried ourselves with a different type of swagger than most other hoods.

Oftentimes I'd reminisce on my childhood to help me get through the rough times. In the module you might not go outside for months with the exception of going to court. My skin complexion was so light I looked white from no sunlight. We'd be stuck in the cell all day with the exception of when we walked to chow or when they allowed us to shower once every 3 days. I used to dwell on various things like how my brothers and I had our favorite T.V shows to watch. Deon loved the 3 Stooges, Gilligan's Island, WWF, and Rifle Man. Pookie loved Benny Hill, The Looney Toons, Speed Racer, Leave it to Beaver, Madd T.V, and Sha-nana, and my shows were Swat, Adam 12, Starsky and Hutch, Pink Panther, Shazam, WWF and Captain Caveman. We all loved to watch shows like Happy Days, Get Smart, Fat Albert, What's Happening, Good Times, Sanford and Son, Different Strokes, The Facts of Life, Bonanza, The Lone Ranger, The Bionic Man, Incredible Hulk, He-Man, Mighty Mouse, White Shadow, The Jeffersons, Tarzan, Kung Fu theatre, The Little Rascals, Welcome Back Carter, Lavern and Shirley, Kojak, Beretta, and Threes Company just name a few. We all were huge NFL fans too. Pookie and Baby Dee were Dallas Cowboys fans while me and Deon were Pittsburgh Steelers fans. Our parents bought us all Jerseys for Christmas one year. Deon had Terry Bradshaw's Jersey, I had Franco Harris' Jersey, and Pookie had Roger Staubach's Jersey.

I remember we used to have candy parties when we had the money to do it. Back then $3.00 could buy you a bag full of candy along with a bag of Laura Scuder potato chips and a Springfield soda. I used to love Chick O Sticks, Big Hunks, The Reggie Jackson candy bar, Jolly Rancher sticks, Reese's Peanut Butter Cups, Laffy Taffys, and Honey buns. In those days kids went outside and hung out at Arcades as well as played sports and other games with each other in the neighborhood. Occasionally we'd play hide and go get it. Hide and go get it was similar to hide and go seek except once you found the person of the opposite sex you had to make out with them. My childhood wasn't all bad. There were some good times too. I used to reminisce on the times I spent with my family during the holidays at my grandparents house.

My father Edward and my uncle Paul really knew how to tell stories that would have everyone breaking out in laughter. Those were times I missed. Losing everything will teach you to have appreciation for the things you do have. While I was in Camp Munz my uncle Paul died of AIDS. He was gay and barely 30 years old at the time. I loved him despite the fact that he was gay. Our family knew he was gay but didn't judge him for it. On the flip side Paul never tried to force us to embrace his homosexuality. We embraced him out of love rather than his condition. Whatever he chose to do behind closed doors in his personal life was on him. But my family wouldn't tolerate him coming around the children flaunting his lifestyle especially in my grandparents home. As a result even though I knew and had heard that he was gay I couldn't tell just by looking at him because he carried himself like a man when he was around family. Thus there was a compromise out of respect. He was the first person that I personally knew who died of AIDS. Everyone else I'd heard of dying from it was celebrities. I still remember his laugh. Paul also smoked crack cocaine. I remember one night he was over at our house. He had been there for a few days because my mother paid him and his boyfriend name Roach to lay down some new carpet in our house.

Paul knew I sold dope. I was asleep in my bedroom when he woke me up claiming that someone outside was looking to purchase a $20.00 rock of cocaine. I gave him the dope to go sell for me and he left. I waited up to about 45 minutes for him to return. I knew something was wrong. Come to find out there was no person outside seeking to buy dope. Paul wanted the dope for himself. When he came back he stood in my bedroom doorway and in a low voice he said, "Boy somebody gone kill yo ass for selling that shit! I damn near had a heart attack when I hit that shit!" I immediately fell out laughing and yelled out, "that's what you get!" as he walked off. This was in "87" when there was a cocaine drought. As a result drug dealers were mixing Vitamin B12 with their cocaine as they rocked it up to increase the amount of it. Dudes would buy a half of a kilo in powder, add the B12 to it and watch it grow from half a kilo to one or two whole kilos depending on how much B12 was mixed in. B12 changed the dope from white to brown. And if they stepped on it too much the dope would be of poor quality. It would literally start melting and shrinking in your hand if it was hot outside. Paul got a dose of that. He tried to work me and got worked. Hilarious. Paul wasn't a coward either. He would beat a dude up too if provoked. One day my Uncle John came on 62nd Street looking for me. He needed some shells for his .38 because some dude had stabbed Paul under the armpit because Paul was beating him up. John was upset about him stabbing Paul and wanted to shoot him. I didn't have any shells but I got a hold of a .357 Magnum from one of my homies and let John borrow it.

Later on he brought it back with 3 bullets missing. John was buff and used to be a member of the 500 club (those bench pressing 500 lbs or more). As kids all of us (me, my brothers, and cousins) were afraid to get whipped by him based on his physical presence alone. But John was a gentle giant of a man and a good father to his children. He had a lot of patience and was a laid back individual. It took a lot to make him angry but once he got upset, like the situation with Paul, watch out. He loved all of his family and wouldn't tolerate anyone doing any harm to us. He opened up his own business and married a younger woman named Kim who had a young daughter named Cashmere from a previous relationship. John raised Cashmere as his own daughter.

John went on to have 3 sons by Kim. Their names are Johnathan, Josh, and Andre. My aunt Paula was Paul's twin. She was beautiful and weight challenged. Back in the 80's she used to live in the Jungles on Coco Avenue and Hillcrest. I used to spend nights over there on some weekends with her son Duane. We used to roam all through the Jungles. I used to tease Paula about her weight and she'd start laughing. I'd call her on the phone and tell her, "Jacquelane called me and asked me when are you going to apply for your membership?" Sitting in a confined cell facing the death penalty for crimes I didn't commit had my mind thinking about all sorts of things. I used to think about my sister Trivette. I remember as a kid growing up she was boy crazy. She got married and had a son by some dude from Rollin 60's. I went to Camp and got out in "89" and learned that she was now gay and getting a divorce. I used to wonder whether her choice was connected to her divorce and heartbreak. I personally never asked her what caused her to go that route. Instead I just respected her decision and didn't judge her despite the fact that I didn't agree with it. I loved her regardless. I hadn't spoken to her since "91" when I dropped off her and her girlfriend in Compton.

She had a son named Keon who was a toddler. I thought about what if I wasn't around to see him grow up and get to know him? Would he even know I existed? On another note I remember the first time I actually rocked up some dope over the stove at 14 years old. I'd seen it done at least a dozen times so I decided to try it myself. I used Baking Soda and it came out like a white cookie. I thought I was the man. But sitting in that cell with my back against the wall I couldn't even think or dream about the future with all of this time hovering over me if I lost.

My biggest fear was my mother dying while I was locked up. I tried not to think about it but when you've been through as much tragedy and pain as I've been through before the age of 21 it's hard to prevent that type of thought from lingering in your mind. Females came and went but my mother would always be there for me because I'm a part of her. Also it was hard calling home back then because I'd have to hear about her and my little sisters financial struggles. They had to move into a shelter and I was ashamed by that. Their struggles made me more determined to succeed with my music so that I could change all of our lives for the better. I didn't want to continue selling drugs just to try to get ahead. I knew that rapping would put some real money in my pocket if I was successful at it. I intended to be successful too. I had the same dream as most brothers from the hood and that was to get my family out of the hood. I had to be strong for all of us. I felt like I couldn't tell my mother how fearful I was of getting found guilty and possibly receiving the death penalty. I knew that telling her that probably would've had negative consequences on her mental and emotional well-being. Therefore I always told her that I was fine and doing good even when I wasn't. I never let her hear or see any vulnerability within me. I threw my dukes up and fought like a champ.

Glynnis was still hanging on by a thread but her heart was with Lewis. He had gone to prison and paroled. Now they are officially together. I knew it even though she tried her best to hide it. My homeboy Slim from 76EC used to come visit me. He was a real homie. We were in Wayside together back in '93. Slim was also the father of my niece and goddaughter Saquilla. Saquilla was Bondie's daughter. I was also in contact with my brother T.C's baby mama named Engla. Engla was also Baby Dee's cousin from New Jersey. She was tall, attractive, and a cool person. She lived in Long Beach at the time. I used to talk to her friend Gayle from New Jersey while in the county jail. She had come to California to visit Engla. Gayle and I were just friends though. She came to visit me too which was cool. Talking to different females on the phone was therapeutic for me because it kept my mind off of my case and my crumbling relationship with Glynnis. Glynnis would catch an attitude if she found out that another female was visiting me. That was ridiculous to me when she had a new love in her life as well as Skillet. I had animosity building up in my heart towards her. I couldn't wait to get out of jail.

CHAPTER TWENTY FOUR

We were getting set for trial. We had the discovery hearing and the D.A gave my attorney the police reports and murder book to those two unsolved homicides on the morning of the hearing. In my opinion the D.A gave my attorney this evidence at that particular time to ensure that he wouldn't have enough time to read through all of the paperwork to adequately prepare appropriate questions for the hearing. For example, the unsolved double homicide occurred in the South Bureau Division's area of the LAPD. However, D.A. Hunter chose not to subpoena the detectives from that Division who investigated the case to the hearing. Instead she subpoenaed a detective from Newton Division to speak on the unsolved double homicide. The detective couldn't say whether or not that unsolved double homicide was gang related because Newton didn't investigate that case. This was subterfuge on the part of the district attorney's office. They didn't want us to find out that the unsolved double homicide was gang related because then they would have to identify the gang alleged to have been responsible which, if it wasn't my hood, would have undermined the People's case against me. How? because the murder weapon used at the gas station was also used in the unsolved double homicide. Thus, it was highly likely that another gang committed the murders I was charged with. D.A. Eleanor Hunter knew what we were looking for and she got one over on us. My attorney didn't ask for a continuance or object and the judge allowed it.

One person I truly missed was Catisha Desmond. She was Deon's ex-girlfriend and a sister to me. When I got released from CYA she took me shopping and bought me some outfits and shoes. Catisha's brothers are Huggie and Reggie. They both are from my neighborhood. My brothers and I were close with all of them. Catisha and Deon broke up when he went to juvenile camp because she had sex with Lil Rat from 62EC and Deon found out about it. He was heartbroken when he learned that news. Though they broke up they continued to still be together and hook up. Their love for each other didn't waver. The last time I saw Catisha was a time when I went on a visit with Lily and Catisha was out there visiting her baby daddy. She came around to my window when her visit ended and was ecstatic to see me. We conversed briefly and she let me get back to my visit. My mother always wished that she had gotten pregnant by Deon and had his child. Thinking of Catisha often got me thinking about her former friend named Shaunice. Catisha brought her to see me after I got out of CYA. Shaunice was my age and dark brown complexioned. She wore glasses which made her look like a plain Jane, but when she took her glasses off the girl was actually fine. She had an athletic build like she played volleyball or took up gymnastics. Our birthdays were days apart as well. I took it slow with her because she was a square. She used to catch the bus to come see me so I knew that she was feeling me. I was feeling her too for a number of reasons. One being that she was the type of female that challenged me to step my game up. I liked that about her.

However, I felt like I couldn't be my usual self around her because she had been a victim of a sexual assault so she sort of viewed relationship matters through that lens. I had never been with a female who had experienced something like that so I didn't know how to really approach her or take charge without her clamming up. For example, one time she came to see me while I was staying with Lil Fish. Me, him, and my bro T.C were on the porch conversing. Shaunice walked up and wouldn't come inside the yard. We all looked at her like "what is she tripping off of?" I went to talk to her to find out what was up and she almost had a nervous breakdown. She started crying talking about she feared my brothers was going to rape her! That shocked me and made me look at her like she was crazy. I tried to convince her that my brothers weren't rapists but that didn't do much to calm her down. I somewhat felt offended by her accusation and by the fact that she was insinuating that I'd allow her to get raped. I forgave her because I didn't think she meant to offend me. But it only made me go even slower with her. She'd call periodically talking to me on the phone and I'd listen but I was doubtful about what she was telling me. I always told her that it's on her to initiate the sex because I didn't want to be falsely accused of doing anything inappropriate with her. The time came where we did go there and she had some fire. They say the crazy ones have the best sex. However, I didn't kiss her during intercourse and she was pissed. I didn't want to do anything that may remind her of when she was assaulted. She alleged that she enjoyed the sex but I wasn't intimate. We broke up behind that. I tried to explain my position but she wasn't trying to hear it. I chose not to fight for that relationship. At times I wondered whatever happened to her. I later learned that her uncle was dating my aunt Rosetta. Small world.

Pookie got out of jail. He was broke but trying to get up on his feet. I spoke to him on the phone. I told him to get a job or do something to get up on his feet and stay out of jail. He said that Pook Dog from 118EC was supposed to be taking him out of town soon. I was concerned about him because although he was older than me some people assumed that I was his older brother due to his character and personality. Lil Ghost used to tell me that his mother-in-law used to question him regarding Pookie being my big brother. His mother-in-law loved me dearly. His wife Netta used to tell me that her mother had a crush on me. I was flattered for sure. Netta is a sister to me who I love and respect. Nevertheless, I was concerned about Pookie's ability to survive and get established on the streets.

I also had a psych evaluation to see if I was fit to stand trial. The psych determined that I was fit after conversing with me. Right after that Twin from Q102 EC started some drama with the 43GC's particularly Fat-Dog. One morning Fat-Dog and Boniac from Venice Shoreline Crips were cracking jokes with one another. Twin intervened and started cracking jokes on Fat-Dog. When Fat-Dog started getting on him, Twin got mad and started fat mouthing. I intervened by telling Twin that he was out of line because he jumped in Fat-Dog's conversation. I also told him that if he's that mad, him and Fat-Dog can fight head up. Twin didn't like that idea because fighting isn't his strong suit. I perceived that he was trying to initiate a feud between the EC's and 42/43GC's to appease the Rollin 60's who didn't want them on the same row with us. I was against that because the issue was childish and because my homeboys were out there getting money with the 42/43's. Thus if a war broke out we would be the ones fighting it on the frontlines. Twin got quiet and got off of the door. However, the issue wasn't over. Later that night C-Rag overheard them talking about stabbing Lil Scrap and Fat-Dog the next morning when the police let us out for showers. Twin didn't let the 62's know what he was planning. Me, Tiny Mont, C-Rag, and Hamburger were all in the cells with 42/43's. Thus his plot was jeopardizing the 62's. Rag shot me a kite informing me about their plot. Twin's cell sat between my cell and Rag's cell. I read the letter and immediately went to work. I wasn't going to let them stab Lil Scrap when he risked his life to save Bear. I also felt like Twin was saying F%@* 62EC so I felt the same way about them. I warned Lil Scrap and Fat-Dog about Twin's plot. In Twin's cell was Twin 1 and 2, Lil Johnny Ray, and Outlaw from 118EC.

I knew Outlaw from our time in CYA but he wasn't claiming 118EC while there. I really thought that he was an imposter. Since they were planning on busting on Lil Scrap and Fat-Dog I helped prepare them. I told them that I can't get involved because I'm from EC. But I refused to let them get ambushed by Twin. The next morning the police told us to strip down to our boxers and shower shoes for showers. They then popped us out of our cells. Twin 1 and 2 both stepped out of the cell fully clothed with burners in their hands while Johnny Ray and Outlaw stood in their doorway with burners. They all were strapped and Johnny Ray dissed 43GC. Me and Tiny Mont stepped out for showers and Lil Scrap stepped out of the cell fully clothed with a burner. Fat-Dog stayed in the cell. The Twins rushed Lil Scrap and poked him as he busted on both of them.

Lil Johnny Ray and Outlaw didn't get involved. The police told everyone to get down as they pushed the alarm. Scrap and the Twins all went to receive medical attention while me, Tiny Mont, and Fat-Dog went to the hole for a week. When we got out of the hole I noticed that at least 8 EC's were missing. I don't know where they went but they were gone. The Twins, Lil Johnny Ray, and Outlaw were still there. I didn't say anything to them. I felt like if they had an issue with what I did we could've lined it up.

I heard that they were communicating with Kiko from 188EC complaining to him about the situation but I didn't care. They jeopardized the lives of S.D's and by right we had a legitimate reason to smash them for it but we didn't. They rushed Scrap and got busted on behind some B.S. because they couldn't control their pride and egos. They all were in the module with me for at least a month afterwards but didn't discuss what happened.

My attorney told me about an alleged eyewitness to the shooting at the gas station named Delphina Cruz. She spoke to the police in 1994. My investigator went and spoke to her and obtained an exculpatory statement from her. They called me out on an attorney/client visit. During this visit O.J. Simpson was also on a visit with his attorney and daughter Arnell. I'd been on a few of these types of visits with O.J. Simpson sitting in the booth next to me. Rothman and my investigator Moore informed me that Delphina Cruz was getting off of the freeway on Gage and Grand when the shooting began.

She was riding in a car with her husband, girlfriend, and girlfriend's husband coming back from a double date. When the shooting began she allegedly saw a few people with guns. They showed her my photo and she said that I wasn't one of the guys she saw that night. However, she alleged that I looked like someone who stole her purse. Rothman was concerned about that part but I wasn't. I wasn't a purse snatcher on the streets and I rather had been accused of snatching a purse than multiple homicides.

Cruz's statement to my investigator was different from the police report she signed. Her police report alleged that she identified me as the guy with the gun. However, the handwriting resembled the penmanship on Clarence Lavan's police report which he never signed. Thus I was convinced that one of the detectives wrote out the contents of the police report and just had Cruz sign it. She probably didn't even read what she signed. Bottom line: the report was fabricated by the detectives. Detectives often write out police reports which further their own agendas by falsifying witness statements and then just having the witness sign it without allowing him/her to read what they are actually signing. This is also dirty police work which is deemed a harmless error in the judicial system. I asked Rothman to call Mrs. Cruz to court along with my other defense witnesses and he agreed that he would. I also wanted him to get in contact with Chilli Moe and speak to him about what Lavan told him about the shooting days later to corroborate what Lil Bow-Low said. His agreement to do so lacked conviction and was unpersuasive.

I called the hood and let my homies (defense witnesses) know that my trial was about to start soon and to be available for when my attorney called them to court. They said that they would be. I also learned that Lil Owl, Biscuit, Dog, Marstein 1 and 2, and Sonny all got busted by the Feds for manufacturing PCP and other crimes. Unbeknownst to me is that they had been under federal investigation since the early part of 1991. What I also didn't know at that time was that it was a joint investigation between ATF and Newton Division. Thus Lil Owl and Biscuit were under investigation when the shooting occurred.

I called Kemo and his wife Nikki answered the phone. Kemo wasn't home. I heard a baby crying in the background so I assumed that they just had a new baby. I was there when they brought home their first child Lil Kemo. Nikki shocked me when she said that she was babysitting the twins Kemo just had with some teenage female. I didn't hate on my cousin but that was bold and wrong. Nikki sensed my silence on the matter and began telling me about how she was feeling. I had love for her because from what I knew about her she was a good woman. I had never heard anything foul about her in all the years I knew her. With that said I had known all along that Kemo played the field but it wasn't my place to tell his wife. I felt like any female dealing with a dude who runs the streets and lives a criminal lifestyle should know that infidelity comes with the territory. Why? Because you're dealing with an individual who doesn't abide by societal rules or etiquette. Instead he's operating from the G-Code or Hustlers Playbook neither of which forbids or frowns on infidelity. This is not to say that an individual who runs the streets can't or won't be faithful. Some can be but most are not. Now that Nikki knew the truth the decision was hers on whether or not she chose to stay or leave. She chose to stay. I left a message for Kemo and told her I loved her and to take care of herself.

CHAPTER TWENTY FIVE

I spoke to my cousin Duane on the phone and he played 2 Pac's album "It's just me against the world." That album stirred up my spirit. The first time I heard "Dear Mama" I was in the module and it was early in the morning. One of the officers brought his radio to work and let us listen to 92 the Beat with downtown Julie Brown for a few hours. I felt like that song was the best one 2Pac had made up until that time and it caused me to become a fan of his music. Listening to the lyrics I felt like he wrote that song for both of us. The songs "So many tears," "Heavy in the game," and "Me against the world" summed up my life in a nutshell. His lyrics inspired me to continue writing. Me and Lil Bow-Low had the module on lock as far as rapping. My skills had improved dramatically over a couple of years. Lil Bow-Low's delivery was similar to Scarface's. He was talented and really could've been something had he put his all into it. However, crack cocaine had him stuck. When I learned that, I was disappointed.

While on the phone with Duane I was able to get in contact with my little brother Shata (pronounced "Shawn-tay"). He's my father's youngest son by a woman named Sandy. He and I hadn't seen each other in years. It was good to hear from him. He was from Acacia Block Compton Crip. He looked out for me. We conversed about my case and he wanted to see me come home. I spoke to Pookie again and he said that he was still waiting on Pook Dog to take him out of state. I told him that I needed Chilli Moe to contact my attorney because my trial was going to start soon and I needed him to come to court. He agreed to do so. Shortly after that I heard that Buckwheat got found guilty for Scottie's murder. Personally, that wasn't any satisfaction to me. I wanted him out of jail but I wasn't the person in control of his outcome. I noticed that I was becoming restless and couldn't sleep for a few days. My eyes would get tired but when I closed them to go to sleep I'd only get about an hour and a half of sleep. I didn't know what was wrong with me but I was fatigued.

I had a dream. In the dream it was night time around 9:00 p.m. I was at the corner of 61st Street and San Pedro standing in the middle of the street facing Avalon. I was lifted up in the air and I started flying down the street real fast but it felt like I was riding a motorcycle. I was driven to the wall of the big alley on 61st and Avalon and then I was let down. I walked across the street to the apartments behind the liquor store where my homeboys used to hang out at. -- I saw 3 of my homeboys sitting on the porch. In the dream I had about $400 on me from a lick I did. I offered to buy them a sack of weed. We began to walk into the big alley to a weed spot they knew of. While walking we came to this building where some dude from Grape Street sold weed out of. One of my homies knocked on the door and the dude opened up. We told him that we wanted to buy a $20 sack of weed. The dude said OK but told us to walk on the side of his building and he would sell us the weed there. We walked on the side of his building and moments later he and another dude came to sell us the weed. There was now only one of my homeboys with me instead of 3. The dude from Grape Street sold me the weed and then the dude with him pulled out a .38 and told me to give him the money and the weed. I looked at this dude but I couldn't see his face because it was blurred. I felt like this was someone I knew from childhood. I was surprised that he was robbing me. I gave him what he asked for and he gave the things to the dude from Grape Street. The dude from Grape Street ran off and this dude cocked back his gun and was about to shoot me.

However, he was close up on me and I reached for the gun, getting my thumb caught between the hammer and firing pin as he squeezed the trigger. The gun didn't go off. Instead it fell to the ground and the dude ran after the dude from Grape Street. I picked the gun up off of the ground and ran behind the dude who robbed me. He was banging on the door trying to get the dude from Grape Street to open the door. I told him that he should have never tried to rob me and then shot him in the back of his head killing him......

I awoke abruptly out of my sleep and contemplated the meaning of this dream. I told my cellmates about the dream. They all just listened. The next morning on April 21, 1995, I called Lily and spoke to her. She told me that Pookie wanted to speak to me so I had her call him on the 3-way. He and I conversed for about five minutes until he put us on hold while he went to go handle some business. After a little over 5 minutes of waiting for him to return I told Lily to let him know I was going to holler at him later. She said OK and I hung up.

The next morning C-Rag yelled down for me to call home. I told him I was good and that I'll call on another date. He urged me to call now because it was important. I thought about it then called my uncle Spark. I asked him what's going on and he was mourning as he told me that Pookie got killed last night! I was devastated. I couldn't even formulate any words. I just hung up. 5 minutes later I called back and asked him what happened. He told me that my brother went with 3 of my little homeboys to do a robbery in the big alley. The situation went bad and he ended up getting killed. This was the dream I had. Based on my dream I was the person who killed my brother. Which meant that I wondered if this whole robbery plot was nothing more than a ruse to lure my brother into a trap to kill him behind his making a statement against me. When I learned what actually happened I was angry. My brother went into this place of business in the big alley owned by some Mexicans after he was persuaded by a certain individual that there was some money inside. Pookie was desperate for some money at the time so he agreed to go.

However, he went inside first and there was a shootout with the Mexicans. Pookie had a .380 which he got from my homeboy. He shot back. The Mexicans shot him 4 times with a 9mm but those injuries were not life threatening. The bullet that killed him was from a .38. One of the dudes with him shot him in the back of the head with a .38 killing him. They didn't get any money because there wasn't any money in there. After Pookie got shot in the back of the head the dudes with him left him at the scene.

My suspicions were never confirmed but it didn't change the way I was feeling. I was hurt for a number of reasons. Most of all because this was another son my mother lost and she didn't have any money to bury him. The trials and tribulations were never ending. I didn't condone my brother's murder and I never ordered it. I knew that Pookie wasn't going to come to court against me and thus his statement would never be allowed to be used against me. I was lying in wait for one of them cats involved to come to the county jail for anything because I was going to smash him if I ran into him. I mourned for 18 months after his death. Family and friends came together to help bury my brother and I'm eternally grateful for it. LaShawn even gave Pookie her burial plot on top of Scottie. That was an act of love and kindness towards my family. My mother and I were thankful to her for it. A couple of days after Pookie's death I was called to the chaplain's office. I already knew that it was to inform me about what I already knew about my brother.

When I got there I was allowed to speak to my mother on the phone. She wasn't doing well despite her attempts to be strong. We conversed and I did my best to comfort her in our time of mourning. When the call was completed I was sitting in the hallway handcuffed waiting for an officer to escort me back to the module. I saw the chaplain and another white man looking at me. They began making light conversation with me which I ignored. But the chaplain pissed me off by saying, "Too bad you're going to spend the rest of your life in prison." I looked at him and said, " That's a lie I'm going to beat this case and walk right out of the door!" They both just looked at me. I restrained myself from cursing him out and spitting on him. His comment got me wondering "was the fix already in?"

When I went to court Rothman got at me with a ton of bullshit. First, he pleaded with me to take the deal because if I did he would get the $54,000 left which was part of the money the court gave him to represent me. But if we went to trial then all he'd receive was $40,000. I told him that I didn't give a damn about how much money he would receive and I wasn't taking no life sentence deal. Second, he told me that he didn't think we needed my defense witnesses or Lil Owl to come to court because all I needed to do was testify and tell my story. I told him that I wanted my defense witnesses called along with Lil Owl because no jury was going to believe my testimony without any other witnesses to corroborate my alibi and innocence. Plus Lil Owl was the only surviving victim so why wouldn't he be called to testify? Third, he told me that I should take the stand and say that I was at the gas station. I told him that he lost his damn mind. If I placed myself at the crime scene then that would be a for sure conviction. I wasn't about to do no dumb ass shit like that especially when I had an alibi and witnesses to support it. He looked at me and said, "with all of these serious charges against you no one is going to believe that you are innocent of everything and didn't do anything." I told him that I didn't care what people think, just call my defense witnesses. Lastly, he told me that his girlfriend thinks I'm guilty. I asked him what he thought. He said he didn't know. Rothman revealed his true colors. He wasn't for me he was against me he didn't give a damn about my life or freedom. He also told me his girlfriend was 30 years old and he had bought her a new red sports car. He was a trick and a sucker. When I got back to my cell I thought about everything he said to me. I wished that I had it in writing.

One thing that stuck out to me is that he violated the attorney/client privilege by discussing my case (pillow talking) with his young girlfriend. Rothman was 62 years old. He could be disbarred for that. My trial was about to start any day so I didn't believe that it was going to be possible to get a new attorney this late in the case. I regret not attempting to get him off my case till this day.

One day I was in the court tank and I ran into Spike from 89EC and East Side Benny from 62EC. Spike was fighting a murder charge due to a gun one of his homies gave him which had a murder on it. Benny had come down from the Pen. I was talking to Spike about my case. He told me that he hoped that I beat the case but if I didn't then when I hit the Pen don't be like so many other dudes who get caught up getting high, playing basketball, catching SHU terms, and just wasting time. He told me to get in that law library and study so I can get this time up off of me. He said that if I don't do it for myself ain't nobody else going to do it for me. I listened carefully to what he was saying and accepted his advice. Benny told me that a lot of my OG homies from EC who had been down for years already heard of me.

When I went back to my cell I thought about what Spike said. I was in the cell by myself and I thought about everything going on in my life. From Pookie and Angie's deaths, to Rothman's egregious ineffective representation of my case, my mother and sisters financial condition, and the fact that I was my mother's last son. I felt the guilt of my brother's blood on my hands and reality set in that I just might lose my trial. I felt like if I got found guilty on top of Pookie's demise it would be a repeat of 1986. I prayed to God to just let the truth come out about what the police did to me in this case because he knew that I didn't have anything to do with it.

Under the pressure of trying to be strong and keep it all together I broke down and cried. Pookie's death caused me to rethink my loyalty to my hood. I told myself that if I got found guilty or beat the case I wasn't going to live the rest of my life gang banging representing something that didn't give a damn about me. If I lost my trial I didn't have anything else to give to the hood, losing my life was enough. I didn't owe anybody anything.

While I was fighting my case I had a few homies look out for me like Sad, Kemo, Fish, and La-La, but that wasn't going to convince me to continue gang banging. Combined I had received less than $150 from them or any other homeboy. I questioned my worth. Everything else I received came from Glynnis, Angie, my hustling selling tobacco, or robbing. I chose to gang bang out of love for my hood and homeboys not for profit. However, my homies started robbing banks, big rigs, and other spots having big money yet my family was broke living in a shelter struggling.

Cats would rather trick money off on a new female they just met, getting high, or a dice game rather than thinking about sending me some money to make sure I was straight. But as soon as I'm talking to them on the phone they're constantly telling me how much they miss me, I'm a real one, etc. East Side Blue once told me that he represented 43GC and did things to put his hood on the map. His hood didn't represent him or put him on the map. I thought that was a profound statement. I spent years on the front line retaliating and putting in work for the set, busting on enemies and getting shot and in reality it was for nothing.

My life wasn't enriched or enhanced from the dirt I did in the name of 62EC. I was broke facing the death penalty while my mother and sisters was living in poverty. Where was the honor in that? I was being true to something that was fake to me. The two and a half years I spent fighting my case could've been spent getting me an associates degree in something that could have led to my having a career. However, I couldn't blame anyone but myself for the lifestyle and choices I made. I knew the consequences of gang banging. I was responsible for the path I chose. I saw Boxer get washed up for a crime he didn't commit. I just didn't think I would ever be in a similar predicament.

Glynnis came to visit me. She had stitches in her finger due to Lewis slamming her hand in the car door. She actually thought it was a sound decision to complain to me about it when we both knew that he was her new man. It was good that I couldn't touch her because I probably would've slapped the hell out of her. In the midst of everything I was going through she had the audacity to tell me about a lover's quarrel she was having with another dude. She didn't have any empathy for what I was going through. The relationship was definitely over.-I needed one last thing from her and that was for her to buy me an outfit for trial. She bought me some Guess Jeans, Timberland boots, and an Eddie Bauer sweater and gave it to my attorney.

I spoke to Nate Ness on the phone. He was excited to hear from me and wanted to know how I was doing. He attended my brother's funeral and was moved by the letter I wrote which was read at the funeral. Nate had a lot of love for me. The trip part is that I never knew he felt that way about me. He told me that I always respected him and never tripped on him. I was beginning to see that the little things a person does can have a big impact on somebody else's life. Nate let me know if I needed anything to let him know. That was amazing because the dudes I ran with everyday never said that to me. Nate was married with two children: Nate Jr. and Talisha. He became a big brother to me and comforted me in my time of grief. He showed me that his words were good. To a person incarcerated all we have to stand on is a person's word. That's what builds trust and respect. If a person's words ain't no good then neither is the person speaking them. Sadly many people don't understand that. I didn't either until I started to mature and grow up.

I went to court and we began to pick the jury and do voir dire. Now I was informed by a few dudes who fought the death penalty that a jury pool for a capital case or LWOP ("Life Without The Possibility of Parole") is supposed to be at least 120 people. Mine was roughly 45 people, many of whom were tired from being bounced off of other trials for two weeks. Thus they were exhausted and ready to get back to their lives. That was a bad sign to me because tired minds don't pay attention. I also saw very few blacks and none of them looked under the age of 35. A good thing happened though. The D.A. dropped the death penalty. As we began to pick the jury I noticed there were more older women than any other demographic. Females tend to be emotional when it comes to violence and will lean towards conviction quicker than men because the facts sometimes go over their heads. The jury members were asked if they could impartially judge someone on trial for murder and attempted murders on police. Some said that they couldn't due to their being related to or being friends with police officers. As a result they were excluded from the jury. While picking the jury members I noticed that the prosecution was filling the jury box with women. My attorney sat back and allowed it while I was able to recognize that having a jury predominantly full of women in a multiple murder trial wasn't in my best interest because women tend to be more sensitive which can sometimes interfere with their judgment. Rather than objectively listening to the facts of a case they may choose to convict just based on the fact that I'm the person charged and there are too many victims thus someone has to pay especially after observing numerous crime scene photos. By the time we finished picking the jury it consisted of 9 women (2 of whom were black) and 3 men (none of whom was black). That didn't look right to me.

When I got back to my cell I thought about that. Baby Pookie was my cellmate. He and I grew close. He went to trial and got a hung jury. Afterwards he and Boogie were offered deals for 12 and 7 years which they took. Rag and Burger got convicted and sentenced to 25 to life each. Cowboy took a deal also on his case. The police moved the EC's, NHC's, Harlems, and 42/43GC's to Denver Row and moved the Hoovers, Gangsters, Compton and Watts, and their allies to Baker Row.

I started my trial on May 10, 1995, just three days after my 22nd birthday. None of the victims' family members came to court. My family didn't come to court either. The courtroom literally consisted of me, my attorney, the D.A., the judge, the court reporter and clerk, and whatever witness was called to testify at court. Rothman didn't call any expert witnesses, instead he relied on the prosecution's expert witnesses. Only Slim came to trial for me. Glynnis came once for a half a day to drop my clothes off and left at lunch break and didn't come back.

The forensic expert's name was Starr Sachs and she testified about the shell casings and the fact that the guns we got busted with didn't match either shooting.Officer David Lott testified as a gang expert and alleged that the 62's and 68's were at war with each other when the shooting at the gas station occurred. This was false. He couldn't point to any previous shootings between them either. He was lying to try to establish a motive for the shooting to help the D.A. Rothman didn't question him much. Lott wasn't an expert in my opinion. Officer Derek Fellows testified to the same things he said at the preliminary hearing. His partner never came to court for some reason. He continued the lie about seeing me behind a truck popping my head up and down and then hearing shots from that location. However, he was contradicted by Detective Berdin who testified that Fellows told him something different when he took down his statement. My cousin Lil Pookie and Tone-Tone never came to court so the D.A. couldn't use their statements against me in court. Baby Dee was in jail at the time on a new beef so they brought him to court. The D.A. played his tape-recorded statements for the jury but he denied ever talking to the police or giving a statement. He also denied that his voice was on the tape. The D.A. was irate. My brother was dead so his statement couldn't be used either. The police shooting case was extremely weak.

As for the murders Leroy Martin testified that he saw me standing by the cashier window observing the scenery 5 minutes before the shooting which the D.A. knew it was a lie. He said that he thought I got out of the red and black car (which was driven by Clarence Lavan). He described me as being in my late 20's to early 30's in age (I was 19 at the time). Rothman asked him why he didn't identify me from the six-packs and live lineup and he claimed that he did when he said that he was 75% sure that I came closest to the guy he saw. He also stated that now there was no doubt in his mind that I was the guy he saw. Rothman contradicted his trial testimony with his previous testimony and he admitted that after the live lineup one of the detectives told him that he should have picked me out because I was at the gas station. Thus to me it's no coincidence that he was now 100% sure that I was the guy he saw. Rothman never pointed out to the jury that Martin identified Lavan standing by the cashier window and he was mistaken about seeing me. Martin also stated that he learned more details from people in the neighborhood about what the shooting was about. He didn't see the shooter or who had the gun in their hand. He said that when I left the cashier's window and walked back towards the red and black car he heard gunshots coming from that direction which he now believed came from the alley instead of the red and black car. The detectives must have convinced him that the shots came from the alley. The problem with that theory is that no shell casings were found in the alley. Martin wasn't credible because me and the D.A. knew that Martin identified Lavan not me. I found it outrageous that my attorney was allowing the D.A. to twist up the facts to secure my conviction. And that D.A. Hunter was culpable in Martin's mistaken identification of me. I was pissed.

Lavan didn't come to trial so some government employee took the stand and read his preliminary hearing transcripts to the jury. I wasn't allowed to cross-examine him. During trial often I'd see jury members falling asleep while witnesses were testifying. This is common in trials that don't make the news. Again, Lavan's trial testimony was the same as his preliminary hearing testimony. The D.A. urged the jury to listen to his tape-recorded statement because that was the best evidence in the case. That was a false statement. The best evidence could only be the witnesses' sworn testimony under oath.

Crook was called to court by my attorney. He testified to standing on his back porch smoking a cigarette when he heard multiple gunshots and seconds later seeing Lil Flux come running through the alley carrying an AK-47 and asking him if he (Flux) could hide inside of his (Crook's) house. Crook said that he told him no and Lil Flux uttered a curse word as he ran off through the alley. He described Flux as short, stocky, and dark skinned. The D.A. tried to coerce Crook into saying that he heard a jeep out in front of his house that dropped Lil Flux off. However, Crook denied that that took place.

Mya Dansby came to court and testified that she was on Gage and San Pedro moments after the shooting when Lil Owl and Junebug drove there and parked. She stated that she called the ambulance for them and she saw me, Kemo, Lil Greedy, Tiny Bubble, and Rodon pull up in two cars minutes later and I wasn't wearing all black clothing and she never knew me to have long hair. Aside from Crook and Mya my attorney didn't call any of my other defense witnesses to testify in court. The D.A. couldn't rebut Crook and Maya's testimony. Officer Rafael Hechavarria testified and confirmed the traffic stop involving Tiny Bubble but he couldn't recall how many people were in the car because his partner Adam Schiffer conducted the traffic stop while he was the backup. He stated that in the midst of the traffic stop he heard "a volley of gunfire" from nearby. He stated that they terminated the traffic stop and sped off to the gas station. In fact they were the first officers to respond to the shooting. His testimony proved that I wasn't making up the story about the traffic stop. However, Rothman didn't call my alibi witnesses to corroborate my alibi when the shooting occurred. Thus the jury never knew my alibi or how Hechavarria's testimony corroborated it. The D.A. quickly pounced on the opportunity to twist up his testimony to her advantage. She persuaded the jurors that Hechavarria was only testifying to show that he and his partner were the first officers to respond to the shooting. When the facts get twisted at trial the wrong person can lose his/her life and freedom.

Detective Schunk testified that on the night that I was arrested he took two photos of me. One with no hat on my head and another with me wearing a beanie hat. He also stated that the reason he put a beanie on my head and took a photo is because at that time he had evidence that the shooter at the gas station wore a beanie. According to police reports the only witness the detectives had spoken to about the shooting at the gas station prior to my arrest was Leroy Martin. Leroy initially identified Clarence and his brother as the suspects so why were two of my photos being placed into six pack photo lineup spreads for the gas station shooting while neither Clarence or his brother's photos were ever placed into six packs for Martin to view? To me this was proof that the detectives were making me the suspect in the shooting. How? Because from the time of the shooting to my arrest there was no evidence to link me to the crime nor did I match Leroy's description of the suspect who got out of the red and black car and went and stood by the cashier's window just before the shooting. It was two days after my arrest that the detectives alleged to have spoken to Crip-Cal who supposedly implicated me as the person bragging about doing the shooting (which Crip-Cal denied and no one corroborated) and a full three weeks after my arrest when they first spoke to Clarence Lavan. So why were the detectives jumping the gun by taking my photos and placing them in six packs for the shooting at the gas station on the night of my arrest? Why the rush? Truth is that they took my photographs and placed them in six packs because they had already presumed that I was the suspect. This was purely in retaliation for the two attempted murders I was charged with against Newton Division LAPD officers. My attorney didn't connect the dots or address any of these issues while Schunk was testifying. Rothman did ask Schunk if he'd spoken to Crook about this case. Schunk confirmed that he had. Rothman asked him if Crook told him what he testified to in court about Lil Flux. Schunk admitted that Crook told him the same things. Rothman asked him if he'd spoken to Lil Flux about this case and Schunk admitted that he had spoken to him about it. Schunk further added that Lil Flux denied any involvement in the shooting so he didn't charge him.

That was strange for a few reasons. 1. There was no police reports or evidence to prove that the detectives had spoken to Lil Flux about this case. 2. Allegedly Crip-Cal also told him that Lil Flux was behind the shooting and Crook testified to seeing Flux running up to his back door from the alley carrying an AK-47 seconds after the shooting and asking if he could hide inside of Crook's house. 3. I denied involvement in the shooting but they still charged me. Schunk acknowledged that my photo was the only photo to appear twice in the 6 six pack photo spreads and the beany he placed on my head while at the police station didn't belong to me. The prosecution attempted to bolster Clarence's identifications of me by alleging that Clarence identified me from both six pack cards A and F. However, when Clarence's tape recorded interview was being played in court the judge stipulated that Clarence stated that "him seeing me in the photo wearing a beanie helped him out a lot in his identification of me because WITHOUT THE HAT he couldn't identify me."

Therefore he didn't identify me from both six packs. My attorney didn't object to either of the witnesses' in-court identifications of me. Rothman urged me to take the stand on my own behalf. I agreed to but shouldn't have because he didn't call my alibi witnesses nor did he prep me before taking the stand. And while testifying he failed to ask me the appropriate questions which would have allowed me to tell my alibi. He advised me to only answer the questions that were asked and for me not to volunteer any information. He knew what my alibi was because he investigated it and found evidence to corroborate it. Thus it was frustrating when he didn't call my witnesses to testify or ask me where I was at the time of the shooting. I felt that was the most important question from a defensive standpoint. I testified that I was not the shooter nor did I have any involvement in the shooting. I was not at the gas station when the shooting occurred, me, Junebug, and Lil Owl was all friends, our hoods was not at war when Junebug and Lil Owl got shot, rival gangs was initially blamed for the shooting, I first became aware of them being the victims when I pulled up on Gage and San Pedro with Kemo, Lil Greedy, and a few other of my homies in two cars and saw Lil Owl's Cadillac parked with bullet holes in it. In regards to the police shooting case I testified that I was out there that night, I was not the shooter, I didn't have a gun, when one of my homies yelled out "it's the police!" I broke and ran. I was not the person popping his head up and down from behind the truck parked in the driveway, I spent the night at one of my homeboys house, and I never ran into Baby Dee that night. The D.A. was unable to refute my testimony so she told the jury that my testimony was self-serving and that I didn't have any alibi witnesses to corroborate my story. I felt like every move my attorney made was just another step bringing me closer to a guilty verdict. I felt betrayed and manipulated.

Lil Owl was called to testify as a prosecution witness. He stated that he never knew me to have long hair, he and Junebug didn't sell drugs in my hood, our hoods were not at war when he and Junebug was shot, we were all friends, he never saw the shooter, and he was shot in his back and shoulder. Those things he testified to were in my favor. But then he turned around and confirmed part of the prosecution's theory by stating that " after the shooting our hoods went to war because the 62's were involved!" I just looked at him with disbelief. The reason why is because I was the only 62 EC gang member on trial for the shooting. Thus the jury could now reasonably infer that I did it. If he didn't see who shot him then he couldn't positively say for certain that the 62's was involved. To me my entire trial was about what the 62's did with the exception of Clarence's bogus identification of me. Lil Owl told my investigator that he didn't believe that I was involved but he didn't say that under oath and Rothman didn't ask him about it.

During the closing argument the D.A. tried to explain away Crook's testimony by stating that Lil Flux was a lookout at the gas station, he was the short, stocky guy with a handgun in the alley Lavan saw, and it was his job to get rid of the AK-47 after I did the shooting. That was totally false. If she truly believed that then why wasn't Lil Flux charged for aiding and abetting multiple murders? The detective testified that he didn't believe Lil Flux had anything to do with the gas station shooting but here was the prosecutor telling the jury that Lil Flux was involved in the murders!

Flux was never placed in any type of lineup for Lavan to view so how was the D.A. certain that he was the lookout? Clearly the police and prosecution weren't on the same page. Sadly, Rothman didn't object to those statements by the prosecution. Thus those lies were allowed to linger in the jury members minds. No witness ever testified to seeing me hand an AK-47 to Lil Flux and his photo was never placed in a six pack photo spread to eliminate him as a suspect.

As to Mya's testimony the D.A. stated that Mya has no reason to lie for me. However, Mya didn't see me during the shooting. The D.A. bolstered Lavan and Martin's identifications by stating that Martin corroborated Lavan's identification of me because he saw me standing by the cashier's window observing the scenery 5 minutes before the shooting.

I couldn't believe what I was hearing. Martin didn't corroborate Lavan's identification. The prosecutor knew that Martin actually identified Lavan as the guy standing by the cashier window before the shooting! Lavan even admitted to being this person at a preliminary hearing. How in the hell was this evidence getting twisted up when it was right there in the police reports and transcripts?

My attorney never argued these points to the jury which also undermined my defense. Photos of Lavan were never shown to

Martin thus the detectives convinced him that he saw me rather than Lavan. The D.A. told the jury that I was positively identified by both witnesses and that they should listen to Lavan's tape because it was the best evidence. In regards to Martin's alleged identification someone needed to explain to me how a witness who admitted to being 75% sure that I CAME CLOSEST to the guy he saw by the cashier's window has somehow made a POSITIVE identification of me?

To back it up for a second prior to closing argument I spoke to Rothman about calling witness Delphina Cruz to testify. The matter went to the judge. Rothman told the judge that I wanted him to call her, but she just tells a different story. It doesn't matter anyway because my client is innocent (I'm paraphrasing.) The judge was willing to postpone the trial for a couple of days until she came back from out of town but Rothman didn't call her to court. He also only asked me ten questions while I was on the stand and he never asked me where I was at the time of the shooting.

Rothman's closing argument was less than convincing. I felt like I was going to lose. The jury deliberated for about 3 days. They asked for read back of me and Martin's testimony. Then on May 18, 1995, they returned verdicts on all counts. They found me guilty of the murders and attempted murder at the gas station. They voted 11 to 1 not guilty on the shooting at the police case then dismissed it in the interest of Justice. My sentencing was in June.

When I got back to my cell I was at a loss for words. I didn't cry but I was numb. Everything I feared came to pass. I let my homeboys on the tier know and they tried to comfort me. I'd never been to prison and all that was on my mind was how long would it take me to get back on appeal. I also learned that Lil Flux got found guilty too. I called Glynnis and officially broke up with her. I knew that she wasn't going to do this time with me and it was time for us to go our separate ways. I had about $250 to my name and two rap albums worth of music I had written. I was headed to prison and I didn't know who was going to be there for me or how I was going to survive financially. My family was in disarray and I didn't know who to trust. It was ugly but I honestly didn't even stress about it. The worst had just happened to me; there was nothing else that could bring me down. I was at rock bottom.

CHAPTER TWENTY SIX

I called Spark and broke the news. He couldn't believe it. I felt bad for my mother because with my conviction she had officially lost both sons. Never in a million years would I ever have imagined that I'd be serving a Life Without Parole sentence for killing Junebug out of all people. The jury got it wrong. My jury was made up of 9 women and 3 men and only 2 blacks. Most of whom were 40 years and older. How in the hell was that a jury of my peers?

What the jury didn't understand is that me and Junebug were from the era of "Coast Love" which began in 1986. It grew stronger in 1987 when we were having football games with the Grape Streets at Jordan High School and Bethune Jr. High School. I was at both games. We were bred to love EC from 1st Street to 190th Street. We didn't include the SOS' and 1200 Bloccs because they never came to L.A. to introduce themselves and get embraced by the homies in L.A. Nevertheless during that era we were all about unity not division. It was the homies who got out of prison or CYA in 1989-90 that brought in the bullshit after Big Bubble and other reputable homies from EC got locked up. When I said that Junebug was my homeboy I meant that.

My definition of homeboy was someone you could trust, who you would ride for, and be there for in the hardest times. A true homeboy wouldn't get jealous of you because you had money. You didn't have to worry about him robbing or killing you. He wouldn't snitch on you. He wouldn't creep behind your back with your girlfriend or wife. This is the code Junebug and I operated from. Lil Owl was part of that era too.

But even if I had been allowed to give my alibi and break this stuff down to the jury it probably wouldn't have mattered anyway. To a predominantly white jury I was guilty just because I was a young black gang member who got busted with assault rifles. To a predominantly female jury I was guilty because they were sympathetic to the victims and felt like someone needed to pay for this crime. I had no problem with the right person paying for the crime. I'm just not that person and there was so much exculpatory evidence that didn't get disclosed in trial due to the fact that my dump truck attorney partnered up with the prosecution to help secure my conviction. Rothman told me that he had polled the jury after the verdict and they told him that Leroy Martin's testimony tipped the scale in the prosecution's favor because he also placed me at the gas station. Only if they knew the truth.

I called my little homeboy Tiny Bam and broke the bad news to him. He couldn't believe it either. Tiny Bam was related to Lil Mont, Rob-Dog, Tiny Mont, and Chivetta. I knew his whole family. I gave him his moniker because he was down and reminded me of myself. I was a big brother to him on the streets. I told him about the game the same way that it was given to me. I took him on his first mission. I loved him with everything inside of me. When fast young girls would come sniffing around me trying to flirt with me I'd go get him and let him holler at them. He was their age. I wasn't trying to have no pedophile jacket even though I was 19 years old.

Some dudes took pride in being cock hounds. They didn't care too much about a girl's age but I didn't get down like that. Me and T-Bam stayed in communication until I went to prison. He hooked me up with a female name Alicia Harris. She was a big breasted light skinned sister from Cudahy, California. She and I became friends but I didn't feel any sparks so I kept the conversation platonic. I conversed with her and Lily to ease my mind from stress.

Baby Pookie was waiting to go to prison. Blink from 118EC and

Lil Ran-Ran from 89EC came to the module right before I left the county jail. Lil No-Good from Rollin 60's beat his kidnap robbery case, got released, and came back to jail 4 months later for a new beef.

On June 6, 1995, I was sentenced to Life Without the Possibility of Parole plus 108 years to life. I had never heard of such a sentence. I found it extremely hard to tell people how much time I received. It seemed surreal. I had been thinking about prison life and thinking about the stories I heard from various dudes telling me how prison was.

The two prisons that sounded the worst were Pelican Bay and Corcoran. Both were notorious for violence. Corcoran was worse because the correctional officers (C/O's) were staging gladiator type fights between black and Mexican inmates in the SHU. For example, they would release one or two black inmates to the SHU yard where they were always outnumbered by the Southern Mexicans (Surenos). Once they hit the yard the Surenos would attack them. The brothers would defend themselves only to get shot by a C/O. The Surenos would never get shot. In fact, the C/O's at Corcoran had recently murdered my homeboy Preston Tate a.k.a. "T-Snake" from 59EC in the SHU in 1994, under the same circumstances. His death was publicized and led to a Federal investigation and a lawsuit. An officer blew the whistle on what was going on. However, none of the officers involved in these incidents were ever convicted because the local community was pro law enforcement. That's another reason why I struggle to trust or honor those in uniform. Some are worthy of respect and honor but many are not. Many are criminals masking as honorable men and women. Many of those who wear uniforms are drug addicts, alcoholics, wife beaters, racists, quick tempered, arrogant, law breakers, thieves, and murderers. Some of them have also been known to operate like gang members or organized criminals. I can never view someone like that as a hero. Taking an oath to uphold and enforce the law means nothing if the person taking the oath isn't honest, upright, and faithful. Nevertheless I was hoping I could avoid those two prisons. On level 4 I was going to have to be on guard at all times and ready to get cracking. This was the big boy league of criminals.

I had heard the stories of prison politics, dudes under paperwork, booty bandits, and the race riots. Thus I prepared myself for whatever may come my way. I planned to leave prison the way I came in. I was

MARLON EVANS

apprehensive about my prospects. My dream of having a rap career was placed on hold. I prayed and asked God to guide me, protect me, supply all of my needs, and to give me the wisdom, knowledge, and understanding to learn the law, prove my innocence, and get my conviction overturned. I intended on using prison as my college university to educate and better myself. I had a lot of anger and bitterness within me that realistically I knew I wasn't ready to get released. I let Nate know what was going on with me too. On June 22, 1995, I was sent to prison (Delano reception center) ironically on Glynnis' birthday.

Chin up and ten toes down as I stepped into the next phase of my life.
"CRYING BLUE TEARS"
Verse
I've been a fan of the game from day 1, back when niggas word and street cred was A-1, was just a young pup when the game was sold, pure gold, told to be bold, respect the G-Code, straight beast mode, I, never knew the things I was learning, would embed my mind like "Mississippi Burning," gold Dana Danes turning, bending corners in Sevilles and Coupe de Villes, Nardi steering wheels, tote steel, we hard to kill, on the real Coast banging so addicted, I'm inflicted, living wicked, in pursuit of mil tickets, I'm with it and can't nobody tell me a thang, on the block trying get change, hand in the dope game, pistol with a long flame, chess player strong game, my brother peddled cocaine, I chose to do the same thang, in the back of my mind heard my parents admonition, them streets get you dead or imprisoned, in hindsight I should've listened, since then niggas messed the game up like a 5 car collision, reminiscing, missing when the game was true, no surprise the tears in my eyes are blue

Hook: I'm crying blue tears for wasted years, reminiscing back when, the game was top ten, now the game sour like a pickle be, niggas tickle me, play hard like my girls nipples be

Verse   two
There was a time when blowing up the set got you booted, rat packed at a meeting and completely uprooted, we was brutal, and busters didn't stand a chance, digging in pants pockets, snatched chains and their watches, gossiping wasn't tolerated, we didn't hear or see no evil stayed solid when interrogated, catching cases doing bids, split wigs, we was kids, had to earn respect, among G's and vets, high signing got you

+184+

handcuffed, stuffed in trunks, sucking on a pump, baller stuck up for his product, kidnapped held for ransom, family cashing out mad dough paid handsome, still blast him, loyalty came with the manual, turned wanna be G's to broken dreams, and empty shadows, but now things changed, so many busters go against the grain, letting snitches kick it and still represent the gang, bow my head in shame, the whole game is new, tears stains, behind Versace tinted frames are blue — Hook

Verse three

Escalades and low riders, nowadays they snort powder, turn the game sour, leave a stench like clam chowder, Sean John and Eddie Bauer, use to be the money and the power, now rings around the collar make me wanna holler, amazed, as if I'm walking in a daze, seeing pink and yellow niggas on trails they never blazed, bumping O'Jays, thinking about the old days, when it was all about unity, patrolling our community, firm continuity before the set tripping, back when we was Jeri Curling and still pistol gripping, something's missing, homies just hit a lick for pounds of weed and hella keys, while real G's forgotten with ease, bro please you seen my mama doing bad, but you never had the decency to help her out or ask, having mad cash, suppose to be my road dog, but now a nigga in the Pen you won't accept my phone call, to hell with all y'all, this the thanks I get, caught life behind the clique, stayed true and never snitched, while you're telling war stories fabricating the truth, just remember the tears in my eyes are blue

—Hook

THE END

"Clay Max" + "Buckwheat"
"Baby Bam"
"Flux"
"Lil Greedy" - M/BL Short
G-Ride
Clarence "Claymax" Mid 30th
69th + Broadway
3rd House on the North side
Off 69th West of Broadway
Back House

9213-41658	MURDER	1391	Phillips, Raymond Gary	12/13/92
9213-41659	MURDER	1391	Broomfield, Henry	12/13/92
9213-41661	MURDER	1391	Hempstad, Moses	12/14/92
9313-02997	MURDER	1391	Smith, Ronald	1/09/93
9213-41660	Att MURDER	1391	Bavis, Donte	12/13/92

BRIEF SYNOPSIS

On December 13, 1992 at approximately 2150 hours, victims Phillips, Hempstad, and Smith were at the Mobil Gas Station located at 343 W. Gage Avenue. Victim's Bavis and Bloomfield had just arrived at the location in Bavis' car, and parked in front of the pay window located on the south side of the gas station. Bloomfield remained in the vehicle while Bavis exited and walked towards the pay window to make a purchase. Victims Phillips, Hempstad, and Smith were standing in different locations within the gas station property. According to witnesses, a Black male suspect walked into the gas station property from Grand Avenue and started spraying the area with gunfire from a semi-auto weapon, fatally wounding victims Phlllips and Bloomfield and critically wounding victims Bavis, Hempstad, and Smith. Victim Phillips sustained multiple gunshot wounds to the face and torso and expired at the scene. Victim Bloomfleld sustained a gunshot wound to the chest and was transported to California Hospital where he expired at 2355 hours." -' Victim Bavis sustained a gunshot wound to both shoulders and was transported to L.A.C. U.S.C. Medical Center where he was treated and was released at a later date.

EXHIBIT 30 - 281

Ex. 39 - 0295

Both victims, Hempstad and Smith, were transported to Martin Luther King Hospital in critical condition, Hempstad from a gunshot wound to the buttocks and Smith from a gunshot wound to the stomach. Hempstead remained in critical condition until December 14, 1992, when he succumbed to his wound. Smith also remained in critical condition until January 9, 1993, when he expired at 0012 hours.

FOLLOW UP INVESTIGATION

On December 13, 1992 at 2215 hours, Detectives Herrera #16502 and Schunk #13040 were contacted and requested to respond to a homicide scene located at Gage and Grand Avenue. During their crime scene investigation, detectives recovered thirty (30) 7.62x39MM brass expended bullet casings which are the caliber of bullets fired from an AK-47 assault rifle. Also during the course of the investigation we found out that victim Henry Broomfield was a member of the 68 East Coast crips gang and rumor on the street was that he had been killed by members of 6 Deuce East Coast Crips gang because Broomfield was selling dope in the 6 Deuce neighborhood. On December 15, 1992 we spoke with Fred Rodney Thomas (8/30/66) AKA "Dee" and Marlon Darrel Evans {5/7/73) AKA "Baby Bam" and "Wimp". Both were members of the 6 Duce East coast Crips gang and had been arrested together on December 14, 1992.

During the time of their arrest Thomas was in possession of an AK-47 Nori rifle which is the same type of weapon used in these murders. Thomas told us that he heard that "Blg Fish " (Gary Singleton) from 6 Deuce East Coast Crips was the shooter. Marlon Evans refused to talk to us.

On December 16, 1992 a Confidentlal Reliable Informant (CRI) stated that the shooting of "June Bug" (victim Bloomfield) was over drugs (narcotics). A non-gang member named Kevin was getting his dope from "June Bug' and was dealing the dope on 59th Street in 6:Deuce's hood and this created a conflict between 6 Deuce East Coast Crip and 68 East Coast Crips.

Consequently "Baby Bam" {Marlon Evans) and three other 6 Deuce East Coast Crip gang members left in a stolen red Jeep Cherokee station wagon and drove to the gas station at Gage and Grand.

According to the CRI, "Baby Bar' had an AK-47 in his possession. The following day the word was that the Swans (blood gang) had killed "June Bug" (victim Bloomfield}. Later that day "Baby Bam" was bragging that he killed "June Bug" not the Swans. We obtained photos of suspects Marlon Evans AKA 'Baby Bam' and Gary Singleton AKA "Fish." We assembled photo display folders and proceeded to the L.A. City Medical Center where we had victim Donte Bavis view the photo display folder.

Victim Bavis could not identify anyone. He said when the first shot struck him, he ducked down and did not see who was shooting at hlm.

EXHIBIT 30 - 282

Ex. 39 - 0296

NOTE: Willie Talos Jr. AKA "Flux" is short and stocky. Lavan further stated that after "Baby Bam" shot the five victims, he walked back to the Jamaicans (victim Phillips) who was laying on the ground, wounded "Baby Bam", then shot victim Phillips two more times. "Baby Bam" then walked up to him (Lavan) and shot at him, missing him, but hit the hood of Lavan's brother's car.

Witness Clarence Lavan's statement was tape recorded on tape # 140915. Witness Clarence Lavan positively identified suspect Marlon Evans as the person he saw shoot the people at the gas station on December 13, 1992.

On January 4, 1993, detectives went to L.A. City Jail and interviewed Little Victor (true name is Victor Sowell). He stated he was afraid of retaliation and refused to identify anyone from the photo display folders.

On January 5, 1993, we met with witness Leroy Martin and showed him photos. He identified the photo of suspect Marlon Evans ("Baby Bam") as looking very much like to be the guy near the cashier's window when the shooting occurred.

EXHIBIT 30 - 284

Ex. 39 - 0298

On December 21, 1992, we contacted Diane at S.I.D. Firearms and requested a comparison of the bullet recovered by Dr. Ortiz from victim Hempstad during the autopsy (December 16, 1992) to test bullets fired from the AK-47 rifle recovered from suspects Fred Thomas and Marlon Evans during their arrest on December 14, 1992, DR# 9213-39544. We also requested a comparison of the bullet casings we recovered at the crime scene. On December 23, 1992 we spoke with Newton CRASH Officers Giles and Lott. They advised that they had spoken to a Black male named John Severin. According to the officers, Severin had knowledge of the murder. Giles and Lott also stated they had spoken to another Black male called "Chili Mo" who is from the 66 East Coast Crlps. "Child Mo" told the officers that he had spoken to a transient named Clarence known as "Claymax," who told him that "Claymax" was present at the gas station when the murder occurred. "Claymax" told "Chili Mo" that a red Jeep Cherokee was used by the suspects.

On December 27, 1992, we spoke with John Severin. He told us that a smoker known as 'Llttle Victor" hustles at the gas station and may have been present when the murder occurred. On December 29, 1992, Detective Schunk received a phone call from the same CRI that investigating officers had interviewed on December 16, 1992. The CRI stated that "Flux" (Talos, Willie Jr., DOB 7/5/66) set up the killing of "June Bug" (victim Broomfield) and that "Baby Bam" (suspect Evans) was the shooter.

At 1730 hours, we spoke to a possible eyewitness by the name of Darryl Jenkins. He stated he was not at the gas station during the shooting, however, Little Victor, "June" (witness Leroy Martin) and Clarence "Claymax" were present during the shooting. According to Jenkins, Little Victor's true name is Victor Saul and he was supposedly arrested by the C.H.P. on 12/24/92.

On January 4, 1993, we located Clarence Lavan AKA "Claymax." He stated he and his brother James were at the gas station when the murders occurred. Clarence Lavan stated he knew all the people who got shot and he also knew the shooter, "Baby Bam." He stated he saw "Baby Bam" the day before the shooting when he bought marijuana from him. According to Lavan, "Baby Bam" was armed with an AK-47 and started shooting at everyone in the gas station. Lavan further stated that "Baby

Bam" (Marlon Evans) is from 6 Deuce East Coast Crip, and came to the gas station in a burgundy Blazer or Jeep Cherokee. The other passenger suspect got out of the red vehicle. The other passenger suspect just stood by the alley while "Baby Bam" was doing the shooting. Lavan described this suspect as being short and stocky and armed with a handgun.
EXHIBIT 30.283
Ex. 39 - 4297

Date/Time of Interview: 12/14/92 0300
Location of Interview: NTN STA
Statement: Leroy Martin
I got to the Mobil Gas Station on Sunday night about 10:00 pm or a little before. I pump gas at the mobile station. I was standing by the gas pumps closest to Gage talking to "June." I saw Raymond, they call him "Jamaican" standing by the corner of the gas station near the window where people pay. Another older, Black guy that pushes a shopping cart was also standing near Raymond closer to the window. A younger Black guy was standing next to the guy that pushes a shopping cart. There was a vinyl over green Cadillac stopped at the pumps closest to Grand, facing towards Gage. There were two young, black guys in the Cadillac. The two guys in the Cadillac did not get out of the car. There was a black vinyl over red, older car parked next to the iron fence, on the west side of the gas station. There were two guys in the black over red car. The driver of the black over red car got out and walked up to the Jamaican and the other two guys that were standing near the pay window. The Jamaican and the young guy (V_2) turned and looked like they were talking to the guy that got out of the black/red car. A few minutes later the driver of the black/red car walked back to his car and got in. right after that I heard shots. I ducked behind the pumps and when the shooting stopped I saw the white/green car take off real fast towards Gage. It looked like the window, I think the back window of the Cadillac was shot out. The Cadillac turned left on Gage and took off fast towards Broadway. I think the last bullet took out the back window of the Cadillac. Right after that the black/red car drove out towards Broadway. The black/red car was driving slow, they did not look like they had been shot at or like they were trying to get away. I got up and saw that the Jamaican, the old guy that

pushed the shopping cart and the young guy that was standing next to them had been shot. The old guy said to call the paramedics because he had been hit. I didn't see any other cars in the gas station and I didn't see anybody walking either. I feel the guy in the black/red car is the one that had to be shooting, because there wasn't anybody else in the lot. The two guys in the Cadillac sort of looked like gang bangers and the guy that got out of the black/red car looked like a gang banger for sure. He looked like somebody that might have just got out of the pen. The driver of the black/red car was a male, black, late twenties to early thirties 5'9" to 6'0", medium build, medium complexion, wearing a dark blue knit cap, blue Levi shirt (light blue) and black khaki pants. He was clean shaven. If I saw him with that cap on I could recognize him. I heard a lot of shots for a long time but I did not see a gun during the shooting, because I ducked down when the shooting started. The black/red car was already parked next to the gas station when the white/green Cadillac pulled in.
-Leroy Martin

Date/Time of Interview: 1/4/93 0935
Location of Interview: Newton Station
Statement: Clarence Lavan

This statement was tape recorded and the below is a brief synopsis of his statement.

Me and my brother James were at the gas station on Gage and Grand. Putting air into James' black/red Dodge car tires. "Lil Al" (Vict. Bavis) and "June Bug" (Vict. Broomfield) were also there. They were in "Lil Al's" Cadillac which was parked in front of the pay window. "Lil Al" was outside the car by the pay window and "June Bug" was sitting in the car. The Jamaican (Vict. Phillips) was there too. As I was talking to "Lil Al" I saw a burgundy Blazer or Jeep Cherokee go n/b on Grand Ave then parked next to the blue apartments behind the gas station. There were three people (susps) in the car. The driver stayed in the car and the two passengers got out. The one with the AK-47 walked over towards Lil Al's car and started shooting at everyone. He shot "June Bug" and drove off and me and my brother hid behind my brother's car. The guy with the AK-47 then walked up to the Jamaican and shot him two more times, then he shot at me, but he missed me and hit the hood of my brother's car. The other guy (susp) had a handgun but he didn't do any shooting. He just stood by the alley. He was short and stocky. The shooter is from 6 Deuce and I bought some marijuana from him the day before the shooting.

1. A, huh?
2. Clarence Lavan: I seen him, yeah. I seen him
3. right there that's him, that's him
4. Detective Herrera: (Untranslatable) the
5. shooting, huh?
6. Clarence Lavan: That's him
7. Detective Herrera: Okay.
8. Clarence Lavan: I seen him.
9. Detective Herrera: Okay. Great.
10. Clarence Lavan: (Untranslatable): hey
11. I to go to jail for ticket or something I
12. got a traffic ticket. And if I go to jail for
13. jay-walk ticket, I'm--I'm dead.
14. Detective Herrera: Okay. Here's--where--
15. where--listen. I know you're afraid to
16. go to court. And ah
17. Clarence Lavan: I don't want to go to court.
18. Detective Herrera: Now, here's the thing. We
19. can relocate you. You know what relocating is?
20. Clarence Lavan: (Untranslatable)
21. Detective Herrera: Get you in a place
22. wherever you want. Even out of state if that's what
23. you want. You and your brother. Your brother was
24. there too, right?
25. Clarence Lavan: I don't want my brother

1. there with me. They're not going to hurt him.
2. Detective Herrera: Did he see anything?
3. Clarence Lavan: No
4. Detective Herrera: He didn't see any of that,
5. okay.
6. Clarence Lavan: (Untranslatable)
7. Detective Herrera: Okay.
8. Clarence Lavan: I'm tired of looking over my
9. shoulder. We don't know how long all
10. this relocating stuff is going to take.
11. Detective Herrera: Oh, it don't take that
12. long.
13. Clarence Lavan: Yeah, but in the meantime,
14. where am I going to rest my head?
15. Detective Herrera: Huh?
16. Clarence Lavan: In the meantime,
17. where am I going to rest my head?
18. Detective Herrera: Well, let me put it this
19. way. We're not going to run and go arrest everybody
20. right now, okay? You know what I mean? Nobody's
21. going to know this yet. Besides, this guy's in jail
22. already.
23. Clarence Lavan: He is?
24. Detective Herrera: (Untranslatable)
25. Clarence Lavan: He--he--I swear he looks

1. just like him.
2. Detective Herrera: That's him, huh? Okay.
3. You want--you want to write this in here. Or do
4. you want--or you want me to write it or--
5. Clarence Lavan: You write it.
6. Detective Herrera: Okay. You tell me what to
7. write.
8. Clarence Lavan: I don't know what to
9. Detective Herrera: Okay. The person in card
10. number one or card A, photo number--have you seen
11. that person before?
12. Clarence Lavan: Yeah (Untranslatable) Where's
13. the guy with the--he had long hair though.
14. Detective Herrera: You said he had a beanie
15. hat.
16. Clarence Lavan: A beanie hat. But
17. they don't wear them right.
18. Detective Herrera: Okay. Remember--
19. remember when I--remember what I told you about the
20. pictures?
21. Clarence Lavan: Uh-huh.
22. Detective Herrera: When they're taken
23. sometimes, you know, the guy may have had long hair
24. at the time. Or--or he may have--when it was
25. taken he had short hair, okay? That--that's the

1. thing. That's why you have to don't worry about the
2. hair, okay?
3. Clarence Lavan: That looks like the guy.
4. Detective Herrera: Well, does it look like it
5. or is it?
6. Clarence Lavan: I think it's the guy.
7. Detective Herrera: Okay. So you want me
8. Write then the person in--in card A, picture number
9. one?
10. Clarence Lavan: (Untranslatable)
11. Detective Herrera: Or do you want to write
12. it?
13. Clarence Lavan: You can write it.
14. Detective Herrera: Okay.
15. Clarence Lavan: Let me look at this picture. This is
16. the guy, man. He's in jail but I've seen him though.
17. Detective Herrera: Oh, yeah?
18. Clarence Lavan: He's in jail but I've seen
19. him, man.
20. Detective Herrera: He is right
21. Afterward this happened.
22. Clarence Lavan: He--he--he--I'm telling
23. the truth, man. I don't see how he can be in jail
24. and I've seen him too, man.
25. Detective Herrera: Huh?

1. Clarence Lavan: How could he be in jail and I
2. seen him too?
3. Detective Herrera: He didn't--he got into
4. jail after this happened.
5. Clarence Lavan: That's him, man.
6. Detective Herrera: Okay?
7. Clarence Lavan: He's from the Deuce.
8. Detective Herrera: He's a Deuce? Have you
9. seen him before?
10. Clarence Lavan: (Untranslatable) That night
11. I did.
12. Detective Herrera: This is the guy who shot
13. June Bug and Lil Al?
14. Clarence Lavan: With A-K
15. Automatic.
16. Detective Herrera: Do you remember what day
17. it was?
18. Clarence Lavan: No, I don't.
19. Detective Herrera: Was it a weekday? Or--
20. Clarence Lavan: It was a Sunday.
21. Detective Herrera; It was Sunday night?
22. Clarence Lavan: Yeah.
23. Detective Herrera: would have been like 13?
24. Clarence Lavan: I don't I'm not sure
25. about the date.

Date/Time of Interview: 2/9/93 1700
Location of Interview: Newton Station
Statement: John Kenneth Severin

On the day (12/13/92) that all those people got killed at the gas station on Gage and Grand I was at home with my little baby boy on the back porch. My father Purvery Severin and my mother Laurence Severin were in their bedroom. At about 9:30-10:00 pm. I heard a lot of shots go off. The shots sounded like they were going across the freeway 1-10 about 1 or 2 minutes later. "Tank" (Will Talos Jr) 6 Deuce East Coast Crips came running up to my back door and asked me to let him inside my house. He had an AK-47 rifle with a banana clip and no stock I told him he could I couldn't let him in with a rifle because my baby was in the house he said, "Fuck it then," and ran off.

Silent Night Detective Agency
P.O. Box 1438
Hawaiian Gardens, CA 90716
(310) 402-4234
December 14, 1994
Ron Rothman
Attorney at Law
1219 Morningside Dr.
Manhattan Beach, CA. 90266
Case name: People versus Marlon Evans
Case number: BA071499
Investigation

Initially Mya Desmond, Demetrius Henson, Kem Gardner, Dante Davis, Larry Anderson, Damon Campbell, and Calvin Dixon were contacted and interviewed regarding their connection to this case as well as their claimed support of his innocence. The relationship between the investigator and the above mentioned appeared to be one of confidence and cooperation.

According to Maya Desmond, she was with the defendant prior to the incident in question and was at the scene just after the shooting occurred and claims the defendant was at the scene during that time.

Demitrius Henson says that on the night in question he was in front of his apartment building talking to friends when he observed a black Jeep International go northbound on Broadway and turn left on Gage. He says a few moments later he heard gunshots coming from the direction the jeep had driven. Henson says he then observed the jeep from Gage onto Broadway going southbound. He says as far as he could tell there was only one person in the jeep and that person did not fit the description of the defendant.

Kemo Gardner says that on the day in question he and the defendant we're together along with several other friends. He says their plan was to go to a club that night and that enroute they were stopped by the police a short distance from the scene of the incident and that during the traffic stop a number of gunshots were heard at which time the officers left them to respond to the shooting scene. He says they too went to the scene to see what happened and then proceeded to go to the club.

Dante Davis, one of the victims at the scene says that he was at the gas station with victim Bloomfield when the shooting started. He says he did not see who the shooter was and in fact does not believe the shooter was Evans in that he and Evans have never had any problems and he has even seen him since the shooting. He goes on to say that once he found out the weapon Evans was arrested for was not the murder weapon nor the gun that shot him he was convinced Evans was not involved.

Larry Anderson says that he was in fact with the defendant on the night in question and does concur with Gardner regarding the police stop occurring just at the time of the shooting.

Damon Campbell, he was arrested for possession of the weapon said to have been the murder of Bloomfield and was also said to have been used against a police officer. He says he was charged and sentenced and has done his time and is now out. He says that Evans was never in possession of the weapon 12/13/92 and does not believe Evans had any involvement in that shooting.

Calvin Dixon is said to have been a confidential informant in this matter according to Dixon he is not and has never been an informant in this subpoenas. He further says that he was also a witness to the traffic stopped on the night in question.

Since my initial contact with these witnesses several attempts have been made to have an in-person meeting with them in order to obtain a tape-recorded statement as well served them with on-call subpoenas. To date neither have made themselves available for live interviews nor has it been possible to serve them personally with a subpoena. Campbell and Anderson have since moved and have left no forwarding address.

This concludes this portion of our investigation, however should any further assistance or additional investigation needed in this matter please feel free to call.

Very truly yours;
Silent Night Detective Agency
Eldridge Moore.
Silent Night Detective Agency
P.O. Box 1438
Hawaiian Gardens, CA 90716
(310) 402-4234

March 5, 1995
RE: People V. Marlon Evans
Case Number: BA071499

<u>Case Update</u>

Per our last report, we indicated that we were unable to contact certain witnesses. Since then we have been able to contact them and secure tape recorded statements as well as their assurance to testify when needed.

- Maya Dansby (213)752-3949 152 ½ E. Gage Ave., L.A.

As per our earlier report, Maya's states that she heard of the shooting then went to the scene to see what had happened. Shortly after arriving the defendant along with several others came up and asked what was going on. She says that at the time Marlon was wearing a black and white plaid shirt and black pants. She says that night Marlon and the others went to a club called the "Name of the Game" on Western and that she was going to go with them but later changed her mind.

Maya says she knows all the victims as well as the defendant and says that to her knowledge there has never been any problems between them. As far as she knew they were all friends and could think of no reason for the defendant to have committed such an act.

- Reuben "Lil Greedy" Jones (213)566-4884 2144 East 101St Street, L.A.

According to Jones, on the night of the incident he and Marlon along with several others were on the way to a club when they were pulled over by police. Jones says there were two cars with them and the police pulled over the car that Larry Anderson was in and that he, Kemo and Marlon were in the other car he says the police approached Anderson's car and began asking questions.

He says in the middle of the questioning, a series of gunshots were coming from nearby. At this time the officer, upon hearing this discontinue the questioning left and apparently responded to the area of the shots upon the officers departure, Ruben and the others also went to see what had happened upon arrival at the scene they saw their friend asked what had happened. Once they saw there was nothing they could do to help they continued on their way.

- Larry Anderson BKG. # 4207752 Wayside Honor Rancho, Med. North

According to Anderson on the night of the incident in question, he and the defendant along with several others were on their way to a club when he was pulled over and questioned by LAPD. He says that during this stop he heard what sounded like a lot of gunshots coming from nearby. Upon hearing that the officers left in such haste, he forgot to return Anderson's driver's license (he received it later in the mail).

Anderson says that he and the others also went to the scene of the shooting then continued on their way.

- John Severin CDC #E93071 CMC, San Luis Obispo, CA

According to the police report, in an interview with Severin on 2/9/93 at Newton station he stated that on the night of the incident, just shortly afterward a friend of his (Willie "Tank" Talos) came to his back door with what appeared to be an AK-47, asked if he could come in, but serve and refused and Hallows left.

During my interview with Severin, he denies ever making such a statement to the police and in fact says Talos never came to his house on the night of the shooting with the rifle any other time. Severin says while he was in custody the police did question him about the incident and had him sign a statement which he never read. He says he was so frustrated over his own arrest, you just signed and initiated where they told him to but had no idea what it was he was signing.

Comments and Observations

In my earlier report it was mentioned that contact was made with Calvin Dixon (an alleged confidential informant) who denies making any statement to police not acting as an informant in this matter. I recently learned that Dixon was murdered on 12/27/94.

Dante Davis has again been contacted and he restates his position that he does not believe Marlon had anything to do with this with his being shot 12/13/93.

This concludes this portion of our investigation, however continuing efforts are being made to contact any additional witnesses. If you have any questions please feel free to call.

Very truly yours,
Silent Night Detective Agency
Eldridge Moore

Silent Night Detective Agency
P.O. Box 1438
Hawaiian Gardens, CA 90716
(213)739-6624
(310)596-3238 FAX

March 9, 1995
RE: People V. Marlon Evans
Case Number: BA071499
<u>Statement of Witness</u>
Ashawnto Ross 8114 ½ S. San Pedro BL. (213)750-8583
According to Mr. Ross, approximately two days following the incident in question, he along with several others including Carlton "Chili Mo" Mosley, were on 62nd Street, when Clarence Lavan approached and said that he saw who shot our "Home-Boy's". He said that he was at the gas station when the shooting occurred and that the shooter was a dark complexion with long reddish braids, short and stocky. He also indicated the shooter was wearing a red shirt, driving a red Jeep. He says he recognized the person as being someone from a "Blood Gang" neighborhood that has a girlfriend that lives in that area. He has seen this person over there on several occasions.

He says he believes Lavan's story in that he continues to repeat the fact that the shooter was a "Blood" that he'd seen before and could identify him. He says that Lavan went on to say that God must have been with him because he was right in the line of fire and did not get shot. He further says that Lavon kept repeating these things over and over as if he was really convinced that this is what had occurred and who he saw.

Ross is currently in custody at LACJ, booking #4300986. He has a violation hearing on 3/10/95 at CCB, Department 114. He says if he is released he can be reached at the above address, otherwise he will be in custody. He says that he is willing to testify in this matter and says that if released he could also assist in locating those who were present when Lavan made the aforementioned statement.

1. Shall be the truth the whole truth and nothing but the
2. truth so help you God
3. The witness I do
4.
5. Donte Bavis,
6. Called as a witness by and on behalf of the people having
7. Then first duly sworn was examined and testified as
8. Follows:
9.
10. The Clerk: Thank you.
11. Please be seated.
12. State your name and spell it
13. the witness Donte Bavis D-o-n-t-e B-a-v-i-s
14.
15. By Ms. Reisz:
16. Q. Do you go by the name of "Little Al" also?
17. A. Yes.
18. the Court: Ma'am one more laugh and you are out.
19. Why don't you go outside right now.
20.
21. By Ms. Reisz:
22. Q. On December 13th, 1992, close to 10:00 in the
23. Evening, did you drive your car in the gas station at Gage
24. and Grand Avenue's?
25. A. Yes.
26. Q. Was there somebody in your car with you?
27. A. Yes.
28. Q. Who was that?

1. A. June Bug
2. Cute. Do you know June Bug's real name?
3. A. Henry Broomfield
4. Q. Were you driving in your car?
5. A. Yes.
6. Q. I'm showing you people's Exhibit 2 and 3 for
7. Identification
8. Is that your car?
9. A. Yes.
10. Q. That's the green, turquoise Cadillac?
11. A. Yeah.
12. Q. When you drove into the gas station, did you
13. Park?
14. A. Yes.
15. Q. Where did you park?
16. A. Right by the window.
17. Q. The pay window?
18. A. Uh-huh.
19. The Court: I know you are not used to being in
20. court but it is important you say yes or no because this
21. lady has to take down everything you say and sometimes it
22. is hard to tell the difference.
23. By Ms. Reisz:
24. Q. Did you get out of the car?
25. A. Yes.
26. Q. What did you do?
27. A. I went to the window to buy a fuel injector

1. Clarence Lavan: Yeah, standing in that--in
2. the dark in the alley. I really couldn't see his
3. face.
4. Detective Herrera: Okay. Card C. Anybody
5. there you recognize?
6. Clarence Lavan: How much did this guy weigh?
7. Detective Herrera: How much did he weigh?
8. Clarence Lavan: How much do he weigh?
9. Detective Herrera: I don't know.
10. Clarence Lavan: This guy had long hair too.
11. That's the only thing that confused me with this guy.
12. This looks like the guy but his hair was longer.
13. Detective Herrera: Okay. Let me show you
14. Card D, okay. Card D. Do you see anybody there
15. That--that might have--that were there that
16. night?
17. Clarence Lavan: No that's not nobody.
18. Detective Herrera: Not any of them were
19. There? One more. Card E.
20. Clarence Lavan: Naugh-uh.
21. Detective Herrera: Nobody. Just in the--in
22. Card A, huh?
23. Clarence Lavan: I've seen
24. this--this one right here.
25. Detective Herrera: Number one in--in card

1. Cleaner
2. Q. You bought that?
3. A. Yeah.
4. Q. Then did you get back in the car?
5. A. Yeah, and somebody started shooting.
6. Q. How close did you get to the car?
7. A. I was sitting in the car. My feet wasn't in
8. The car.
9. Q. You hadn't completely gotten in?
10. A. Yes.
11. Q. Where was June Bug?
12. A. On the passenger side.
13. Q. Had he remained seated in the car when you
14. Went to the pay window?
15. A. Yes.
16. Q. Where were the shots coming from?
17. A. I don't know.
18. Q. What did you do?
19. A. I ducked.
20. Q. What was the next thing you did?
21. A. I ducked in the seat, and the shots started
22. Getting louder, and I ducked, and June Bug said, "Let's
23. go."
24. Q. Then what happened?
25. A. I turned the wheel. He grabbed the gas pedal
26. with his hand.
27. Q. Was June Bug laying down, and he put his
28. Hands on the accelerator?

1. A. Yeah. He was leaning towards me.
2. The Court: he was leaning towards the door?
3. The Witness: we were leaning towards each other.
4.
5. By Ms. Reisz:
6. Q. Were you ducking down below the windshield
7. Part?
8. A. Yes.
9. Q. Did June Bug reach down with his hand and put
10. Is it on the accelerator?
11. A. Yes.
12. Q. And that's how the car got the gas?
13. A. Yes.
14. Q. Were you shot?
15. A. Yes.
16. Q. When?
17. A. From the first three shots I was hit..
18. Q. Was that when you were inside your green
19. Cadillac?
20. A. Yes.
21. Q. Where were you shot?
22. A. On the shoulder.
23. Q. Anywhere else?
24. A. In the back.
25. Q. Anywhere else?
26. A. In the head.
27. Q. So you were shot in which shoulder?
28. A. The left.

1. Q. When you were shot in the back, was that
2. Above your waist?
3. A. I was ducking, and it came across an
4. Angle
5. Q. The middle?
6. A. On the side.
7. Q. Is that below the shoulder?
8. A. Yeah, right with the shoulder, even with it.
9. Q. Is that on the right or left side?
10. A. Right.
11. Q. And your head was hit?
12. A. I had a lump.
13. Q. Did you feel a bullet graze your head?
14. A. No.
15. Q. Did you feel a lump?
16. A. When I went to the hospital, I felt it.
17. Q. What did you do once you started up the car?
18. A. Just drove. We drove, and we was both ducked
19. Still, I got up, and I ran into some parked cars.
20. Q. What street did you drive out of the gas
21. Station on?
22. A. To Gage.
23. Q. Where did you drive?
24. A. To Gage and San Pedro.
25. Q. Did you stop there?
26. A. Uh-huh, yes.
27. Q. When you stopped there, what was the reason?
28. A. I stopped. I wanted help.

1. Q. Why?
2. A. I wanted some help.
3. Q. What was Henry Bloomfield's condition when
4. You stopped?
5. A. He wasn't talking.
6. Q. Did you see what his physical condition was?
7. A. No. He had a coat on. I couldn't tell.
8. Mr. Rothman: I didn't hear.
9. The witness: He had a coat on. I couldn't really
10. Tell.
11.
12. By Ms. Reisz:
13. Q. You said he wasn't talking?
14. A. No.
15. Q. Was he breathing?
16. A. Yes.
17. Q. How was he breathing?
18. A. Like--
19. Q. Was it a labored breathing?
20. A. It was heavy.
21. Q. Was it hard for him to breathe?
22. The Court: Well, did you get that?
23. Ms. Reisz: Well, he was breathing for us.
24.
25. By Ms. Reisz:
26. Q. I see in people's 2, in the pictures marked,
27. That the car was shot up.
28. Where was your car when it received those

1. Injuries?
2. Mr. Rothman: You mean where was the car?
3. The Court: I thought it was interesting that the
4. car received injuries.
5. The Witness: The gas station.
6.
7. By Ms. Reisz:
8. Q. What damage did your car sustain?
9. A. Bullet holes.
10. Q. Where were those located?
11. A. The windshield.
12. Q. The front or back?
13. A. The front and back and passenger side.
14. Q. Did the body of the car receive damage, as
15. well?
16. A. Yes.
17. Q. Where?
18. A. The trunk, mostly by the door, though.
19. The Court: Which door?
20. The Witness: The passenger side, the right side.
21.
22. By Ms. Reisz:
23. Q. Was that where June Bug was sitting?
24. A. Yes.
25. Ms. Reisz: And I believe people's 17 is the next
26. Exhibit.
27. The Court: Yes.
28.

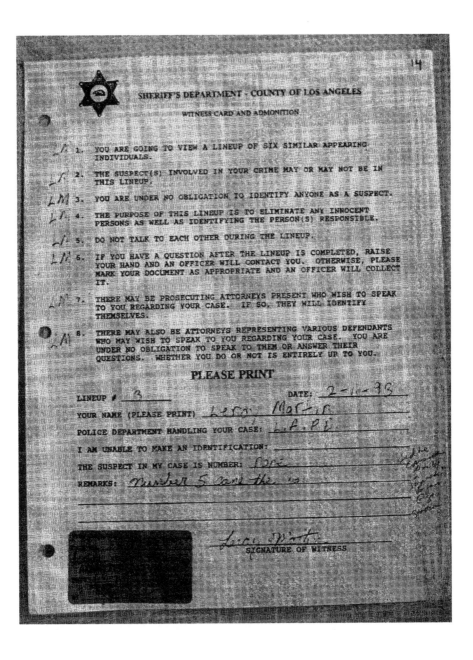

14

SHERIFF'S DEPARTMENT - COUNTY OF LOS ANGELES

WITNESS CARD AND ADMONITION

1. YOU ARE GOING TO VIEW A LINEUP OF SIX SIMILAR APPEARING INDIVIDUALS.

2. THE SUSPECT(S) INVOLVED IN YOUR CRIME MAY OR MAY NOT BE IN THIS LINEUP.

3. YOU ARE UNDER NO OBLIGATION TO IDENTIFY ANYONE AS A SUSPECT.

4. THE PURPOSE OF THIS LINEUP IS TO ELIMINATE ANY INNOCENT PERSONS AS WELL AS IDENTIFYING THE PERSON(S) RESPONSIBLE.

5. DO NOT TALK TO EACH OTHER DURING THE LINEUP.

6. IF YOU HAVE A QUESTION AFTER THE LINEUP IS COMPLETED, RAISE YOUR HAND AND AN OFFICER WILL CONTACT YOU. OTHERWISE, PLEASE MARK YOUR DOCUMENT AS APPROPRIATE AND AN OFFICER WILL COLLECT IT.

7. THERE MAY BE PROSECUTING ATTORNEYS PRESENT WHO WISH TO SPEAK TO YOU REGARDING YOUR CASE. IF SO, THEY WILL IDENTIFY THEMSELVES.

8. THERE MAY ALSO BE ATTORNEYS REPRESENTING VARIOUS DEFENDANTS WHO MAY WISH TO SPEAK TO YOU REGARDING YOUR CASE. YOU ARE UNDER NO OBLIGATION TO SPEAK TO THEM OR ANSWER THEIR QUESTIONS. WHETHER YOU DO OR NOT IS ENTIRELY UP TO YOU.

PLEASE PRINT

LINEUP # 3   DATE: 2-11-93

YOUR NAME (PLEASE PRINT) Leroy Martin

POLICE DEPARTMENT HANDLING YOUR CASE: L.A.P.D

I AM UNABLE TO MAKE AN IDENTIFICATION: _____

THE SUSPECT IN MY CASE IS NUMBER: none

REMARKS: Number 5 look the cl___

_____

SIGNATURE OF WITNESS

LOS ANGELES COUNTY SHERIFF'S DEPARTMENT

WITNESSES ONLY!

1. *Larry Martin*
2. _____
3. _____
4. _____
5. _____
6. _____
7. _____
8. _____
9. _____
10. _____

11. _____
12. _____
13. _____
14. _____
15. _____
16. _____
17. _____
18. _____
19. _____
20. _____

NOTABLE INCIDENTS:

No STATEMENTS

No WRITTEN OBJECTIONS RECEIVED

WITNESS WALKED ON STAGE.

EACH SUSP PUT ON A BLUE KNIT CAP - WIT
STOOD ON THE STAGE IN FRONT OF #2

PHOTO IDENTIFICATION REPORT

DETECTIVE
SCHUNK, P.
HERRERA, G.

LOCATION
1126 W
65ᵀᴴ Pl.

COMMENTS OF WITNESS: *I fully understand the admonition read to me regarding th...*
ADDITIONAL COMMENTS REGARDING PHOTOGRAPHS –

THE PERSON IN PHOTOGRAPH # 3
"F" LOOKS A LOT LIKE THE GUY I SAW ... IR
THE CASHIERS WINDOW ON THE NIGHT T... T
THE SHOOTING HAPPENED. I DID NOT SEE HIM
WITH THE GUN BUT I SAW HIM NEAR THE
BLACK AND RED CAR AND NEAR THE CASHIERS
WINDOW. I'M ABOUT 75% SURE THAT THE
GUY IN PHOTO # 3 ON CARD # F IS THE GUY
I SAW THAT ~~NIGHT~~ I SAW THAT NIGHT.

Larry Martin   L.M   1-5-93   10:55 A.M.
SIGNATURE OF WITNESS   INITIALS   DATE   TIME

1. By Ms. Reisz:
2. Q. Do you recognize the person in people's
3. Exhibit 17?
4. A. Yes.
5. Q. Who is that?
6. A. Henry.
7. Q. Henry Bloomfield?
8. A. Yes.
9. Q. What happened to Henry as you were seated in
10. Your car, having pulled over?
11. A. He was just breathing.
12. Q. Did the paramedics come?
13. A. Yes.
14. Q. Do you know where they took him?
15. A. No. They took him out of the car first, and I
16. didn't see him no more.
17. Q. Pardon me?
18. A. They took me out the driver's side, and they
19. Took him out and took me in another ambulance.
20. Q. They took you to the hospital in the
21. ambulance?
22. A. Yes.
23. Q. Which hospital?
24. A. General.
25. Q. How long were you in the hospital?
26. A. Seven days.
27. Ms. Reisz: Nothing further.
28. The Court: Cross.

1. Mr. Rothman: Thank you.
2.
3. Cross Examination
4.
5. By Mr. Rothman:
6. Q. Have you made a full recovery from the
7. injuries you sustained?
8. A. Yes.
9. Q. The gentleman seated to my right, do you know
10. him?
11. A. Yes.
12. Q. How long have you known him?
13. A. For about 10 years.
14. Q. You guys grew up in the hood together?
15. A. Yes.
16. Q. Do you know someone by the name of June Bug?
17. A. Yes.
18. Q. And who would that be?
19. A. That's Henry Bloomfield.
20. Q. And you knew June Bug for a long period of
21. Time, too?
22. A. Yes.
23. Q. Would you describe the relationship at the time
24. of the shooting and before the shooting, the relationship
25. between you and Mr. Evans.
26. A. It was normal.
27. Q. It was normal?
28. You were friends?

1. A. Yes.
2. Q. Good friends?
3. A. Yes.
4. Q. How about the relationship between June Bug
5. and my client? Would you know what that was?
6. A. Normal, too.
7. Q. It was normal?
8. A. Yes.
9. Q. Were they also good friends?
10. A. Yes.
11. Q. Do you know of any reason why my client would
12. want to injure either you or June Bug?
13. A. No.
14. Q. If a witness were to come in here and testify
15. that there was some animosity over something between
16. June Bug and my client, would you know anything about that?
17. A. No.
18. Q. If there had been a problem, wouldn't you
19. have known about it, being that close to both of them?
20. A. Yes.
21. Q. Is there any question in your mind as to
22. that?
23. A. No.
24. Mr. Rothman: Thank you.
25. I have nothing further.
26.
27.
28.

1. Redirect Examination
2.
3. By Ms. Reisz:
4. Q. What gang are you from?
5. A. East Coast.
6. Q. Which set?
7. A. Six-eight.
8. Q. Six-eight?
9. A. Yeah.
10. Q. Is the defendant a member of a gang?
11. A. Yes.
12. Q. What gang is that?
13. A. East Coast.
14. Q. Which set?
15. A. Six-deuce, 62nd street.
16. Q. And your testimony is there no problems
17. Between six-eight and six-deuce in December of 1992?
18. A. No.
19. Mr. Rothman: I asked him about a conflict between
20. Two individuals, and I didn't mention any intergang
21. warfare.
22. The Court: Reword your question.
23. Mr. Rothman: Thank you.
24.
25. By Ms. Reisz:
26. Q. My question is: Where there problems between
27. Six-eight and six-deuce in December of 1992?
28. A. No.

1. A. I don't know if that's his real name, but
2. everybody calls him Moses.
3. Q. When you first talked to the police, did you
4. Tell them that you thought maybe the people in the black
5. and red car did the shooting?
6. A. Yes.
7. Q. Why did you say that?
8. A. Because that was the only other car--the
9. Reason why I thought that it was them doing the shooting is
10. Because I didn't see no one shooting at their car, but I
11. Seen someone shoot--I seen the green and white Cadillac
12. being shot at.
13. Q. So you were assuming that since the only car
14. you saw was the green and black car, that maybe--the red
15. and black car, that maybe the shooting came from there?
16. A. Yes.
17. Q. But, in fact, you didn't see where the
18. Shooting came from?
19. A. I didn't see who had the gun and who was
20. Doing the shooting, but I knew what direction the shooting
21. Was coming from.
22. Q. And that was Grand Avenue, shooting in
23. the direction of the pay window?
24. A. Yeah, on the side.
25. Ms. Reisz: Thank you.
26. Nothing further.
27. The Court: Cross.
28.

1. Cross Examination
2.
3. By Mr. Rothman:
4. Q. Mr. Martin, you saw the gentleman seated to
5. my right at the gas station near the cashier's window?
6. A. Yes.
7. Q. Do you know who he is?
8. A. No.
9. Do you know him from the neighborhood?
10. A. No.
11. Q. Had you ever seen him before that night?
12. A. No.
13. Q. And you saw him, apparently, at the cashier's
14. Window.
15. When you saw him, what was he doing, if
16. Anything?
17. A. Observing the scenery.
18. Q. He was standing there?
19. A. Yeah.
20. Q. Did he have anything in his hands?
21. A. He had his hands behind him.
22. Q. Show us.
23. A. Like you are doing.
24. Me. Rothman: With my hands behind me.
25.
26. By Mr. Rothman:
27. Q. Did it appear that he had anything in his
28. hands?

1. A. The way he was looking, yeah.
2. Q. But you don't know what it was he had in his
3. hands?
4. A. No.
5. Q. How long was it between the time you saw him
6. standing there and the shooting started?
7. A. How long?
8. Q. How long a period of time elapsed in minutes
9. or seconds?
10. A. Three minutes, two minutes.
11. Q. Two or three minutes?
12. A. Yes.
13. Q. And what were you doing during that two or
14. three minutes?
15. A. Standing, talking to someone.
16. Q. And during the time you were standing and
17. talking , did you look over to see where he was?
18. A. Yeah.
19. Q. Why did you do that?
20. A. Just ordinary observing, being there, looking
21. around.
22. Q. You didn't anticipate that anything was going
23. to happen? You were just kicking back and looking around?
24. A. Yeah.
25. Q. And did you have occasion to see him again
26. during that two or three minutes?
27. A. No. When I seen him the first time, I was
28. wondering why he was standing there, because he wasn't

1. paying for nothing from the window, and he wasn't nobody I
2. see there, because I have been there more than once.
3. Q. So when you looked back, he was gone?
4. A. Yeah.
5. Q. Did you see where he went?
6. A. Back the same--toward the red and black
7. Car, back that-a-way, because he didn't walk out
8. forwards.
9. Q. When you say back towards the red and black
10. car, did you see him walking out of a car when went to
11. the cashier's area?
12. A. No.
13. Q. So the first time you saw him he was near the
14. cashier's window?
15. A. Yeah, and I assumed he got out of the red and
16. black car.
17. Q. You just assumed that? You didn't see it?
18. A. Yeah.
19. Q. Was there anyone else in the red and black
20. Car?
21. A. No. I don't know how many people was in the
22. red and black car, but I seen him, I thought he had
23. got out of the red and black car.
24. Q. Whether or not he got out of it, at some
25. point, he was at the cashier's window?
26. A. On the side.
27. Q. Standing there, and then you saw him leave,
28. right, walk away?

1. A. No. I seen him stand there and be standing
2. There, and when I looked around, I didn't see him standing
3. there no more, but I never seen him leave.
4. Q. My question is: You said that you thought he
5. Went back to the red and black car.
6. Is the reason you thought he went back to the
7. red and black car because you thought he got out of the red and
8. black car?
9. A. Yeah.
10. Q. So you don't really know where he came from
11. Or where he went. THose are thoughts you formed.
12. Is that a fair statement?
13. A. Yeah.
14. Q. Did anything else happen in the period of
15. Time between the time you looked at my client and the
16. Shooting started? Did anything else go on that you saw in
17. the gas station area?
18. A. No, other than before I seen him, the red and
19. black car drove in and parked over there on the side.
20. The green and white Cadillac came in and
21. Parked at the gas pump to get gas, and then I looked over,
22. And seen him standing there. I looked, you know, to see
23. Was he buying something at the window, but he was standing
24. there, looking around, observing the scenery, and I started
25. back talking to who I was talking to.
26. Q. With respect to the red and black car, do you
27. know what kind of car that was?
28. A. No, I don't know what kind of car.

1. Q. Would you know--if someone said it was a
2. Dodge, would you say, "okay," or you don't know?
3. A. Yeah, I think it was.
4. Q. How many people were in the car?
5. A. I never seen how many people was in the car.
6. Q. Did you ever seen anybody standing near that
7. car at any time?
8. A. Yeah.
9. Q. When was that?
10. A. Eight before the shooting.
11. Q. And what did you see right before the
12. shooting?
13. A. I seen him standing by the cashier's window.
14. I seen the Jamaican headed toward the car, you know,
15. Because he would go up to and ask them people could he
16. wipe their windows.
17. The Court: Toward what car?
18. THe Witness: The red and black car.
19.
20. By Mr. Rothman:
21. Q. When the Jamaican started toward the red and
22. black car, how far was he from it?
23. A. Him?
24. Q. Forget him. We are talking about the red and black car and the
Jamaican.
25. How far was the Jamaican from the red and
26. black car?
27. A. Two feet.

1.   A. I am a detective for the City of Los
2.   Angeles. I am currently assigned to the Narcotics
3.   Group, South Bureau.
4.   Q. Were you assigned to investigate a
5.   shooting of some police officers that involved the
6.   arrest of Mr. Marlon Evans, the defendant in this
7.   case?
8.   A. Yes.
9.   Q. And you were the investigator in that
10. case?
11. A. Yes.
12. Q. In connection with that case at the
13. shooting of the officers, were some casings
14. retrieved at the scene?
15. A. Yes, they were.
16. Q. And when My. Evans was subsequently
17. Arrested, was he arrested with some weapons?
18. A. Yes.
19. Q. After the arrest of Mr. Evans, did you
20. ask that the weapons be analyzed with some casings
21. or ballistics information that was retrieved from
22. your crime scene?
23. A. Yes, I did.
24. The Court: Can you specify for me, the crime scene we're talking
about is November 22, 1992; is
25. that right?
26. My. Rothman: Yes.
27. Ms. Hunter: Yes.

1. My. Rothman: Your honor, could I suggest to
2. Expedite this, there are two shootings. Could we
3. Refer to the first one that occurred on November
4. 22nd as the fellows shooting, involving officer
5. fellows. And the one that occurred on December
6. 13th as the Gage Street shooting.
7. The Court: That would be fine.
8. Mr. Rothman: That would help me and I am
9. sure help the people, too.
10. The Court: Miss Hunter, we're talking at
11. this point about the fellows shoot.
12. Ms. Hunter: Yes, this is the investigating
13. Officer on the fellows shooting.
14. The Court: All right.
15. Q. By Ms. Hunter: In any event, did you
16. --that evidence was retrieved from the crime
17. scene and the guns that were retrieved from this
18. defendant, did you ask that there be an analysis
19. prepared?
20. A. Yes, I did.
21. Q. Okay. Do you recall offhand when that
22. Analysis was prepared or do you need to look at the
23. report?
24. A. I would need to look at the reports. I
25. don't have the dates.
26. Q. I am going to show you a copy of the
27. analyzed evidence report. Calling your attention
28. to the top--

1. The Court: And the defendant was arrested on
2. December fourteen; is that correct, detective?
3. The Witness: I apologize, your honor, I
4. wasn't able to review any reports. I just come--
5. Mr. Rothman: Would stipulate that that is
6. the date of his arrest.
7. The Court: THat when he was arrested certain
8. Weapons were found in association with his arrest;
9. is that correct?
10. The Witness: That's correct, sir.
11. The Court: And that is what we're talking
12. about. Okay.
13. Mr. Rothman: Is the report that you are
14. looking at page one or two, that D R 92 thirteen
15. three nine five four four in the upper right hand
16. corner?
17. The Witness: No.
18. Mr. Rothman: Which one?
19. The Witness: The request was 12-15-92, D R
20. 92 thirteen four one six five eight.
21. Mr. Rothman: Okay, thank you.
22. Q. By Ms. Hunter: And when was that
23. request made?
24. A. On 12-15-92 and was an analysis done on those
25. two items.
26. Q. Yes. Was also--were some other--
27. were some other evidence also analyzed in
28. connection with these two guns found?

1. A. Yes, Detective Herrera had a Homicide
2. Investigation and we thought there might be
3. connected so we requested--I believe he actually
4. did the request, comparisons between guns that were
5. recovered compared to the casings found at his
6. murder scene and also the casings founf at the
7. Fellow Shooting.
8. Ms. Hunter: And, your honor, for the record
9. that is the December thirteen, Gage.
10. The Court: That would be the Gage Shooting,
11. What we're calling the Gage Shooting?
12. Q. By Ms. Hunter: And when did the
13. analysis come back?
14. A. According to the reports, January 27,
15. 1993.
16. Q. Okay. And what were the results of
17. that analysis?
18. A. That the weapon--the two weapons, the
19. AK47 and the Emblem Carbine were not used in the
20. shooting.
21. The Court: In either shooting or just the Fellows Shooting?
22. The Witness: In either shooting, your honor.
23. The Court: All right.
24. Q. By Ms. Hunter: Now at sometime in 94
25. Were you contacted by the defense in this case to retrieve the
evidence that had been booked in?

1. A. Yes.
2. Q. Okay, approximately when were you
3. contacted?
4. A. It would have been within the last four
5. months. I should estimate maybe two months ago.
6. Q. And when you went to go retrieve the
7. evidence that was in connection with your November
8. 22nd crime, what did you learn?
9. A. I learned that all the evidence had
10. Been destroyed.
11. Q. In connection with your crime?
12. A. Yes.
13. Q. And when you say all, are you referring
14. to both the guns and the casings that were
15. retrieved from your crime of November 22nd?
16. A. That is what I was advised, yes.
17. Q. Had you ordered that at all?
18. A. No, I did not.
19. Q. At the time--prior to the time that
20. they had been destroyed, did you know whether or
21. Not they had any type of--I am sorry, strike
22. That.
23. Nothing further at this time.
24. The Court: All right, Mr. Rothman.
25. Mr. Rothman: Thank you.

1. Cross Examination
2. By Mr. Rothman:
3. Q. Officer Biczo, do you recall having a
4. conversation with a ballistics expert named Parker
5. Bell on November 14, 94: Does that refresh your
6. memory?
7. A. Would that be the defense ballistics
8. expert.
9. Mr. Rothman: Yes, for the record, your
10. honor, I am referring to Mr. Parker Bell who is
11. seated in the courtroom.
12. The Court: Yes.
13. Mr. Rothman: Yes.
14. The Witness: Yes, I do recall having a
15. conversation with him.
16. Q. By Mr. Rothman: Do you recall in that
17. conversation that he indicated to you that on
18. September 6 he had had contacts with Detective
19. Herrera regarding the same evidence?
20. A. Because my understanding, it was
21. Regarding some different evidence.
22. Q. But as far back as September of last
23. year Mr. Bell was actively pursuing attempts to
24. obtain this evidence for evaluation, was he not?
25. A. I only know the time that he contacted
26. me, sir.
27. Q. All right.
28. The Court: And that was about the November

1. 14th of 94?
2. The Witness: That sounds about right, your
3. honor.
4. The Court: All right.
5. Q. By Mr. Rothman: Detective Biczo, am I
6. pronouncing it correctly?
7. A. Biczo, yes close enough, Biczo, yes.
8. Q. Property that is taken in by the
9. LAPD is held by the property room in connection
10. with the case. Before that evidence is destroyed
11. there is a system by with the property room
12. contacts one of the officers involved with the
13. case, either in writing or orally, and makes a
14. determination as to whether the case is still
15. active and whether the evidence is needed: is that
16. a fair statement?
17. A. That is the way it is supposed to work,
18. yes.
19. Q. All right. And would it be a fair
20. statement that in this case, if there had been a
21. positive match, that it would have been essential
22. evidence that you and the prosecutor would want?
23. A. I would consider essential evidence
24. here regardless, but, yes.
25. Q. In other words, it is your position
26. that it should be kept whether incriminating or
27. exculpatory until the case has been terminated?
28. A. Yes.

1. Q. Do you know who was contacted in
2. connection with this case to make a determination
3. of whether if could be destroyed or not?
4. A. No, I do not.
5. Q. Do you have any idea where the system
6. broke down?
7. A. I found out what serial number issued
8. destruction notice or gave approval for that.
9. However, I spoke with that individual and he said
10. he never did it and someone put his serial number
11. on the card.
12. Q. There is a serial number on the release
13. card but the person whose serial number that is,
14. denies giving permission: is that what you are
15. saying?
16. A. That's correct.
17. Q. Who is that individual that denies--
18. A. That was my former supervisor Detective
19. Dennis Scherr. I believe it's S-C-H-E-R-R.
20. Q. I notice that on the second page of the
21. property report item 21 refers to a barrel shroud.
22. Did you personally observe that item, do
23. you have an independent recollection of that?
24. A. I do not believe I saw that.
25. Q. It is described as a black metal found
26. in driveway.
27. Just for purposes of this hearing, what
28. Would your understanding be of a barrel shroud?

1.   Los Angeles, California; Tuesday, May 16, 1995; 9:25 A.M.
2.   Department No. 104 Hon. Robert J. Perry, Judge
3.   Appearances:
4.   (As previously noted.)
5.
6.   (Carmen R. Young, CSR, Official Reporter.)
7.
8.   (The following proceedings were held in open
9.   court of the presence of the jury:)
10.
11.   The Court: Let's go on the
12.   record outside the presence of the jury. This is people versus Marlon
13.   Evans. All parties are present.
14.   There are a couple of matters that we
15.   want to conclude that we have discussed outside the
16.   presence of the jury.
17.   First as to the transcript, exhibit 53,
18.   I noted that I heard, when I listened to the tape on
19.   page 80 at line 13, that the phrase that is identified
20.   as untranslatable should read, "I couldn't identify him
21.   without the hat."
22.   It presently reads, "I untranslatable
23.   identify him without the hat." What I'm going to do is
24.   make that correction on the transcript so that the
25.   transcript that's in evidence will read, "I couldn't
26.   identify him without the hat."
27.   Mr. Rothman: Can I inquire how your honor is
28.   going to convey that to the jury?